JOLLY ROGER

THE STORY OF THE
GREAT AGE OF PIRACY

FRANCISCVS DRAECK NOBILISSIMVS EQVES ANGLIÆ AN° ÆT SVÆ

THE FATHER OF MODERN PIRACY

[*Frontispiece*

JOLLY ROGER

THE STORY OF THE
GREAT AGE OF PIRACY

Patrick Pringle

DOVER PUBLICATIONS, INC.
Mineola, New York

Published in Canada by General Publishing Company, Ltd., 30
Lesmill Road, Don Mills, Toronto, Ontario.

Bibliographical Note

This Dover edition, first published in 2001, is an unabridged republication of the original edition published by W. W. Norton and Company,
Inc., New York, 1953.

Library of Congress Cataloging-in-Publication Data

Pringle, Patrick.
    Jolly Roger : the story of the great age of piracy / Patrick Pringle.
        p. cm.
    Originally published: New York : W. W. Norton, 1953.
    Includes bibliographical references and index.
    ISBN 0-486-41823-5 (pbk.)
        1. Pirates. I. Title.

G535 .P72 2001
910.4'5–dc21
                                                    2001028920

Manufactured in the United States of America
Dover Publications, Inc., 31 East 2nd Street, Mineola, N.Y. 11501

CONTENTS

LIST OF ILLUSTRATIONS

INTRODUCTION

AS trade followed the flag, so the black flag followed trade. Probably piracy began soon after prehistoric man paddled his first dug-out: it continued until the twentieth century. As Philip Gosse has pointed out, a complete history of piracy would begin to resemble a maritime history of the world, and it is outside the scope of a single volume.

This book deals only with the most flourishing era in the history of piracy, which began in the reign of Queen Elizabeth I and ended in the second decade of the eighteenth century. To avoid having to keep repeating this definition, I have taken the liberty of calling the period the Age of Piracy.

Most of my pirates were born in England or Wales. There is nothing curious in the fact that the English and Welsh excelled at piracy at a time when they led the world in other maritime activities.

I have had to leave out the pirates of the Far East, partly because one book is hardly enough for the pirates of the West, but mainly because the history of Asiatic piracy cannot be written by one who has not got access to Chinese State Papers and who could not read them if he had.

I have modernized the spelling and punctuation of quotations where the original form seemed likely to irritate the reader.

I wish to thank the staffs of the Public Record Office and the Reading Room of the British Museum for all their help, and also Mr. Clinton Black, keeper of the Colonial Archives at Spanish Town, Jamaica, for generously carrying out researches that otherwise would not have been made.

CHAPTER ONE

Abominable Brutes

PIRATES have been stripped of their glamour. No one believes any longer in the romantic conception of a ship-load of hearties, immensely brave and daring and rather jolly: it is not supported by any historical evidence. So pirates have been degraded from swashbuckling adventurers to common criminals. Even in schoolboy literature they are portrayed not as enviable heroes but as despicably bloodthirsty, ferocious villains.

"For the most part," Raymond Postgate has written, "pirates were abominable brutes. They have no right to the romance with which later writers have invested them. There was sometimes chivalry or wit to be found among the highwaymen, but the records of Blackbeard, Kidd or Morgan are tedious stories of revolting cruelty and dishonest greed."

I have quoted this opinion because it is fairly typical of the popular conception of pirates to-day. Like the romantic conception, it is unsupported by evidence, and it seems equally far from the truth. Whether or not the stories of Blackbeard, Kidd, and Morgan are tedious is a matter of opinion; it is a matter of fact that one of these three was not a pirate at all; it is a matter of conjecture whether another of them was a pirate; and there is no evidence that any of them was revoltingly cruel. I shall try to give fairer pictures of these and other pirates and alleged pirates later in this book. Meanwhile it seems necessary to consider how pirates in general have incurred this bulk charge of abominable brutality.

Hundreds of books (not counting fiction) have been written on pirates. With a few notable exceptions, such as the works of Philip Gosse, these have been based mainly on two 'standard' books, the 'classics' of pirate literature: *Bucaniers of America*, by A. O. Exquemelin (Amsterdam, 1679; first English translation, London, 1684); and *A General History of the Robberies*

and Murders of the Most Notorious Pyrates, by Captain Charles
Johnson (London, first edition, 1724; fourth edition, enlarged,
1726). Together these two works cover the most important
periods of the Age of Piracy.

Little is known about either of the authors, but both books
have been proved to contain much accurate information. Unfortunately this fact has been over-emphasized, especially in
Encyclopædia Britannica and the *Dictionary of National Biography*,
with the result that it has often been assumed that both works
are entirely true instead of only partly true. Yet there is
no need to take them on trust. Although not all the information given in them can be verified, much of the same ground is
fully covered in the Calendar of State Papers and in Admiralty
and Colonial Office documents preserved in the Public Record
Office. By comparison with official records it can be seen, for
example, that Johnson is more reliable on pirates of the
seventeen-twenties than on pirates of the sixteen-nineties. This
is hardly surprising.

There is no mystery about the sources of Exquemelin's
information. He was a buccaneer himself, and sailed under
Morgan. He did not like buccaneering, and he hated Morgan.
Johnson, on the other hand, probably was not a pirate, but he
knew some pirates and used their stories. He also made use of
reports of trials and other similar publications, and almost
certainly had access to unpublished documents as well.

All written history is selective, and it is not difficult to discover these authors' canons of selection. Both these ' classics '
were written for entertainment. They were not serious histories; they were meant to be popular. From this point of
view they were highly successful. Each ran through many
editions and impressions. For both Exquemelin and Johnson
tried, with success, to give the public what it wanted. It
would be unreasonable to expect this to coincide with what is
wanted by a twentieth-century historian in search of the truth.

It is said in Fleet Street that only bad news is news. The
worse the news, the better the ' copy '; similarly, the best-
selling pirates were the worst ones. There were scores to
choose from, and Johnson openly revealed his method of
selection in the title of his book.

Single sources of information, however authentic and accurate, are rarely satisfactory. Books written for popular enjoyment need to be treated with especial caution. Imagine, for example, the case of a historian of the future writing on crime in Britain in the twentieth century. Suppose that his only source of information was a complete file of back numbers of our most popular Sunday newspaper, which is as justly renowned for its accuracy as for its specialized brand of news. The historian would have plenty of material. He would have an embarrassment of embarrassing but true facts to work on. But his study would hardly be a balanced picture of twentieth-century crime.

Sex and sadism have probably always been the most popular subjects of entertainment, vicarious as well as actual. In our own age sex is the more fashionable, although discriminating film censorship has recently given sadism a boom. In the late seventeenth and early eighteenth centuries, on the other hand, sadism seems to have had a greater market appeal. Pornography was not ignored, but in popular esteem the naked ran a poor second to the dead. In the popular literature of the period sexual incidents were usually related in catalogue fashion, and seductions and rapes were described with almost Biblical terseness. There were none of the lingering bedroom scenes that pander-writers excel in to-day. This seems to have been due to popular taste rather than lack of imaginative writing, for the pander-writers of the period lingered with equal salacity over torture scenes, which were described in considerable physical detail. The taste in vicarious entertainment then seems to have been for physical pain and human destruction. To-day the preference seems to be for physical pleasure and human procreation. After reading Exquemelin and Johnson, I am inclined to hope it will not change again, in spite of the efforts of the Hays Committee.

Giving the public what it wanted, both Exquemelin and Johnson piled on the atrocities. It seems probable that the pirates they selected were the most atrocious they could find. The probability becomes almost a certainty when Johnson's book is compared with official letters from the Governors of British colonies in the West Indies. These letters confirm

Johnson in many particulars, but there is nothing like the same emphasis on atrocities.   There was no reason for the Governors to play down this or any other disreputable side of pirate behaviour, for most of their letters were in the form of impassioned pleas to the Council for Trade to persuade the Government to send out warships to destroy the pirates.

In popular literature the division between fiction and non-fiction was not so sharp then as it is to-day.   Books about high-waymen and pirates were not subjected to any close scrutiny or liable to lose sales as a result of literary condemnation.   There was no *Times Literary Supplement* with a corps of omniscient reviewers.   Popular writers could get away with—well, murder.

The value of the histories of Exquemelin and Johnson is further weakened by the authors' conscientious observance of the convention that a writer on criminals had to be a moralist as well as an historian.   This convention is not entirely dead to-day.   It may help to reduce crime, although that is extremely doubtful; certainly it does not make for good history.

In the seventeenth and eighteenth centuries biographers of criminals usually professed that their only object in writing about such dreadful persons was to deter others from falling into similarly evil ways.   They simply wanted to prove that crime did not pay.   This was an even more difficult task then than it is to-day, for in fact crime paid well.   Piracy especially was highly profitable and not very hazardous.   In the three peak periods, each of which lasted several years, dishonesty was much the best policy for the ordinary seaman.

Another literary convention of the period was that criminals came from the lowest class of society.   In so far as poverty caused crime this was correct; but there were no grounds for assuming that honesty went hand in hand with birth, wealth, and high office.   To observe this convention Exquemelin not only suppressed the fact (which he must have known) that Morgan always carried privateering commissions signed by the Governor of Jamaica, but he even falsified the facts about Morgan's parentage.   Johnson, in his first edition, daringly suggested that Blackbeard had the support of the Governor of North Carolina, but later retracted this with an abject apology, although the accusation was well founded. Johnson was careful not to make the same 'mistake' when he came to write on the Red Sea pirates, nearly all of whom bought commissions and pardons from one or other of the Governors of the American colonies. Neither of the two 'classics' of pirate literature gives any hint of the fact that a large number of the most notorious pirates had the blessings of colonial Governors.

It is not the fault of Exquemelin and Johnson that their works have been credited with canonical authority for the last three centuries. Writers like Andrew Lang and Lord Macaulay deserve stronger censure for their blind faith in the magic label 'contemporary.' Even worse 'crimes' against the pirates were committed by those writers who exaggerated or distorted piratical characteristics and incidents found in Exquemelin and Johnson. Historical falsification of this sort was commonest in the nineteenth century, when even a Lord High Chancellor was among the culprits. Twentieth-century writers have drawn much less on their imaginations, although those who have not troubled to go back to primary sources have perpetuated many of the earlier embellishments.

There is, I think, one other important reason for the popular vilification of the pirates. This is the common error of judging men of a past age by the moral fashions of the present.

Historical novelists often show this failing, and they cannot be blamed very much. It is much easier for them—and easier for their readers to understand—if historical characters and events are taken out of their moral context and interpreted by present-day values. Makers of historical films do this quite regularly and shamelessly; and while much unreasonable fuss may be made if the heroine of a Hollywood 'Biblical' has a 1953 hair-do, little comment is made on the more important anachronism that she has been endowed with the morality, outlook, and even habits of an emancipated woman of the twentieth century.

Pirates have suffered from this in popular histories as well as fiction. When Raymond Postgate called them 'abominable brutes' he was presumably judging them by modern British standards of brutality. He did not mention that, by the same standards, they lived in an abominably brutal age. As it is

impossible to judge, or even understand, the pirates outside
their moral context, I shall end this chapter with a brief account
of the behaviour of their law-abiding contemporaries on the
high seas and of their law-enforcing contemporaries at home.

The most important part of the Age of Piracy was also the
age of the African slave trade. The facts about this traffic
have sometimes been obscured rather than enlightened by the
propaganda of well-meaning sentimentalists, who also have
made the mistake of judging the past by their own moral
standards. My object here is not to criticize, but simply to
state a few facts about the Middle Passage. These are especially relevant to the study of piracy because many pirates were
recruited from slavers.

One common misconception about the slave trade is that the
traders had no regard for the health of the negroes on the
Middle Passage. In fact this concerned them very much, and
they made great efforts to reduce mortality; for a dead slave
was an unsaleable slave, and a sickly slave fetched a lower price
than a healthy one. Indeed, it was more in the traders'
interests to look after the slaves than to care for the crews of the
ships that carr᾽ᵊd them, which were expendable; and it is not
surprising that seamen often complained that their welfare
was cared for less that that of the ship's cargo.

Two factors made the conditions for the slaves worse than
they should have been from an economic point of view. One
was the cupidity of the traders, whose profit depended on the
number of slaves still alive at the end of each voyage. The
other was the cupidity of captains, most of whom surreptitiously
shipped additional slaves as a private investment. The result
was considerable overcrowding.

According to the Royal African Company, which held a
monopoly at the time, the mortality in 1679 was twenty-five
per cent. This was a rough average. An outbreak of infectious disease, such as smallpox, made the figure much higher
on a single voyage.

The most reliable evidence about conditions on slavers dates
only from the end of the eighteenth century, shortly before the
abolition. It is reasonable to suppose that conditions were at
least no better earlier in the century.

A convincing picture is painted by a surgeon named Alexander Falconbridge, who served on a number of slavers and wrote his testimony in a book entitled *An Account of the Slave Trade on the Coast of Africa* (London, 1788). Nearly forty thousand slaves a year were being transported at this time, and Falconbridge says that the mortality was often one-half or even two-thirds of the total cargo.

Male slaves, according to Falconbridge, were usually fastened together in pairs, with handcuffs on their wrists and irons riveted on their legs. They seem to have been packed like sardines. " They are frequently stowed so close as to admit of no other position than lying on their sides, nor will the height between decks, unless directly under the grating, allow them to stand." Except for brief daily exercise, the slaves had to lie in their own filth for the whole voyage. Every morning the dead were thrown overboard and the living hosed with seawater. Their food was usually adequate, and refusing to eat was a serious offence. Falconbridge reports having seen " coals of fire, glowing hot, put on a shovel and placed so near their lips as to scorch and burn them "—with a threat to make them swallow the hot coals if they could not take food. Falconbridge adds hearsay evidence of a captain who had molten lead poured on hunger strikers.

Another surgeon, James Arnold, giving evidence before a parliamentary commission in 1789, described a voyage under a captain named Williams, who wielded the cat tirelessly and " seemed to find a pleasant sensation in the sight of blood and the sound of their moans." On this ship the cat was used to make the slaves dance as part of the keep-fit programme. Once the slaves tried to revolt, and were brutally punished. One man who hid in the hold was dislodged by pouring down boiling fat, which removed most of his skin. Two corpses were beheaded, and " the two gory heads were successively handed to the slaves chained on the deck, and they were obliged to kiss the lips of the bloody heads. Some who refused to obey were unmercifully flogged by the captain and had the bloody part of a head rubbed against their faces." Not wanting to jettison any of his valuable cargo, Captain Williams did not execute any of the rebels, although one boy of about fifteen who got a

B

fractured thigh was condemned as unsaleable and thrown overboard alive.

Male and female slaves were kept apart, and in practice the
relations of the crew with female slaves were at the discretion
of the captain.   Sexual intercourse was often allowed, for it was
an amenity that was much appreciated by the crew and cost the
captain nothing.   According to Falconbridge, ordinary seamen
were usually allowed intercourse if consent was given, while for
officers consent was unnecessary.   According to Arnold, Captain Williams reserved the youngest and prettiest girls for his
own use, and if they refused he had them flogged into submission.

While it usually paid captains to keep the slaves alive, there
were exceptions to this.   In 1783 the ship *Zong* carried about
four hundred and forty slaves, of whom sixty died and many
more became very ill.   The captain had one hundred and thirty-
two of the sick men thrown overboard, on the grounds that " if
the slaves died a natural death, it would be the loss of the
owners of the ship; but if they were thrown alive into the sea,
it would be the loss of the underwriters."   After the voyage the
underwriters refused to pay, so the owners took them to court.
The case for the owners was that the insurer was liable in a case
of " jetsam or jetson, i.e. a plea of necessity to cast overboard
some part of a cargo to save the rest."   The captain's excuse
was that there was not enough drinking-water to go round.
This was probably untrue, but it could not be disproved, and
the court ordered the underwriters to pay.

It is sometimes said that until Wilberforce roused the public
conscience the morality of slave-trading was not questioned.
This is incorrect.   The Quakers—who in matters of humanity
seem usually to be about a hundred years in advance of other
religious bodies—condemned the slave trade as early as 1727,
and in 1761 excluded from their ranks all who participated in it.
George Fox had denounced the trade as early as 1671.   And in
1734 Captain Snelgrave, who had commanded several slavers,
published a book in defence of the slave trade.

It is ironical that slave-dealing, which is to-day statutory
piracy, was in the Age of Piracy virtually a royal prerogative.
The trade was a monopoly vested in a company founded by

the Duke of York, whose principal shareholders were members of the royal family, and whose president at one period was King George I.

Sadists are not usually fussy about their victims, and under men like Captain Williams the crews of slavers had as bad a time as the slaves. Arnold says that Williams flogged his men until they were " a gory mass of raw flesh." Falconbridge reports a case of a captain with a peculiar sense of humour who used to force his men to swallow cockroaches alive. If a man revolted, he was flogged and his wounds were rubbed with beef-brine. Falconbridge tells also of an elderly sailor who complained about the water ration. An officer knocked out his front teeth and had an iron pump-bolt fixed in his mouth so that he had to swallow his blood. William Richardson, a mariner who wrote a diary that is reliable as far as it can be checked, served on a slaver whose captain " would flog a man as soon as look at him." Richardson says this captain " flogged a good seaman for only losing an oar out of the boat, and the poor fellow soon after died."

Conditions were little better on other merchant ships or in the Royal Navy. Captains had powers of life and death, and used them. Floggings were brutal. For example, in 1704 Captain Staines of the *Rochester* inflicted six hundred lashes on one of his crew, using a tarred rope one inch in diameter. A still more brutal punishment was keelhauling, or dragging a man right under the keel of the ship so that he was lacerated by the points of encrusted shells. Other punishments included ducking from the main yardarm and towing in a rope astern. The punishment for drawing a weapon in a quarrel or mutiny was the loss of the right hand. A man caught blaspheming or swearing was forced to hold a marline-spike in his mouth until his tongue was bloody. The punishment for using obscene language was the same, the offender's tongue sometimes being scrubbed with sand and canvas.

These punishments were legal. As John Masefield has pointed out, " on the whole they were no more cruel than the punishments usually inflicted ashore. Indeed, if anything, they were rather more merciful." There is much evidence to support this view.

Throughout the Age of Piracy the standard punishment for felony was execution. All hangings were carried out in public. The favourite place in London was Tyburn, almost on the present site of Marble Arch.

Death by hanging was not instantaneous. The drop was not long enough to break the neck of the condemned man, so that for some time after he had been hanged he entertained the crowd by performing a convulsive dance in mid-air. Relatives were allowed to pull the man's legs to hasten his release from pain. In fact this labour was unnecessary, for the man lost consciousness almost as soon as he was hanged, and pulling his legs did not make his death any quicker. This was not generally realized at the time, and it was common for a condemned man to tip his executioner beforehand on the understanding that he would make it quick.

Towards the end of the eighteenth century the Government decided to abolish " Tyburn Fair," as it was called. The decision was unpopular—and therefore, by modern standards, undemocratic. It was against the will not only of the majority of the people, but also of men of culture like Dr. Johnson. " They object that the old method drew together a number of spectators," he said. " Sir, executions are intended to draw spectators. If they do not draw spectators, they don't answer their purpose. The old method was most satisfactory to all parties: the public was gratified by a procession; the criminal was supported by it. Why is all this to be swept away? "

It was not only the procession that gratified the public. Most spectators took up positions at Tyburn itself, where they could see the actual execution. Grand-stands were erected, and seats in these and at windows of overlooking houses were sold in advance. Despite the much smaller population, the crowds were greater than at Cup Finals to-day. The record attendance was estimated at two hundred thousand. Women were just as enthusiastic as men, and took their children with them, perhaps for fear that they might get up to mischief if left alone. Nor did these people attend merely to reflect on the sins of the wicked and to fortify themselves against temptation. They went to enjoy themselves. Samuel Richardson, who attended Tyburn in 1741, found that " the face of everyone spoke a kind of mirth, as if the spectacle they had beheld had afforded pleasure instead of pain."

It would be agreeable to think that we have become so much more civilized that a public execution to-day would not draw a crowd at all. But it is difficult to believe this in an age when people queue up to catch a glimpse of a murderer, and when the bald official announcement posted outside the prison gates after an execution draws quite a throng of gapers. A few years ago one of our Archbishops, in supporting the retention of the death penalty, said he thought that public opinion was against abolition. I am sure he was right.

It was in 1783 that the Government flouted public opinion and abolished Tyburn Fair. This meant the end of the processions, but not of public executions. These continued outside Newgate, and were witnessed by as many people as could find room. Crowds began to assemble on the evening before, and amused themselves during the night by drinking, dancing, and fornicating in the streets. The privileged classes bought window-seats for £10, and it was their custom to watch the show over a champagne breakfast.

In 1788 a new gallows was introduced, which robbed the spectacle of some of its attractions. The use of a falling trap-door caused the prisoner to drop far enough to break his neck, and the convulsive dances went out of the programme. But the crowds still found the entertainment worth watching. In 1807 a crowd estimated at forty thousand went to see two men and a woman hanged, and twenty-eight spectators were killed in the crush.

Public executions continued in England until 1868.

During the Age of Piracy persons convicted of treason were hanged, drawn, and quartered. The condemned man was dragged on a sledge to Tyburn, and hanged in the normal way, " but not till he was dead." To make sure that he did not die before his time he was usually cut down after only a few minutes' suspension. The executioner then laid him on a stone block or table, cut off his penis and testicles, ripped open his belly, and pulled out his entrails, which had to be burnt " before his eyes." The law insisted that " while yet alive he be disembowelled." This was often a messy business, for unless the executioner was quick the prisoner recovered consciousness during the operation and resisted as well as he could. Finally the man's body was cut or torn into quarters, which were displayed in various public places.

It is hardly necessary to add that executions of traitors drew the biggest crowds. Perhaps the most famous display of this kind was during the week following the conviction of the regicides in 1660. The celebrations were held at Charing Cross, and graced with the presence of His Majesty Charles II.

Treason included forgery and coining and the murder of a master by his servant. During the eighteenth century some of the more gruesome details of this punishment were omitted, but it was not until 1814 that disembowelling was abolished and the penalty was reduced to hanging till death supervened.

Female traitors were not subjected to this form of punishment, as, according to the official explanation, " the decency due to their sex forbids the exposing and publicly mangling their bodies." They were therefore burnt alive. Sometimes— but not always—they were strangled before the flames reached them. Female treason included the murder of a husband. (It was not treasonable for a man to kill his wife.) The last case of a woman being burnt alive for coining was in 1789.

The punishment for refusing to plead in court was " pressing." A typical sentence (dated 1657) read as follows :

" You shall go to the place from whence you came, and there being stripped naked and laid flat upon your back on the floor, with a napkin about your middle to hide your privy members, and a cloth on your face, then the Press is to be laid upon you, with as much weight as, or rather more than, you can bear. You are to have three morsels of barley-bread in twenty-four hours; a draught of water from the next puddle near the gaol, but not running water. The second day two morsels and the same water, with an increase of weight, and so to the third day until you expire."

This punishment was not abolished until 1772, although rom 1714 it was more generally replaced by screwing the thumbs with whipcord in open court. A case of pressing occurred in 1726.

Although all felonies were capital offences, minor thieves who could prove their literacy were entitled to "benefit of the clergy" and got off with a branding. The condemned man was branded with a large "T" (thief) with a red-hot iron " in the most visible part of the left cheek, next the nose." This ancient 'privilege' was not abolished until 1829.

A milder punishment (for misdemeanour) was the pillory. This was a frame erected in a public place with holes for the head and arms. The prisoner was placed inside, and his ears were nailed so that he could not move his head. There he was exposed to public ridicule and bombardment. There were many cases of death, the last in 1756 (caused by a stone). Loss of sight was common. This punishment was not abolished until 1837.

Public whippings could be ordered by a Justice of the Peace in cases of vagrancy and begging, and by any clergyman for offences against public decorum. The insane were given therapeutic whippings to bring them to their senses. Men, women, and children were treated alike. They were stripped from the waist up, and tied to the whipping-post or made to run through the streets at the cart's tail. The law stated that they should be "whipped until the body be bloody."

One of the most famous public floggings was that of Titus Oates. After being twice pilloried he was whipped from Aldgate to Newgate, and then, two days later, from Newgate to Tyburn. According to a contemporary, "He received upwards of two thousand lashes. Such a thing was never inflicted by any Jew, Turk, or heathen. Had they hanged him they would have been more merciful; had they flayed him alive it is a question whether it would have been so much torture."

The public whipping of females was stopped in 1817. For men it continued until 1850.

Whereas most of the atrocity stories of the pirates are apocryphal, the above catalogue of legal severities is taken from authentic records. The examples could be multiplied; but perhaps those given will suffice to indicate the way in which the law was administered in England during the Age of Piracy.

It is in this context that the alleged atrocities of pirates and other outlaws should be considered.

CHAPTER TWO

Big Business

ENGLISH piracy dates from the beginning of English maritime history. It flourished in the Middle Ages, survived Henry VIII's creation of a Royal Navy, and increased as that Navy was allowed to deteriorate under Edward VI and Mary. When Elizabeth I came to the throne it was, as G. M. Trevelyan has said, " so general as to be scarcely disreputable."

Two things favoured the growth of English piracy in the sixteenth century. One was international politics. The other was privateering.

Privateering was a close relation of piracy. It would greatly simplify matters for the historian if a clean division could be made between the two, for both continued until the nineteenth century. Privateers were used in the Napoleonic Wars, although Nelson wanted them abolished and anticipated later judgments by calling them little better than pirates. It is very difficult to distinguish clearly between the two occupations, and impossible to give a short definition of either.

According to the *Concise Oxford Dictionary*, a privateer was an " armed vessel owned and officered by private persons holding commission from government (letters of marque) and authorized to use it against hostile nation, especially in capture of merchant shipping." This was the accepted definition in 1856, when privateering was outlawed by most of the civilized nations under the Declaration of Paris. In the sixteenth century the word had quite a different meaning.

English privateering dates back at least to the thirteenth century. What were called " commissions of reprisals " were granted by Edward I to owners of merchant ships that had been illegally plundered. These commissions gave the owners wide powers of redress. If, for example, an English ship was plundered by a French ship, the English owner could obtain a licence to recover his losses by plundering any French merchantmen he could take. These commissions were issued in peacetime as well as in war. Thus privateering originally was nothing more than legalized piracy.

Later privateers were simply private men of war, fitted out by gentlemen adventurers who obtained letters of marque authorizing them to plunder all shipping belonging to the King's enemies. They were wartime auxiliaries to the Royal Navy. However, even in the seventeenth century privateers were still sometimes commissioned in time of peace.

Privateers cost the Crown nothing, and were even a source of revenue. Costs were borne out of the plunder, and the King took a proportion of the profits. The crew were not paid any wages, but each man had a share of the loot. Their duties were the same as on pirate ships, and, in fact, privateers were manned mainly by seamen with piratical experience. As Captain Johnson said, " War is not the harvest season of pirates ; those who are naturally of a rambling turn of mind then find employment in privateering."

At the beginning of the sixteenth century the English Channel was infested with French as well as English pirates. The merchant shipping of both countries suffered, and Henry VIII and Louis XII made a treaty for the purpose of suppressing the Channel pirates. For his part, Henry signed the first Act of Piracy, and created a new type of official, called the Vice-Admiral of the Coast, to enforce it. It was not enforced very strictly, and English and French pirates carried on until the outbreak of the next war between the two countries, when they either joined their respective Navies or, more commonly, served on privateers. When the war ended little attempt was made on either side of the Channel to stop them from going back to their old ways. They were too valuable a naval reserve to be destroyed. The deterioration of the Tudor Navy removed the only possible means of destroying them.

In the reigns of Edward VI and Mary a few attempts were made to control piracy. For example, in April 1547 the Lord High Admiral, Lord Seymour, led an expedition against a pirate named Thomessin, who had seized the Scilly Isles and was using them as a base for his attacks on the shipping of all nations. The expedition was successful from Lord Seymour's point of view, as he succeeded in coming to an understanding with Thomessin whereby the two men shared control of the islands and of the spoils. Lord Seymour continued to devote some of his time to piracy until he was executed for treason in 1549.

In the second half of the sixteenth century English piracy took on a new political significance. Edward VI was succeeded by Queen Mary; Protestants were persecuted and burnt at the stake; and England was in danger of losing her independence to Catholic Spain. At the same time Spanish ships, sailing to and from the Netherlands, were the favourite prey of the Channel pirates.

It would be false to suggest that the pirates acted from motives of high idealism. Plunder was what they wanted, and Spanish shipping was the most profitable prey. But piracy against Spain was endowed with moral sanctions, and was supported by many honourable and honest men of good family and influence, especially in the west country. To them piracy was more than respectable. It was as much a positive protest as Wyatt's rebellion—and a good deal more effective. In the minds of many Englishmen religion and patriotism were almost synonymous, and both found expression in the irregular sea-war waged by the pirates against Spanish ships.

Spain then was regarded by Mary's opponents much as our own generation regarded Nazi Germany. Spain preached a hateful ideology and tried to impose it by force. The Spanish Army, second to none, threatened to dominate the continent of Europe, and only the Channel saved England from the fate of the Netherlands. As Mary allowed the Navy to fall into decay, England's only defence seemed to be in her pirates.

The result of this growing feeling was that the pirates received exceptional support from such Protestants as were able to retain their influence. At the same time young men of good families fitted out ships and personally threw in their lot with the pirates. Other men of good family expressed their idealism more soberly, meeting the needs of their pockets as well as their principles by organizing piracy from behind the lines.

The Queen was powerless to suppress it, for she lacked the strong Navy that was needed for effective policing of the Channel.

This was the position when Elizabeth I came to the throne, and England's policy changed towards both Rome and Spain. Nothing changed for the pirates, except that their irregular sea-war received some measure of covert official support.

From the beginning of the reign of Elizabeth the Spanish Ambassador in London spent much of his diplomatic time in lodging protests against the English pirates. The Queen professed sympathy and promised to try to suppress them. She even made some half-hearted attempts to do so, but was never in much danger of succeeding. She had inherited a weakened Navy, which was quite inadequate to deal with the swarms of pirate ships in the Channel (their number was estimated at four hundred in 1562); besides, the trade was already in the hands of big business.

Elizabethan piracy was controlled by a remarkable network of big syndicates, financed and directed by lords lieutenants and sheriffs and high naval officers and Government officials. Its records are filled with the names of famous and distinguished men. Sir Richard Grenville, William Hawkins, and many other eminent Elizabethans appeared before the Privy Council on charges of piracy. They were all acquitted.

The pirate magnates did not normally take a personal part in operations. They put up the money, provided the ships and provisions, and arranged port facilities by bribing local officials, from the Vice-Admiral downwards. Plymouth, Southampton, and many smaller ports were controlled by one or other of the big syndicates.

The pirates thus had nothing to do except take the prizes and bring them into port. The syndicates acted as receivers and arranged for the disposal of the plunder. They also took the main share of the profits, the usual arrangement being four-fifths for the syndicate and one-fifth for the captain and his crew. Certainly these earnings were less spectacular than those of the free-lance pirates, but the men had regular work, no capital outlay or worries over the sales side of the business, and almost complete security from the law. The syndicates

even arranged for their accommodation in lodging-houses
when in port.   One pirate captain normally stayed with the
local Sergeant of the Admiralty.

The biggest of the combines was controlled by Sir John
Killigrew, a relative of Lord Burleigh, the Queen's first minister.
Sir John was Vice-Admiral of Cornwall.   He inherited the
syndicate from his father and his uncle, who had built it up
into a flourishing concern.   Killigrew's mother, who was the
daughter of a famous Suffolk ' gentleman pirate,' continued to
take an active part in operations.   Another relative, Sir John
Wogan, Vice-Admiral of South Wales, handled the Welsh
branch, while the Irish branch was managed by Sir Thomas
Norris, Deputy President of Munster.

The headquarters was at Falmouth, the family seat of the
Killigrews.   Their house of Arwennack was connected with
the harbour by a secret passage.   The only other building near
was Pendennis Castle.   This was armed with a hundred
cannon, and in the wrong hands it would have been a serious
threat to the pirates.   Fortunately there was no danger of this,
as Sir John was hereditary Royal Governor of the castle.

There does not appear to have been any pirate promoters'
union, but it seems that the big syndicates had a definite
understanding among themselves about not encroaching on
one another's preserves.   Co-operation of this sort was easy and
logical, for whoever controlled the port controlled the area.

For several years the pirates of Cornwall and Devon, encouraged by the gentry, enjoyed almost complete immunity.
Nor did they have to confine their attentions to foreign shipping.
Although they attacked mostly Spanish ships sailing to and
from the Netherlands, they also plundered English coastal traffic
and English fishing-vessels returning from Newfoundland.
Few pirates were captured, and those that were generally
either escaped from prison or were acquitted when they stood
trial.   Most prison governors and warders were in the pay of
the syndicates, and local juries were easily bribed.

There were several independent gentlemen pirates who
worked outside the big combines.   One of these, Sir William
Godolphin, followed Lord Seymour's example by making himself uncrowned pirate king of the Scilly Isles.   Another was

Sir Thomas Stukely, a cousin of John Hawkins. The Queen gave Stukely a licence to explore and colonize in Florida; but when he was at sea he decided, in his own words, " to make the sea my Florida." He went to Ireland, which had some of the best pirate bases at the time. For two years he plundered French, Spanish, and Portuguese shipping, and the English Ambassador in Madrid confessed that Stukely's exploits made him " hang my head for shame."

Another gentleman pirate was Thomas Cobham, son of Lord Cobham, Lord Warden of the Cinque Ports. He is said to have been a ruthless captain. The story goes that on one occasion, after taking a ship in the Bay of Biscay, he had all the prisoners, including non-combatants, sewn up in sail-cloth and thrown overboard. Eventually Cobham was outlawed, caught, tried, and convicted. The Spanish Ambassador, da Silva, who was being criticized by his superiors for his failure to persuade the Queen to act, was able to write to his King with the news that Cobham had been " condemned to be taken to the Tower, to be stripped naked to the skin, and then to be placed with his shoulders resting on a sharp stone, his legs and arms extended, and on his stomach a gun, too heavy for him to bear, yet not large enough immediately to crush him. There he is to be left till he dies. They will give him a few grains of corn to eat, and to drink the foullest water in the Tower." But Cobham never received this or any other punishment.

In 1564 Queen Elizabeth seems to have made her first serious attempt to stop the pirates. Unwilling to spend any money herself, she commissioned a private enterprise under the command of a Devonian, Sir Peter Carew, who was himself an experienced pirate. " Forasmuch as that the coast of Devonshire and Cornwall is by report much haunted with pirates and rovers," she wrote, Carew was " to cause one or two apt vessels to be made ready with all speed in some ports thereabout." The crews were to take " their benefit of the spoil and be provided only by us of victuals."

The expedition was a failure. Carew could not find any pirates off Cornwall and Devon, so to try to get some spoil for he crew he sailed to the Irish Sea. Here he found Stukely, and a brief engagement followed.   Carew got the worst of it and withdrew.

Contemporary with the big west-country combines was another large piratical confederation which operated farther east.   It was less aristocratic, less English, and, on paper, less illegal.   It was called the " Beggars of the Sea," and was founded by Dutch Protestants who had escaped from Holland and formed themselves into a resistance group.   They swore to continue the fight against Spain wherever and however they could, and William of Orange issued them with letters of marque against all Catholic shipping.   Their ranks were swelled by French Huguenots with similar authorizations from the Prince de Condé.   English seamen joined this Protestant confederation, and the Earl of Warwick countersigned some of the commissions issued by the Prince de Condé.   English Channel ports were used as bases, and for three years the " Beggars " enjoyed the sympathy and support of the English people and were secretly aided by Elizabeth.

I have described the " Beggars of the Sea " as a piratical confederation.   Technically they might be called privateers; but it seems to me unreasonable that an English seaman plundering Spanish ships at one end of the Channel, under the orders of the Vice-Admiral of Cornwall, should be called a criminal, while an English seaman plundering Spanish ships at the other end of the Channel, with the authority of a foreign monarch in exile, should be called an honest man.   This is a typical example of the difficulty of separating privateers from pirates.

The Protestant confederation came to an abrupt end when Elizabeth signed a treaty with France and agreed to withdraw her support from the Huguenots.   Dover was closed to the " Beggars," and in 1573 Sir William Holstock, Controller of the Navy, went out with two men-of-war to disperse them.

In the same year Elizabeth sent the Earl of Worcester to France with a christening present of a golden salver for the daughter of Charles IX.   On the way from Dover to Boulogne the ship was seized by pirates.   The Earl of Worcester escaped with the salver, but was robbed of £500, and about a dozen of his attendants were killed or wounded.   This incident was followed by a general round-up of pirates, and several hundreds were arrested. Only three were hanged. Many others were not brought to trial at all, but were simply pressed into the Navy.

The administration of justice in Elizabeth's reign was not gentle. Most crimes against property were capital offences, and even petty thieves were executed. But pirates were a privileged criminal class, in spite of the fact that their robberies were considerable and were always accompanied by violence and sometimes by murder. The main reason for this, and for the comparatively mild police measures taken against them, was simply that Elizabeth could not afford to destroy them. England's defence still lay in her pirates until a strong Navy could be built.

In the expectation of war with Spain, Elizabeth was strengthening her Navy. The best recruits available were the crews of pirate ships, who were good seamen with battle experience. It would have been silly to hang them when they could serve usefully on men-of-war.

When Elizabeth needed men to make up her naval establishment she ordered stronger measures to be taken to capture pirates. Thus in 1581 Lord Howard of Bindon, Vice-Admiral of Dorset, closed Lulworth to the Killigrew combine, and built a castle overlooking the harbour. The Killigrews lost some men but not their business, which was not seriously affected by this restriction. This was typical of Elizabeth's limited offensive against the pirates. She wanted enough of them caught to man her own ships, and was content to let the rest remain at sea until they were needed. Merchants who suffered from their depredations complained, but they had little chance of redress unless they had some special influence. Fortunately for the commerce of the country, the pirates still took mostly foreign prizes, especially Spanish; although even here they sometimes came up against influence. An instance of this occurred early in 1582.

It was on New Year's Day when a storm drove a Spanish-owned ship into Falmouth. The ship anchored directly opposite Arwennack, and Lady Killigrew saw it from her drawing-room window. She made inquiries and was told there was a valuable cargo on board. Sir John does not seem to have been at home at the time, so his mother took personal command of operations.

While waiting for the weather to clear, the owners, Philip de Orozo and Juan de Charis, went to Penryn and put up at the local inn. They were still there on the night of January 7, when a Killigrew boat filled with armed men put off from the shore. It was steered by Lady Killigrew herself. The pirates boarded the ship, killed the crew, and threw them overboard. Two of Lady Killigrew's servants, Kendal and Hawkins, took several bolts of Holland cloth and two barrels of pieces of eight back to Arwennack, while the other pirates took the ship with the rest of its cargo to their Irish base.

The Spanish owners immediately complained to the Commissioners of Piracy for Cornwall. The President of the Commissioners was Sir John Killigrew, and he could find no evidence to implicate any known person. But the Spaniards had some influence in London, and as a result of their complaint the Earl of Bedford, a Privy Councillor, ordered Sir Richard Grenville and Edmund Tremayne to inquire into the matter. The result of the inquiry was that Lady Killigrew, Hawkins, and Kendal were arrested, tried, and sentenced to death. Hawkins and Kendal were actually executed, but Lady Killigrew was reprieved at the last moment.

This was an exceptional case, and it did not affect the future operations of the big combines. Piracy off Devon and Cornwall continued unabated until one day in 1588, when a pirate named Fleming saw a fleet of tall ships sailing up the Channel. He immediately went to Plymouth and surrendered to the Lord High Admiral in order to report the arrival of the Spanish Armada.

The Armada was defeated by a combined fleet that included privateers and pirates as well as the Royal Navy. The belief that England's defence lay in her pirates was proved well founded, and Elizabeth had reason to be thankful that she had not tried to destroy them. Ironically, the decline of piracy in the English Channel dates from the defeat of the Armada. War with Spain took away most of the pirates' prey; and in any case seamen who could escape the press gangs had good prospects of lucrative employment in officially authorized privateers.

LORD SEYMOUR OF SUDELEY

A brother-in-law of Henry VIII. In 1547 he was appointed Lord High
Admiral, married Catherine Parr, and entered piracy. Executed in 1549.

o my most gratious
Soveraigne, that represents the ...
Kinge of Heaven, whose mercy
is aboue all his
works.

iue leaue I humblie
beseech your Grace) to mee your owne (creature
(being newly re-created and restored by your
gracious Pardon to that life which was forfeited to the Lawe)
humbly to offer with a faithfull, loyall, obedient, & a thankfull
harte to your Maties fauor, this, as some oblacon for my offences,
and a perfect signe of the true and harty acknowledgment I
make of your Highnes grace, vnto mee. I am so far from
Iustifying, my owne errors, that I can scarce affoord them
those reasonable excuses, which might be perhapps allowable
in an other man. As that I fell not purposely, but by mis
-chaunce into those Courses, being, in them, euer stroue to do
all the seruice I could to this State and the Marchaunts.
As that where there were 30 Saile of Piratts in Mamora:
I suffered none to goe in or out, but with condicon not to
disturbe any your Maties subiects; I made peace with
Sally

FROM AN EX-PIRATE TO HIS KING

The first page of the manuscript of a treatise entitled " Of the Beginnings, Practises, and Suppression of Pirates ", by Henry Mainwaring. Mainwaring was England's leading pirate from 1612 until his retirement in 1617. He was knighted in 1618 and appointed a Gentleman of the King's Bedchamber. Later he became Lieutenant of Dover Castle and M.P. for Dover.

There are few records of the activities of the combines in the last decade of the sixteenth century, but it seems that the syndicates died slowly. It is certain Killigrews' was still active in 1597, for in that year a pirate captain returning to Falmouth was surprised to find a squadron of men-of-war anchored in the harbour. This situation called for the personal intervention of Sir John, who was rowed out to the flagship and called on the senior naval officer, Captain Jonas. A hundred pounds changed hands, and the S.N.O. obligingly went ashore and left the pirates to unload their cargo.

A year later Killigrews' failed, and English Channel piracy stopped almost completely. Not for the first time and not for the last time, war had killed piracy by making it legal.

CHAPTER THREE

Her Majesty's Pirates

THE preceding chapter was, perhaps, notable mainly for its omission of reference to the most famous of the Elizabethan irregulars who fought against Spain before war broke out in 1588. Many pirate historians have left them out altogether, for Elizabethan heroes like Sir Francis Drake are not usually considered to have been pirates—at least, not in England. There's the rub.

I have mentioned that under British law, slave-trading, which used to be legal, is now statutory piracy. This is typical of the way in which the definition of piracy has changed from age to age. It has also varied in different countries at the same period in history. All this makes it immensely but fascinatingly difficult to discover who were pirates and who were not.

The easiest course for the historian is to choose his pirates subjectively on the grounds that the issue is a matter of opinion. Another way is to leave out all the ' doubtfuls ' because his book has got to be selective anyway. Both methods seem evasive; and it is surely unreasonable to leave out Drake simply on the grounds that space does not permit. If he was a pirate, then he was the greatest of them all.

There is another reason why the Elizabethan sea-dogs deserve attention here. Whether or not they were pirates themselves, they were in a sense the ancestors of modern piracy. It is impossible to understand the later pirates without considering their inheritance.

Coleridge, in his *Table Talk*, acquitted the Elizabethan sea-dogs from the charge of piracy on the grounds that " no man is a pirate unless his contemporaries agree to call him so." This looks a sensible rule, for it is based on the sound principle that a man of one age should not be judged by the legal and moral fashions of another; but it ignores the fact that laws and morals vary in place as well as time. By contemporaries Coleridge presumably meant compatriots, or he would not have spoken of their agreement.

Paul Jones was considered a pirate by his contemporaries in England, but in America he was hailed as a naval hero. Sir Francis Drake was a naval hero in England, but his Spanish contemporaries regarded him as a very bad pirate. Which of the contemporaries should we believe—the compatriots of the accused or the compatriots of his victims?

In the case of Drake the verdict of history—or rather of historians—only emphasizes the disagreement. Usually the answer depends on the nationality of the historian.

The Spanish case against Drake is straightforward. At a time when England and Spain were at peace, he attacked and plundered Spanish merchant shipping. That was piracy.

The English defence cannot be put so briefly; and when it is put it is often confused by a catalogue of Drake's undoubted virtues. He is stated to have been a man of great daring and endurance, a fine captain and a brilliant navigator; and he is credited with other qualities that are considered virtues by some, such as religious zeal and patriotism. All this can hardly be disputed, but it is irrelevant. Some full-blooded pirates could fairly claim the same qualities. The fact that Drake was a great man does not acquit him from the charge of piracy.

Another point advanced in Drake's favour is that he was remarkably humane in an age of inhumanity. He never hurt a woman or an unarmed man, and indeed in the *Golden Hind* adventure he does not seem to have slain a single Spaniard. Again, all credit to Drake, but this, too, is irrelevant. Robbing without violence is still robbery; and, as will be shown, many proven pirates were equally humane.

The real defence is that Drake was not a pirate, but a privateer. The argument now becomes semasiological.

In Drake's day, according to the usual English version, a pirate was a sea-robber who stole from all and held authority from none. He plundered ships of all nations indiscriminately. He sailed under no national flag himself, and was, indeed, outside the law of his own nation. A privateer, on the other hand, sailed under a national flag and only seized ships of an enemy nation. Drake fulfilled these conditions, and was therefore not a pirate, but a privateer.

As I have tried to show, to divide pirates and privateers in this fashion involves a great deal of over-simplification. Moreover, it is easy for the Spanish to pick holes in the argument. It can be pointed out that Drake had no right to regard Spanish ships as hostile, because Spain and England were not at war; and that Drake sailed without letters of marque or any credentials at all, but was simply an uncommissioned private adventurer.

These facts are indisputable, but they need qualification. I have already mentioned that a declaration of war was not a prerequisite of a privateering expedition, and when Drake sailed, Spain had committed many hostile acts against English shipping which earned reprisals. There was already what we would now call a ' cold ' war between the two countries. It was not very cold—wars cannot really be classified like watertaps—and probably the old-fashioned description of undeclared war is more suitable.

The main scene of the struggle was in the approaches to the Spanish Main. In 1494 Spain and Portugal had agreed to divide the undiscovered world between themselves, and a line had been drawn down the map to demarcate their respective preserves. The Pope had blessed the agreement. England, not yet a great seafaring nation, was excluded; and as she had not been consulted when the agreement was drawn up, and as, in Elizabeth's reign, she no longer recognized the authority of the Pope, England had every right to dispute it. Hitherto it had been generally understood among the nations that possession of territory involved physical occupation. There was certainly no precedent for the claim to sovereignty over lands that had not even been discovered.

The whole of the New World came within the Spanish sphere of influence, and Philip of Spain made it clear that he meant it to remain there. Foreigners were not only denied the right to seek colonies for themselves; they were not even allowed to trade with the New World. All trespassers were prosecuted. If they were Protestants, justice was dispensed by the Inquisition. Every English ship that tried to trade with the West Indies or America was liable to be seized; every English sailor on board was in danger of torture and death. England was not going to get a place in the American sun if Spain could prevent it.

John Hawkins tried to get peaceful co-operation with the Spanish, and had his answer at San Juan de Ulua. Drake was with him then, and if a personal justification for reprisals was needed he had his own score to pay off.

It is true that Drake did not sail under letters of marque when he plundered the *Cacafuego*; but he sailed under the English flag, and when he returned home the Queen of England knighted him for his exploits and accepted the gift of jewels that she knew to be stolen and wore them in her crown. She had not sent him, but she rewarded him for having gone. It is possible that she had, as a private individual, secretly taken shares in the expedition. It is certain that the next time Drake sailed he carried the Queen's commission authorizing him to try to repeat his plundering exploits, although England and Spain were still technically at peace.

There remains one further Spanish objection to the argument that Drake was not a pirate. It is simply that the distinction between pirate and privateer was an English one, and did not exist under Spanish law or custom. There was no such thing as a Spanish privateer, and Spain did not recognize the legality of privateering by any other nation. Therefore English privateers were simply Her Majesty's pirates.

This argument is hardly discussible. In the sixteenth century international law was even more primitive than it is to-day, and there was no International Court of Justice to adjudicate on national rights on the high seas.

It is difficult to strike a balance between the opposing points of view. Considering all the circumstances, the Spanish contention that Drake was a pirate seems reasonable; while from the English point of view it is equally reasonable to say, with J. A. Williamson, that he " was levying war in the character of a privateer and was morally not a pirate."

At the same time it is worth remembering how narrowly Drake missed being a pirate even under Coleridge's definition.

The *Golden Hind* got back to England in September 1580, and it was not until the following April that Elizabeth went to

Deptford and knighted Drake.   In the meantime his fate had been in the balance.   Elizabeth was not the only one who hesitated whether to call him hero or villain.   Although the fact is often glossed over nowadays, Drake had powerful opponents in England.   His actions were condemned on both political and moral grounds by some of Elizabeth's advisers, including Lord Burleigh.   There is much evidence to support Stow's assertion that there were many to raise a clamour against him, " terming him the master thief of the unknown world."

There is no reason to think that Elizabeth was concerned with the morals of the matter.   Drake was a political issue to her. The King of Spain, through his Ambassador in London, had demanded the return of the loot and the punishment of Drake. What Elizabeth had to decide was whether or not to risk war with Spain by defying this demand.

The overpowering argument in Drake's favour was the value of his loot.   Conservatively it was estimated at £1,500,000— enough, says Stow, to " defray the charge of seven years' wars, prevent and save the common subject from taxes, loans, privy seals, subsidies and fifteenths, and give them good advantage against a daring adversary."

Elizabeth weighed it up, and finally decided in favour of Drake (and the loot).   The decision taken, there was nothing half-hearted about the way she carried it out.   She went aboard the *Golden Hind* to give Drake his knighthood; and the Spanish Ambassador, after warning her that this might lead to war, was told " quietly, in her most natural voice, as if she were telling a common story, that if I used threats of that kind she would fling me into a dungeon."

So Drake was absolved—in the eyes of the English.   The belated authorization given by his sovereign did not make him any less of a pirate in Spanish eyes, and this point of view must be respected.   In our own times the fact that certain German Generals did nothing worse than carry out the orders of their legal Government—for which they, too, were publicly honoured by their legal Head of State—did not stop us from hanging them as criminals.

The English and Spanish will probably go on disagreeing about Drake as long as the two nations exist as independent states; but about one thing, at least, there can be no difference of opinion. Guilty or blameless, Drake was exonerated simply because he had been highly successful in his plundering and because the political wind happened to blow in his favour. If he had brought back less loot, or if Elizabeth had considered it inexpedient to offend Spain just then, Drake would probably have been executed as a pirate.

I have gone into the case of Drake at some length because it has an important bearing on the later history of piracy. Nothing shows more clearly the impossibility of drawing a sharp line between privateering and piracy—between lawful and unlawful seizure of ships and goods. In sanctioning Drake's depredations after the event Queen Elizabeth established a precedent that was remembered long afterwards.

Nearly forty years later Sir Walter Raleigh, when discussing his proposed voyage to Guiana to look for El Dorado, mentioned the possibility of raiding the Mexican Plate Fleet. Bacon protested that this would be piracy, and Raleigh replied: " Did you ever know of any that were pirates for millions? They only that work for small things are pirates." Raleigh was unlucky. His crew refused to attack the Plate Fleet, and he returned home without plunder at a time when the political wind was blowing the wrong way. He had no gold to offer to offset the King's inclination to appease the Spanish; and he lost his head.

CHAPTER FOUR

Jacobeans and Carolines

" AFTER the death of our Most Gracious Queen Elizabeth, of Blessed Memory," wrote Captain John Smith of Virginia, " our royal King James, who from his infancy had reigned in peace with all nations, had no employment for those men of war, so that those that were rich rested with what they had; and those that were poor, and had nothing but from hand to mouth, turned pirates."

Elizabeth died in 1603, and King James immediately set to work to make a lasting peace with Spain. Privateering was stopped, and all letters of marque were called in. Warships were laid up. At the same time English seamen were forbidden to take employment on foreign ships. The men who had fought and plundered the Spanish for so many years were thrown on the labour market.

It was a buyers' market. Full employment after a war is a modern phenomenon. In 1603 the ports were full of unemployed sailors, and owners of merchantmen found long queues for every berth. Wages were cut sharply, and in some cases waived altogether. There were seamen ready to sail for the food alone, bad as it was. The alternative was to starve.

Some, in desperation, trudged inland, looking for any other kind of work. They found themselves tramping in step with the disbanded Army, which had swollen the inland labour market after the conquest of Ireland. And there was little chance for a seaman to get a job in a town. Certainly he could not learn a craft, for entry was controlled by the closely guarded guild system. Once a sailor, he was told, always a sailor; go back to the sea. Closed shops were invented long before trade unions.

The seaman's last resort was to join the Navy. According to Raleigh, men " went with as great a grudging to serve in His Majesty's ships as if it were to be slaves in the galleys." But

40

after the peace with Spain even the Navy did not want them. So for many seamen there was only one alternative to unemployment, poverty, and even starvation. This was piracy.

For some of the crews of privateers this merely meant returning to their pre-war employment. For all who had served on privateers the change in occupation was very slight—much slighter than the change from privateering to service in the peacetime mercantile marine. Piracy offered a greater choice of prey, a higher share in the profits for the ordinary seaman, and a little more risk. The last factor was inconsiderable.

" The privateering stroke," complained the Rev. Cotton Mather a century later, in one of his famous " hanging sermons " to pirates in Boston, " so easily degenerates into the piratical." Captain Johnson had the same thought in mind when he described privateering as " a nursery for pirates." It has been said that war makes thieves and peace hangs them. I think it can also be said that every age gets the criminals it deserves. King James got pirates.

John Ward was a typical Jacobean pirate. He had been serving on a privateer when the Spanish War ended, and after a period of unemployment he managed to get into the Royal Navy. Pay was ten shillings a month, and conditions were very poor. Ward grumbled, and his shipmates grumbled ; and when, in Portsmouth harbour, they saw a small bark and heard rumours of great treasure on board, they stole a boat and rowed out and seized the vessel. There was no treasure on board, but they could not return now. With Ward as captain they sailed down the Channel, hoping for the best.

Off the Scilly Isles the pirates met a tall French ship of eighty tons, armed with five guns, which they managed to take by a stratagem. Boldly putting back into Plymouth, they made up their crew from unemployed seamen, and then sailed for the Mediterranean, taking two prizes on the way. At Algiers they offered to serve under the Dey, but he disliked the English and sent them away. They had better luck at Tunis, where the Dey granted them harbour facilities in return for a half-share in their plunder. Ward and his men agreed to attack all Christian shipping except English merchantmen.

About the same time a Dutch sea-captain, Simon de Danser, made a similar arrangement at Algiers, and eventually he and Ward joined forces. After only a year the King of France sent a special mission to Tunis to protest against the activities of Ward. But the English pirate's most valuable prizes were Venetian ships, and he gained enough treasure to be able to build a palace in Tunis second only in magnificence to the palace of the Dey himself. In 1611 the traveller William Lithgow reached Tunis and dined and supped with Ward several times.

Piracy based on the Barbary coast had begun with the expulsion of the Moors from Spain in 1492. At first it was simply anti-Spanish; by extension it assumed the proportions of a holy war against all Christian nations. The Barbary corsairs, or Sallee rovers, went to sea in galleys and took not only plunder but also slaves. Those who could get the money were ransomed; of the others, the men were put in the galleys and the women in the harems and brothels. The Moors committed many atrocities, but more than one Protestant who had the misfortune to experience captivity under both the Moors and the Spanish expressed a preference for Mohammedan methods.

In the sixteenth century, under the leadership of two Turkish brothers called Barbarossa (Redbeard), the Barbary corsairs terrorized the Mediterranean. A united effort could probably have suppressed them, but at this time the European Powers were struggling among themselves for control of the Mediterranean, and each sought to use the Barbary corsairs as a weapon against the others. They paid tribute for exemption and curried favour generally. There was an English consul in Algiers in Elizabeth's reign, and England and France each entered into treaties with the corsairs.

This was not unreasonable, for in fact the corsairs had powerful State backing. Tunis and Algiers were outposts of the Turkish Empire, and the younger Barbarossa was both Viceroy of Algiers and High Admiral of the Sultan's fleet. The corsairs were not breaking their own laws, but were acting under Government orders. They were what the English would have called privateers. It is absurd to label them pirates and yet

exonerate Drake, who had much less authority for his depredations with the *Golden Hind*.

Men like Ward can be branded as traitors and renegades, but
it is difficult to blame them for what they did. Encouraged
in plundering merchant shipping during the war, and reduced
to poverty afterwards, it was only natural that those who were
able should make for the Mediterranean, where they could
earn a good living by privateering under a different flag.

The main advantage of the Barbary coast to English pirates
was that it afforded them protection in harbour and immunity
on land. Pirates could usually look after themselves at sea, but
they had to have shore refuges with facilities for disposing of
their loot and cleaning and refitting their ships. Such facilities
had almost ceased to exist in England since the decline of the
west-country syndicates, and King James, in pursuit of his
policy of friendship with Spain, took steps to see that they did
not reappear.

The Moors, for their part, welcomed these hardy English
seamen, who repaid their hosts by teaching them European
methods of ship-building. It was Danser and Ward who first
showed the Moors how to build sailing vessels instead of oared
galleys. A change of this sort can only be compared with the
later change from sail to steam. Its effect was tremendous—
and very costly for England. No longer confined to the
Mediterranean, the Barbary corsairs burst out into the Atlantic,
and even sailed into the English Channel, plundering English
coastal villages and carrying off the inhabitants. They continued to ravage English shipping until the nineteenth century.

John Ward represented one class of Jacobean pirates. There
were others much higher in the social scale, comparable with
the Elizabethan gentlemen adventurers. One of the most
famous was Sir Francis Verney, a graduate of Trinity College,
Oxford. According to one story he had a nagging wife, who
drove him to sell his estates and go abroad. After wandering
about Europe, and spending his fortune, he joined a relative,
Captain Philip Gifford, who commanded a company of two
hundred English adventurers under the Pretender to the throne
of Morocco. After the Pretender's defeat Gifford and Verney

turned pirates, using Algiers as their base and plundering English shipping. Eventually Verney was taken prisoner by Sicilians, and spent two years as a galley slave. William Lithgow found him dying in a hospital in Messina in 1615. While in Algiers, Verney is accused of having " turned Turk and worn the turban in the habit of the Moors." The same charge was made against Ward and many other English seamen who settled in Tunis and Algiers. It is doubtful if this symbolized any religious conversion. Perhaps in their own country Tunisians and Algerians are criticized for wearing European clothes when in Europe.

Another famous gentleman pirate was Captain Peter Eston, or Easton, part of whose story is told by Sir Richard Whitbourne in his *Discourse and Discovery of Newfoundland* (1622). Eston was a pirate admiral rather than a captain, and in 1610 he commanded a fleet of forty ships, which held up Bristol Channel traffic at the mouth of the Avon. Soon afterwards he went to Newfoundland with ten ships to replenish his crews. At Harbour Grace he stole five ships, a hundred pieces of ordnance, and goods worth over £10,000, and enlisted five hundred English fishermen. He robbed French, Flemish, and Portuguese shipping in the vicinity, and pillaged the shore.

Whitbourne's story is that he was captured by Eston and held prisoner for eleven weeks. He claims that he pointed out to Eston the wickedness of his ways, and so impressed the pirate that he begged Whitbourne to go to England and use his influence to get him a King's pardon. Whitbourne agreed, at the same time refusing a heavy bribe for his services.

Whitbourne's story sounds a bit far-fetched, but it is a fact that shortly afterwards a royal pardon for Eston was issued. It came too late. Once away from Whitbourne's influence, Eston sailed to the Azores, intercepted and plundered one of the ships of the Spanish Plate Fleet, and took his own fleet into the Mediterranean.

The Duke of Savoy had just declared Villefranche and Nice free ports: all criminals were granted asylum, and bonded warehouses were opened for the storage of their plunder. Leghorn had been declared similarly free to pirates by the Grand Duke. Eston chose Villefranche, where he bought a palace, in which he was reputed to have kept a hoard of gold worth £2,000,000. He spent the rest of his life in luxurious retirement.

The most famous of all Jacobean pirates was Sir Henry Mainwaring, the son of an old Shropshire family. Educated at Brasenose College, Oxford, he matriculated at twelve and gained his B.A. three years later (1602). After working first as a lawyer and then as a soldier, he took to the sea, and in 1611 received a commission from the Lord High Admiral to try to capture Eston. He failed in this, but in the following year the Lord High Admiral gave him letters of marque authorizing him to plunder Spanish shipping in the West Indies. Mainwaring sailed in a small but fast ship of a hundred and sixty tons, called the *Resistance*. When nearly at Gibraltar he called the crew on deck and said that he did not think it necessary to go all the way to the West Indies to find Spanish plunder. The crew agreed, so the *Resistance* sailed to Marmora, on the Barbary coast, which Mainwaring had chosen as his base.

Mainwaring was a very successful pirate, and before long he had a fleet of about thirty captured Spanish ships. Although he had already exceeded the terms of his commission he would not allow his crew to plunder any English shipping. This was not a great sacrifice, as Spanish ships were more attractive plunder.

Mainwaring's fame spread, and the King of Spain first threatened and then offered the English pirate a high command in the Spanish service with a large bounty. Another offer came from the Dey of Tunis, who proposed an equal partnership if Mainwaring would renounce Christianity. Mainwaring refused both offers. He was a patriotic pirate.

The extent of Mainwaring's fame can be judged from the account of a pirate-chasing expedition undertaken by Sir William Monson and described in *Naval Tracts*. Monson was sent to the Irish Sea to try to catch some of the pirates who were preying on Scottish shipping. Eventually he sailed into Broadhaven, which at that time, he said, was " the well-head of all pirates." The local chief, a man named McCormac, was a notorious receiver of stolen plunder, and Monson decided to try to catch him by a stratagem. He sent some of his crew ashore and told them to say that the great Captain Mainwaring had arrived. The name worked like magic, and Monson was received with the greatest hospitality. He got all the information he could from McCormac before arresting him.

Mainwaring was no longer able to return in safety to England, so, like Eston, he recruited his crews mainly from the fishing-banks of Newfoundland. According to the Records for 1614:

" Captain Mainwaring with divers other captains arrived in Newfoundland the 4th June, having eight sails of war-like ships, one whereof they took at the bank, another upon the main of Newfoundland, from all the harbours whereof they commanded carpenters, mariners, victuals, munitions and all necessaries from the fishing fleet after this rate—of every six mariners they take one, and the one-fifth part of all their victuals: from the Portugal ships they took all their wine and other provisions, save their bread: from a French ship in Harbour Grace they took 10,000 fish; some of the company of many ships did run away unto them. They took a French ship fishing in Carbonear, and so after they had continued three months and a half in the country taking their pleasure of the fishing fleet, the 14th September 1614, they departed, having with them from the fishing fleet about 400 mariners and fishermen: many volunteers, many compelled."

Those who were " compelled " were not necessarily unwilling recruits. Seamen like to be compelled to serve on pirate ships, so that if they were caught they could use this in their defence.

Newfoundland suffered so greatly from the pirates that in 1615 a Vice-Admiralty Court was set up there with authority to try and punish pirates on the spot. This was the first Vice-Admiralty Court to be set up outside England; but it was only a temporary expedient to meet a crisis.

After this trip Mainwaring returned to Marmora and found that the Spaniards had seized the port and were firmly in possession. He let them keep it, and sailed to Villefranche, where he was joined by another aristocratic pirate, Walsingham.

Mainwaring continued to prosper at the expense of Spain, taking booty worth half a million Spanish crowns in six weeks. Spanish merchant shipping was brought to a standstill, and the King sent five warships with orders to rout out the pirates and bring back Mainwaring dead or alive. Sailing from Cadiz the squadron met Mainwaring with only three ships, but the Spanish were decisively beaten. The King of Spain then offered Mainwaring a free pardon and a salary of 20,000 ducats a year to command a Spanish squadron. Mainwaring refused.

Both the French and Spanish Ambassadors in London were complaining about Mainwaring, and at length King James sent an envoy to the Mediterranean with an offer to Mainwaring of a free pardon if he promised to give up piracy, and a threat to send a fleet strong enough to crush him if he refused. It is doubtful if the threat could have been carried out, but Mainwaring accepted the offer and sailed to Dover with two ships. In 1616 he was pardoned under the Great Seal on the grounds that he had " committed no great wrong." An amnesty was granted to all who had served under him.

Mainwaring now took up pirate-hunting. He began his new career by chasing Barbary corsairs, who were becoming increasingly daring. They sailed freely in the English Channel, and on one occasion captured the whole of the returning Newfoundland fishing fleet. Mainwaring found three of their ships in the Thames as high up as Leigh, where he boarded them and released Christian captives.

For this and other exploits Mainwaring was knighted in 1618 and was appointed a Gentleman of the King's Bedchamber. For a time he was a courtier and personal friend of the King. Tiring of this life, in 1620 he accepted the appointment of Lieutenant of Dover Castle and Deputy Warden of the Cinque Ports. A year later he was elected Member of Parliament for Dover. He was deposed from his office at Dover Castle on the grounds of " neglect of duty, attempts at fraud, keeping low company, and running into debt," but reinstated after the intercession of Prince Charles, who testified that he was " a discreet and able gentleman and worthy of some good employment." He ended his career as a Vice-Admiral.

In his spare time Mainwaring wrote a book entitled *Of the Beginnings, Practices, and Suppression of Pirates,* which he dedicated to the King. The manuscript is in the British Museum. It is a fascinating work, telling the whole story of piracy, especially in the Mediterranean, at the time when the author was active.

Mainwaring explained what made seamen turn pirates, and how many of them were driven to the trade by hunger and unemployment. He called Ireland "the nursery and storehouse of pirates," attributing this partly to the good bays and harbours and also to a "good store of English, Scottish, and Irish wenches, which resort unto them, and these are strong attractions to draw the common sort of seamen thither." Mainwaring also described other pirate haunts and the customs and tricks of the trade. He explained how they operated and gave advice on how to catch them. Respectfully, and quite seriously, Mainwaring advised the King against granting pardons to pirates. He said these acted as incentives, as pirates "do generally assure themselves of a pardon," and "to this they usually add that if they can get a thousand pounds or more, they doubt not but to find friends to get their pardons for them." Yet he advised that captured pirates should be treated with clemency, not out of kindness but because, he said, they were good seamen and could well be used as galley-slaves to patrol the English coast.

Little attempt was made to carry out the recommendations of Sir Henry Mainwaring, and in 1623 a pirate named John Nutt, a refugee from the press gang, commanded a fleet based on Torbay. He does not seem to have been molested by the authorities until the King, in need of men for the Navy, ordered Sir John Eliot, Vice-Admiral of Devon, to press seamen in his command. Nutt heard of this, warned seamen of the press, and gave employment to as many as he could use. He paid them wages and commission, which was unusual on pirate establishments at that time.

A warrant was issued for Nutt's arrest, and Eliot tried to catch him. But Nutt always had a strong armed bodyguard when he was ashore, and could not be taken. However, he was willing to come to terms, and he wrote to Eliot offering £300 for a pardon. Eliot had to go on board Nutt's ship in Torbay harbour to negotiate. After a lot of haggling he promised to obtain the pardon for £500.

Nutt duly surrendered, only to find that he had been tricked, for the pardon provided by Eliot was already out of date,

THE BUCCANEER LOLONOIS

According to his biographer, Exquemelin, "an infamous, inhuman creature". See next picture.

ATROCITY PICTURE

From Exquemelin's lurid history of the buccaneers. According to the text, Lolonois both extracted and gnawed his victim's heart ("like a ravenous wolf"), but the artist used his imagination. So, probably, did Exquemelin.

Nutt was arrested and taken to London. Fortunately he had influence with Sir George Calvert (later Lord Baltimore), the King's principal secretary, who had Eliot arrested and Nutt not only pardoned but given £100 as compensation. Nutt returned to Torbay and continued his piracies. Later another warrant was issued for his arrest, and Captain Plumleigh was sent with one royal ship and two ' whelps ' to take Nutt on the Irish coast. Plumleigh found the pirate commanding twenty-seven Barbary vessels, and was lucky to escape alive. Nutt continued his piracies for another three years.

There was no significant change in piracy when James I was succeeded by Charles I. It continued to flourish, and very few pirates were ever captured.

Privateering also flourished, in peace as well as in war. Although James I usually frowned on attacks on his Spanish friends, he had no qualms about the robbery of non-Christians. He freely connived at piratical expeditions to the Red Sea and the Persian Gulf, and took a share of the plunder from the Mogul fleets. Charles I, who succeeded his father in the year 1625, put these expeditions on a sounder basis. In 1630 he granted a commission to Captain Quail of the *Seahorse* to go to the Red Sea " to make purchase [i.e. plunder], as well as anywhere else, of any he could meet with that were not friends or allies of His Majesty." The profit from this voyage was estimated at between £20,000 and £30,000.

Four years later two more ships sailed with a royal commission empowering them to " range the seas all over and to make prize of all such treasure, merchandise, goods, and other commodities, which they shall be able to take of infidels, or of any other prince, potentate or state not in league or unity with us beyond the line equinoctial." Both ships were ordered to wear the colours appointed for the Royal Navy, and " all our other loyal subjects " were enjoined to give them any assistance they might need. This commission implied the broadest definition of privateering I have come across.

The first prize taken in this expedition was a native-owned ship from Surat sailing with a pass, or safe-conduct, issued by the East India Company at Bombay. The pretext for the seizure was that the President of the Company had omitted to sign the pass when issuing it. According to the Company's report, His Majesty's pirates persuaded the native captain and crew to tell them where their treasure was hidden by " binding their fingers together with wire and putting lighted matches between them until their fingers were burnt to the bone." This method of persuasion was successful, and much treasure was revealed.

This seizure led to native reprisals being taken against the East India Company, whose officers did not approve of the King's piracies in their waters. The Company tried to seize the offending ship, and the captain and other officers were eventually arrested. But they were never tried, and the King and the promoters made about £30,000 out of the venture. The East India Company had to pay the natives more than this in compensation, but their protests were unheeded in London.

Official and unofficial piracy in the Eastern seas continued throughout the seventeenth century, but until the last decade it was mainly spasmodic and unorganized. The East India Company, which invariably suffered reprisals from the natives and had to pay compensation, kept up a running war against pirates. The Company made a virtue of this, but its own slate was hardly clean. East Indiamen themselves were the pioneers of piracy in these waters.

I think it is worth mentioning here that piracy in Eastern waters was often characterized by behaviour that may well be described as abominable brutality. Murder and rape were common, and victims were often tortured into revealing where they had hidden their jewels. Often, atrocities of this kind were committed by pirates who had a clean record in their treatment of captives in western waters, and it is clear that different standards prevailed west and east of Suez. This apparent inconsistency of conduct was not peculiar to pirates. In 1604, for example, Edmund Scot, the Agent of the East India Company at Bantan, reported how he tried to persuade a captured Javan Admiral to supply information.

" Because of his sullenness and that it was he that fired us, I caused him to be burned under the nails of his thumbs, fingers and toes with sharp hot irons, and the nails to be torn off, and because he never blinshed at that we thought that his arms and legs had been numbed by tying, therefore we burned him in the hands, arms, shoulders, and neck. . . . Then we burned him quite through the hands and with rashpes of iron tore out the flesh and sinews. After that I caused cold screws of iron to be screwed into the bones of his arms and suddenly to be snatched out. After all that the bones of his fingers and toes to be broken with pincers. . . . Where all the extremity we could use was but in vain, I caused him to be put in irons again, where the amits or ants, which do greatly abound there, got into his wounds and tormented him worse than we had done, as we might well see by his gesture. . . ."

There seem to have been two reasons for the exceptionally brutal behaviour of Englishmen in the Eastern hemisphere. One was simply that their victims were not Christians. It has been noted that King Charles I's commission of 1634 specifically mentioned " infidels." Over half a century later the English chaplain who attended the execution of some pirates at Wapping Old Stairs reported that one of them " expressed his contrition for the horrid barbarities he had committed, though only on the bodies of heathens." Another English chaplain (the Rev. Paul Lorrain, Ordinary of Newgate), reporting the execution of Darby Mullins, one of Captain Kidd's men, said that the condemned man admitted that he had been guilty of swearing and profaning the Sabbath, for which he was very penitent, but added that " he had not known but that it was lawful to plunder ships and goods belonging to the enemies of Christianity." In 1701, an officer of the East India Company wrote in a pamphlet entitled *Piracy Destroyed* that " one of the old hardened pirates said they looked on it as little or no sin to take what they could from such heathens as the Moors or other Indians were." Other evidence confirms that in the seventeenth century offences such as robbery, torture, rape, and murder were considered much less serious when committed against heathens or Mohammedans than against Christians.

The other reason for English barbarities in the East seems to be simply that the " Moors "—a term that included Indians and Armenians as well as Arabs—had a different-coloured skin. This is probably easier for us to understand, as colour prejudice has outlived religious prejudice. Even to-day there are many

persons in the world who find it hard to believe that dark-
skinned persons are entitled to equal human rights. The
myth that civilization and character derive from hereditary
pigmentation dies hard. Rightly or wrongly, but very understandably, most of the peoples of Asia still think that we would
not have used the atomic bomb against other whiteskins, even
the Nazi barbarians.

In the Age of Piracy the whiteskins' superiority complex was
far stronger that it is to-day. The pirates themselves had been
taught to regard coloured peoples as inferior. The only
coloured persons many of them had ever seen were the African
slaves that were shipped like cattle on the Middle Passage or
flogged into submission on the West Indian plantations.
How these slaves were regarded even as late as 1783 is revealed
in the remarks of Lord Mansfield in the Court of King's Bench
in the case of the *Zong*, which was mentioned earlier. Regard-
ing the throwing overboard of the living slaves, Lord Mansfield
said: " The matter left to the jury was whether it was from
necessity, for they had no doubt (though it shocks one very
much) that the case of slaves was the same as if horses had been
thrown overboard."

There are still allegedly civilized countries to-day where the
rape of a white woman by a coloured man is regarded (by the
whites) as a more serious offence than the rape of a coloured
woman by a white man. Pirates who had, when honest seamen, been allowed to use female slaves as ship's comforts,
doubtless regarded such rape as no offence at all.

I have tried to sketch in this part of the pirates' moral
context because I shall return to piracy in Eastern waters later
in this book.

CHAPTER FIVE

Brethren of the Coast

BUCCANEERS, according to some purists, were not pirates. They were hunters of wild cattle and pigs, who cured their meat on a wooden hurdle or framework over a fire. They learned the process from the native Carib Indians, who called the hurdle a *boucan*: hence their name. The same purists admit that many buccaneers took up piracy; but going to sea meant giving up buccaneering.

By the same argument hypocrite means actor, blitz means lightning, to aggravate means to increase the gravity of, and muscle means little mouse; and it is ' wrong '—whatever that may mean—to use any of these words in a different sense. Perhaps it is better to assume that words mean what most people think they mean, not what they ' ought ' to mean or meant originally.

Etymology apart, however, it is correct to say that the majority of buccaneers were not pirates, although many of them never even saw a *boucan*. They were first organized as a kind of Resistance Movement against the Spanish. They were irregulars of the kind that are to-day called partisans or patriots by their political sympathizers and terrorists or thugs by their political opponents. Later they got regular commissions as privateers. Those who served Britain continued the work of the Elizabethan sea-dogs, and the result was the British West Indies.

The defeat of the Armada broke the sea-power of Spain, and with it went the Spanish monopoly in the New World. The Spanish clung to their closed-shop policy, but could not enforce it effectively. They kept a firm hold on Cuba, the eastern part of Hispaniola (Santo Domingo), and Puerto Rico, as well as parts of the American mainland (Spanish Main); but they could not prevent other seafaring nations either from trading with or from settling in other parts of the New World. In the early years of the seventeenth century the British, French, and Dutch all got footholds in the West Indies.

The early buccaneers had already arrived by then. At first they were mostly runaway Frenchmen—political and religious refugees and other escaping criminals. Somehow they got to the West Indies, where they went native. They had no alternative, for the Spanish did not want them. Many went to the western part of Hispaniola (Haiti), which was thinly settled but quite well stocked with wild cattle and pigs. The buccaneers kept to the hills and the woods, and remained nomads rather than settlers.

Strange and wonderful stories are told about these early buccaneers, and all sorts of reasons are given for their unwillingness to till the soil and build settlements in the conventional colonial manner. Probably the correct reason is simply that they were not conventional colonists. They were in hostile territory, and had no home Government to support them. They arrived without arms or equipment, and could only survive by keeping clear of the Spanish. They did not build new homes, simply because they lacked the means to defend them.

The buccaneers did not have to worry much about the uncivilized Indians. The Spanish had neutralized them. According to Las Casas, in twenty years the Spanish had succeeded in reducing the native population of Hispaniola from at least a million to a few thousand; but this certainly was an exaggeration.

The establishment of the first sponsored non-Spanish colonies brought new recruits to the buccaneers. They had already been joined by occasional deserters from ' interloping ' trading ships and by shipwrecked mariners who did not want to meet the Spanish; now their ranks were swollen by runaway slaves from the plantations.

White slaves, not black; although they were not called slaves. They were indentured servants, or bondsmen; but most of them had been kidnapped, and their masters bought and sold them like slaves. They fetched good prices, too. The plantations were short of labour, and the importing of " black ivory " had not yet been properly organized. Their em-

ployers, or owners, had powers of life and death over them, and
that often meant death. According to Exequemelin, who
suffered personally, floggings were brutal and numerous.
Here is his description of how a planter treated a bondsman
who ran away and was recaptured:

" No sooner had he got him, but he commanded him to be
tied to a tree; here he gave him so many lashes on his naked
back, as made his body run with an entire stream of blood;
then, to make the smart of his wounds the greater, he anointed
him with lemon-juice, mixed with salt and pepper. In this
miserable posture he left him tied to the tree for twenty-four
hours, which being past, he began his punishment again,
lashing him, as before, so cruelly, that the miserable wretch
gave up the ghost."

I shall shortly throw some doubts on Exequemelin's reliability,
especially in atrocity stories; but other accounts suggest that he
may not have been exaggerating here.

Many of the bondsmen who escaped were Englishmen from
the sugar plantations of Barbados, which was one of the
first English settlements in the West Indies. The buccaneers
were joined also by French, Dutch, Portuguese, and various
other Europeans. They became cosmopolitan and increasingly
numerous. About 1630 some of them went from Hispaniola to
the neighbouring island of Tortuga. It was uninhabited at the
time, although of course Spain claimed possession.

While the buccaneers seemed contented with a diet of meat
and fruit, and were not over-particular about clothing, they
had to trade to get arms and ammunition for their hunting.
In return they could offer hides, tallow, and dried meat;
and non-Spanish ships were glad to make the exchange.
Naturally the Spanish did not like this, and in any case they
were getting worried about the growth of the buccaneers; so
they decided to wipe them out. They took Tortuga without
much difficulty, but the buccaneers slipped back to the hills
and woods of western Hispaniola. The Spanish abandoned
Tortuga, and the buccaneers returned.

Spanish oppression continued, however. Such buccaneers
as were caught did not return alive, and the wild cattle
were slaughtered in an attempt to cut off their food supplies.

It was the start of a war that the Spanish were soon to regret.

The buccaneers took to the sea. At first they had only native canoes and home-made boats or dug-outs. In these they attacked and captured small Spanish craft—and then went after bigger prey. Before long they were in possession of Spanish ships, and used them to prey on other Spanish ships. They got a new name. The English form was freebooters. The French took this into their own language as *flibustiers*, and the English took it back as filibusters. In Spanish it meant pirates.

Realizing that their only chance was in unity, the buccaneers formed the self-styled " Confederacy of the Brethren of the Coast." They fortified Tortuga with captured Spanish arms, and defended the coast with captured Spanish ships. They gave up hunting wild cattle. They had not got the time. Besides, buccaneering was more profitable than curing meat over *boucans*.

The first buccaneer of whom any sort of record exists was Pierre le Grand, a native of Dieppe. He may not have been great, but he was certainly brave—and wise.

Pierre went to sea in a small vessel with only twenty-eight men. They were afloat for a long time without taking a prize, and their provisions had nearly given out when they sighted one of the ships of the Spanish Vice-Admiral's fleet. It was separated from the others, and they decided to try to take it.

They waited till dusk, and then sailed in. Before attacking, according to Exquemelin, they swore an oath to fight to the last. To make sure they kept it Pierre " ordered the surgeon of the boat to bore a hole in the sides of it, that their own vessel sinking under them, they might be compelled to attack more vigorously, and endeavour more hastily to board the ship."

Pistol in one hand and sword in the other, they climbed up the sides of the ship. They were in luck, for the watch was evidently asleep. Before the alarm could be raised some of them reached the great cabin, where they found the captain and other officers playing cards. Others took the gun-room, killing all who resisted. The fight was short, and the Spanish soon asked for quarter.

It was a brave, desperate deed, but not exceptional. The plunder was good, and after the share-out Pierre le Grand and some of the others decided to retire from buccaneering and sailed back to France. But the success of this exploit brought the buccaneers many new recruits. The buccaneers became such a menace to Spanish shipping that the Vice-Admiral detailed two men-of-war to try to destroy them.

Tortuga was now firmly established as a buccaneering base. Ships of the French West India Company called there regularly to trade, and the island became almost a French colony. A Governor was sent out from France. He did not pretend to exercise any authority over the buccaneers, but he was empowered to issue them with letters of marque for privateering against the Spanish. There was no official war on at the time, but irregular war was a permanent condition in the West Indies. It was a strange conflict. English and French colonists generally sank their religious and political differences, and took little heed of the shifting alliances in Europe. In the West Indies the fight was between Spain and the rest.

The French were the first to realize that the buccaneers could be a useful weapon. They had the strong double motive of revenge and gain. The Governor of Tortuga did not worry about his King's share of the loot taken, and issued letters of marque freely to buccaneers of all nationalities. The buccaneers usually accepted these commissions, which gave them some sort of backing and were useful for trading purposes; but they kept their independence, and each expedition was a private enterprise. Articles, mainly financial, were drawn up and agreed upon in advance.

The first article was simple: " No prey, no pay." The next article laid down how prize money was to be divided. Exquemelin gives a detailed account of the usual share-out, which can be expressed in tabular form. The sums are given in pieces of eight. It would be pointless to try to give an exact contemporary equivalent for this currency, as the relative prices of goods have changed so much. Very roughly a piece of eight may be considered as equivalent to a U.S. dollar at the present rate of exchange.

	Pieces of eight
To the captain, " for his ship "	Not stated; presumably dependent on the ship
Salary of the carpenter, or shipwright, " who careened, mended and rigged the vessel " .	100 to 150
Salary of the surgeon (including allowance for medical supplies)	200 to 250
Provisions and victualling (estimated) . .	200
Disability pensions:	
Loss of right arm	600 (or 6 slaves)
Loss of left arm	500 (or 5 slaves)
Loss of right leg	500 (or 5 slaves)
Loss of left leg	400 (or 4 slaves)
Loss of eye	100 (or 1 slave)
Loss of finger	100 (or 1 slave)
Balance to be divided as follows:	
Captain	5 or 6 shares
Master's mate	2 shares
Other officers	" Proportionately to their employ "
Ordinary seamen	1 share each
Boys	½ share each

According to another version, compensation for loss of both eyes was 1,000 pieces of eight (or ten slaves). " Slaves " in this context meant servants captured from Spanish ships.

No pension was awarded to dependants of men killed in action, but the ordinary shares were paid to the next of kin.

The scale of compensation for injuries differs in some respects from insurance standards to-day, which usually class limbs together. There is no need to explain why the buccaneers set such a high value on their right arms.

These articles are of some importance, because they outlived the buccaneers and, indeed, lasted throughout the age of piracy. Similar articles are quoted by Captain Johnson, and these have been enthusiastically requoted by later historians as colourful examples of eighteenth-century pirate lore. As a matter of fact they were not even invented by the seventeenth-century buccaneers. They were simply copied from the articles used on ordinary privateers.

I have been unable to discover what proportion of the buccaneers sailed with privateering commissions issued by the French Governor of Tortuga, but it hardly matters. The island was not under effective government, and the commissions were of doubtful validity; and later, when the

Governor was temporarily forbidden by his Home Government
to issue commissions, he went to the trouble of procuring
for " his " buccaneers letters of marque signed by a Portuguese
Governor.   It seems probable that the buccaneers accepted
commissions when they were offered, and sailed without them
if they were not.   If they were caught by the Spanish they were
executed whether they had commissions or not, and it is unlikely that buccaneers worried much about such legal niceties.
Articles similar to those described above were used by all
buccaneers, whether technically privateers or pirates.

Exquemelin says that the division of spoil was " very
exact."   All plunder had to be put in the common pool.   " They
take a solemn oath to each other not to conceal the least thing
they find among the prizes; and if any one is found false to
the said oath, he is immediately turned out of the society."
He was lucky if he got out alive.   In buccaneer societies felons
usually received the normal punishment prescribed by contemporary British law.

There was probably as much honour among buccaneers as
in other communities.   Exquemelin says the buccaneers were
" very civil and charitable to each other "—although he gives
some examples of disputes showing little charity or civility.
They were generous when in funds, and profligate in port.
Taverns and brothels were opened to provide them with
entertainment and relieve them of their money.   " Such of
these pirates will spend two or three thousand pieces of eight in a
night, not leaving themselves a good shirt to wear in the
morning.   I saw one of them give a common strumpet five
hundred pieces of eight to see her naked."

Exquemelin's generalizations are curiously inconsistent with
his accounts of particular incidents.   He says that the buccaneers treated their captives decently.   "As soon as these
pirates have taken a prize, they immediately set ashore the
prisoners, detaining only some few, for their own help and
service;   whom, also, they release after two or three years."
This is completely contradicted by the greater part of
Exquemelin's book, which is crammed with lurid atrocity
stories.

Exquemelin published his book on the buccaneers shortly

after the third Dutch War, and it has been suggested that his
account of Henry Morgan was influenced by national prejudice.
I doubt if there is much truth in this.   One of the first members
of his rogues' gallery was a compatriot named Roche Brasiliano,
who hated the Spanish so much that " he commanded several
to be roasted alive on wooden spits, for not showing him hog-
yards where he might steal swine."   Another villain was Jean-
David Nau, of Sables d'Olonne, better known as Lolonois.
A former slave from the sugar plantations, Lolonois won the
favour of the Governor of Tortuga, who gave him not only a
commission, but also a ship.   Before long he commanded a
fleet of eight ships, and with an army of four hundred men
sacked the Spanish towns of Maracaibo and Gibraltar on the
Spanish Main, gaining great loot.   This was the first big
combined operation in the history of the buccaneers, and in this
respect, at least, Exquemelin had reason to call Morgan " a
second Lolonois."   But the Frenchman's atrocities are
unique even in Exquemelin's lurid history.   He never took a
prisoner.   He slew brutally and indiscriminately.   He used
the rack to force victims to reveal the hiding-places of their
treasures, and pulled out their tongues if they still refused to
speak.   Once, in a rage, " he drew his cutlass, and with it cut
open the breast of one of those poor Spaniards, and pulling out
his heart began to bite and gnaw it with his teeth, like a ravenous wolf."

Andrew Lang, who seems to have believed every word that
Exquemelin wrote, came to the conclusion that the buc-
caneers were " the most hideously ruthless miscreants that ever
disgraced the earth and the sea."   Lang, of course, had the
Victorian's belief in man's moral as well as material progress.
A twentieth-century writer could not afford to be so smug.
Still, it was a big statement even for one who never knew
twentieth-century barbarism.

I think Exquemelin probably exaggerated his atrocity
stories; I think it is equally likely that he did not invent them.
But the buccaneers can only be fairly judged against their own
environment, which was not a Victorian drawing-room.   By
Victorian standards it could probably be called hideously
ruthless.

I have already tried to show the common severities of the law in England at the time of the buccaneers, and the normal treatment of seamen on both naval and merchant ships. I must add here that torture, although never recognized by English common law, was used in England as a means of extracting confessions until the Commonwealth. In Scotland it was legal and used until 1708. In France judicial torture was not abolished until 1789. In the seventeenth century torture was probably used most by the Spanish, who took the Inquisition with them to the New World. Most buccaneers were Protestants, or heretics.

Sensational writers have depicted the Spanish Inquisition as the last word in human cruelty, and the Inquisitors have been credited with diabolical ingenuity in devising new tortures. Both charges were unfounded. They probably derive from the greatest enemy of historical truth—judgment of the past by the moral fashions of the present. The Spanish Inquisition also can only be judged within its contemporary context.

At the time of the Inquisition judicial torture was a normal part of all the legal systems of Europe that had adopted Roman law. The Inquisitors, far from inventing new refinements, used only a few of the numerous methods in vogue among the secular authorities, such as the water-torture, the pulleys, and the rack. These were by no means the cruellest or the most dangerous to life, although by present-day standards they were still cruel.

The object of judicial torture was to make people talk. It was used to force evidence from witnesses and confessions from persons accused of crimes that were difficult to prove by other means.

Heresy was a very difficult crime to prove, and it was natural and logical for the Inquisition to follow the example of the secular courts and use torture.

It was equally natural and logical for the buccaneers to use torture for a similar purpose—to make their prisoners talk. They wanted them to confess where they had hidden their treasures. Some of the buccaneers had been in the hands of the Inquisition, and all knew its methods. It is not surprising that Lolonois put Spaniards on the rack. Neither the Inquisition nor the secular courts nor the buccaneers used torture as a punishment. All of them may have enjoyed inflicting it. Exquemelin seems to have enjoyed writing about it. Doubtless his readers shared his vicarious pleasure.

The history of criminal violence closely parallels the history of judicial violence. Crime has been most brutal when the law was most brutal. Each reduction in the physical severity of punishment has been followed by a corresponding reduction in the physical violence of criminals. It has been said that statistics can be used to prove anything, so perhaps it may be false to assume that corporal punishment is an incentive to crimes of violence, and that capital punishment stimulates the crime of murder.

Soldiers are usually more brutal than civilians, and the Spanish conquistadores had set an example in atrocities in the New World. Nor did they confine their barbarities to the Amerindian ' savages.' In 1604 the Venetian Ambassador in London reported that " the Spanish in the West Indies captured two English vessels, cut off the hands, feet, noses and ears of the crews and smeared them with honey and tied them to trees to be tortured by flies and other insects."

In the New World, as in the Eastern Hemisphere, punishments were harsh even by contemporary European standards, especially when the victims were non-Europeans. As late as 1700 a French priest, Père Labat, reported that in Barbados, in the event of a revolt on the plantations, " the slaves who are captured are sent to prison and condemned to be passed through a cane mill, or be burnt alive, or be put into iron cages that prevent any movement and in which they are hung up to branches of trees and left to die of hunger and despair. The English call this torture ' putting a man to dry.' " As France was at war with England when Labat published his book he may be thought prejudiced in his criticisms; but he was not criticizing. " I admit that these tortures are cruel, but one should be careful before blaming the inhabitants of an island, no matter what nationality they may be, for being frequently compelled to pass the bounds of moderation in the punishment of their slaves. For it must be remembered that the object of these punishments is to make the slaves fear and respect their masters."

Labat's book reveals him generally as pious, kindly, and humane.

So long as Britain was ruled by the Stuarts, the English buccaneers had no official help from their own country. They could choose between sailing with French commissions or without any commissions at all. Even this choice disappeared in 1654, when the Spanish reoccupied Tortuga. They held the island for a while, and then suddenly withdrew their troops. They needed them elsewhere, for the struggle for the New World was approaching a climax. The reign of the Stuarts was over in Britain, and Cromwell demanded respect for British rights in the West Indies. The Spanish Ambassador told him bluntly that to ask for liberty from the Inquisition and free sailing in the West Indies was to ask for his master's two eyes, so Cromwell sent an expedition to attack Hispaniola.

The expedition was led by Colonel Venables and Admiral Penn. Only three thousand men sailed, and the attack was a miserable failure. As a consolation prize the British took possession of a smaller island, thinly populated and weakly garrisoned. It was called Jamaica, but few people knew and fewer cared. It was hardly worth taking, and there was little hope of holding it.

Edward Long, the historian of the West Indies, wrote in 1774: " It is to the buccaneers that we owe the possession of Jamaica to this hour." This opinion is still valid. Although Cromwell had the foresight to send a naval squadron to protect the island, its main defence was in the buccaneers. The first Governor was empowered to issue privateering commissions, and the English buccaneers were welcomed into the port of Cagua. Later, as Port Royal, this became known as the " wickedest city in the world."

Both the ships of the British Navy and the buccaneers more than paid their way. Both were authorized to take prizes and sack Spanish towns on the mainland, and much plunder was brought into Jamaica. In 1659 three naval frigates under Commodore Myngs attacked a Spanish town and returned with treasure worth over a quarter of a million pounds.

The Restoration brought about a cease-fire from the naval guns. While in exile Charles II had agreed to cede Jamaica to Spain if he became king, but he broke this promise. Still, he restored the Stuart policy of friendship with Spain, much to the alarm of the colonists in Jamaica. In February 1662 the Governor had to publish a proclamation announcing the cessation of hostilities and calling on all captains at sea with his commission to return at once. The proclamation had a limited circulation, and with the connivance of the Governor the buccaneers ignored it.

A few months later a new Governor, Lord Windsor, arrived. He had instructions to secure free trade for English ships, if possible by agreement, otherwise by such means as he found necessary. He tried to negotiate with the Spanish, but was rebuffed; so he ordered an attack on Santiago, the second largest town in Cuba.

The expedition was commanded by Commodore Myngs in the frigate *Centurion*. He had a fleet of eighteen ships, mostly buccaneers, and a force of nine hundred men. The town was captured and ransacked, and with difficulty Myngs restrained his motley crew from burning it to the ground. The plunder was considerable; and, according to custom, the King received one-tenth and his brother the Duke of York, as Lord High Admiral, one-fifteenth. Britain and Spain were not at war.

Further expeditions followed, with Mings still in supreme command, while the buccaneers were under the general orders of an elderly man named Captain Edward Mansfield. Then, in August 1663, the Governor received orders from London to break off hostilities. At about the same time Myngs was told to return home with all naval ships in preparation for the coming Dutch war. Jamaica was left defenceless—in theory.

Deprived of their commissions, the buccaneers made the easy transition from privateering to piracy, and continued to bring large booty into Jamaica. The Governor encouraged them as far as he could, and pointed out to the Privy Council, " If we forbid them our ports they will go to others, to the French or Dutch, and find themselves welcome enough." As Britain was now on the verge of war with both France and Holland, while Spain was as hostile as ever, Lord Windsor was understandably worried.

VICE-ADMIRAL SIR CHRISTOPHER MYNGS

As Commodore of the Jamaica Squadron, Myngs led a combined force of warships and buccaneers in plundering raids against the Spanish while Britain and Spain were at peace. The Spanish regarded this as piracy.

SIR HENRY MORGAN

Unlike Drake, Morgan never plundered without a legal commission.

In 1664 another new Governor was appointed. He was Sir Thomas Modyford, a rich planter from Barbados, and he began in the usual way by issuing a proclamation banning all hostilities with Spain. Hostilities continued. In the following year Modyford was authorized by the Lord High Admiral to issue privateers with commissions against Holland. He sent an expedition of ten ships under Colonel Edward Morgan to seize Curaçao. The attack failed, and Morgan was killed. As the men were on the usual " No prey, no pay " terms, they refused to undertake any more such expeditions. They preferred to operate independently against the Spanish, whose ships and towns were richer and easier to take. Modyford, explaining this to the Home Government, added: " I had no money to pay them, no frigates to force them; the former they could not get from our declared enemies, nothing could they expect but blows from them, and (as they have often repeated to me) will that pay for sails or rigging? "

Britain was at war with France now, and English buccaneers received tempting offers from Bertrand d'Ogéron, the new French Governor of Tortuga. But they remained loyal, and at last Modyford got authority to commission privateers against the Spanish " as should seem most to the advantage of the King's service and the benefit of the island." In February 1666 Modyford persuaded the Jamaican council to grant to Captain Edward Mansfield and his " parcel of ships and privateers " letters of marque against Spain, this being " the only means to keep the buccaneers from being the enemies of Jamaica," and " the only means to force the Spaniards in time to a free trade." Under the Great Seal of Jamaica, Modyford thus granted a free charter and commission to the Brethren of the Coast, only reserving the usual fifteenth and tenth of the plunder for his royal masters. Britain and Spain were still not at war.

Hesitating to use his new powers too quickly, Modyford told Mansfield to begin operations by taking Curaçao. The " Admiral " sailed with six hundred men, who quickly told him they had no intention of making another attack on Curaçao. Mansfield sent a message back to Modyford explaining his men's attitude and quoting them as saying that " there was more profit with less hazard to be gotten against the Spaniard, which was their only interest." As the company included French, Dutch, Greeks, Portuguese, Amerindians, and negroes, as well as English, this self-interest was hardly surprising. Modyford was not a bit surprised. It is doubtful whether either he or Mansfield ever expected the attack on Curaçao to be made.

Having sent the message, Mansfield did not wait for further instructions, but at once sailed to Costa Rica, where his men made a ninety miles' march inland before being forced to return to their ships. Next they took the island of Santa Catalina, or Old Providence, which had a splendid harbour and was a useful base for attacks on Spanish shipping and the Main itself. With the plunder taken in Costa Rica the buccaneers returned to Jamaica, where Modyford congratulated Mansfield and sent a garrison to hold Santa Catalina. To the Lords of Trade in London he wrote: " I have as yet only reproved Mansfield for doing it without his Majesty's express orders, lest I should drive them from that allegiance which they make greater professions of now than ever. Neither could I without manifest imprudence but accept the tender of it in his Majesty's behalf."

However, Santa Catalina was soon recaptured by the Spanish, and in 1667 Mansfield died. He had been elected by the buccaneers, and it was not in Modyford's power to appoint his successor. He had to accept the buccaneers' own choice of their new " Admiral."

They chose the late Colonel Edward Morgan's nephew Harry.

CHAPTER SIX

Morgan

IN the eyes of the Spanish, who did not recognize the legality of privateering, Sir Henry Morgan was as much a pirate as Sir Francis Drake. British pirate historians have been less consistent. Many who have exonerated Drake have condemned Morgan. If pirates and privateers could be plausibly separated from each other, the judgment should be reversed. Like Drake, Morgan sailed under his nation's flag and plundered only the Spanish; unlike Drake, Morgan always carried a privateering commission.

The only discernible reason for the defamation of Morgan's character is Exquemelin's *Bucaniers of America*, on which most British versions of Morgan's career have been based. Exquemelin called Morgan a pirate, and omitted to mention his commissions from the Governor of Jamaica.

Exquemelin cannot be blamed for all the false stories about Morgan that are still being rehashed to-day. The Dutchman never said Morgan was hanged at Tyburn. That was an embellishment of the British crime-does-not-pay school of the eighteenth century. Later his place of execution was changed, but the legend that he was punished for his misdeeds persisted. In 1890 the American author Howard Pyle observed that " it seems a very fitting epilogue to the comedy of fate that Morgan should have died in the Tower of London for the very deeds for which he was knighted." Pyle was doubly wrong. Morgan was not knighted " on account of his attack upon Panama," and he was never imprisoned in the Tower, but died in his bed in Jamaica.

Henry Morgan's origins are obscure. Apparently he was the son of a Welsh farmer and small landowner, but how he got to the West Indies has never been discovered. One theory is that he was a member of the Venables expedition; another is that he ran away to sea, became a bondsman on Barbados, and escaped and joined the buccaneers at Tortuga. He may have been a pirate in his youth; at least, there is no proof that he was not. But it can be said with certainty that on all the exploits for which he has become famous he carried letters of marque issued by the Governor of Jamaica. The extent to which he may have exceeded the terms of his commissions may be judged from the facts. These are given in great detail in the Calendar of State Papers.

Morgan probably commanded a buccaneer ship in the Myngs expedition against Santiago in 1662. There is no definite evidence that he served under Mansfield, and Exquemelin's statement that Morgan was his " Vice-Admiral " in 1666 is unconfirmed. The first reliable information about him dates from 1667, when he was elected Mansfield's successor. He was then thirty-three.

In May of that year Britain signed a treaty with Spain at Madrid, under which each country guaranteed not to interfere with the other's trade. There seems to have been some difference in interpretation of the treaty, although this was not immediately apparent. As the West Indies and America were not specifically included, the Spanish assumed that they were excluded; as they were not specifically excluded, the British assumed they were included. A copy of the treaty was sent from London to Sir Thomas Modyford, with instructions to withdraw his commissions for privateering against Spain and an assurance that in future British rights in the West Indies would be properly observed. Sir Thomas received the instructions and the assurance just after he had learned that a Spanish expedition was being prepared in Cuba with the object of seizing Jamaica. He at once wrote and told the Government what he thought of the treaty, and then summoned his Council.

As there were no naval ships stationed at Jamaica, the island's only means of defence was the use of the buccaneers. As there were no funds for paying them, their services could not be retained unless they were allowed to seek plunder. Competition for their services was becoming keener. They were being ardently wooed by the French Governor of Tortuga, who lent them money without interest, declined any share in

their loot, and freely issued commissions against the Spanish—
and against the British.

The Council of Jamaica unanimously passed a resolution
authorizing the Governor to grant a special commission to
" Colonel " Henry Morgan " to draw together the English
privateers and take prisoners of the Spanish nation, whereby
you may gain information of that enemy to attack Jamaica, of
which I have frequent and strong advice."

With this commission Morgan carried out his first great raid
on the Spanish. He sailed with about seven hundred men,
English and French, and twelve ships, and planned at first to
attack Havana. However, some of his men who had been
prisoners in the town warned him that it was strongly defended,
and suggested instead an attack on Puerto del Principe. Fifty
miles inland, it was not the best place for seeking intelligence
about the reported Spanish expedition against Jamaica; but
it was the second richest town in the island, and was said to be
undefended. Morgan agreed that it was a better objective
than Havana.

The buccaneers landed on the coast and began their march
inland. The people of Puerto del Principe were warned of
their approach, and after hiding their treasures they formed a
militia and took up strategic positions outside the town.
Morgan's men avoided the ambush but had to fight bitterly for
the town, taking it house by house. When the fighting was
over some of the prisoners were tortured by the buccaneers, and
eventually admitted that seventy men in the town had recently
been taken away by the Spanish press-gang for service in the
forthcoming expedition against Jamaica. Having gained this
information, Morgan had accomplished his mission; but his
men still had to draw their pay, so they tortured more prisoners
until they revealed where they had hidden their treasures.

When the plunder was shared out it was found to be greatly
below expectations. Exquemelin, whose account of this
raid is fairly reliable, said that " it caused a general grief to see
such a small purchase, not sufficient to pay their debts at
Jamaica." Morgan pacified his men by promising them much
larger booty if they would sail to the mainland of Central
America and attack the town of Puerto Bello. At the same time

they would be able to rescue some Englishmen who were known to be confined in the dungeons there.

This was a very daring project. Puerto Bello was a large port, and all the treasure from Peru passed through it. It was defended by three forts, and said to be impregnable. Drake had found it so. Morgan's men were not enthusiastic, and said they thought an attack from the sea would have little chance of success. Morgan agreed, and said he proposed to attack from land. His plan was accepted by the English but not by the French, who left the expedition.

Reaching the coast some thirty miles from the port, the buccaneers left their ships some way out and paddled to the shore in canoes. Marching on the city, they made a surprise attack on the first fort, or castle, but had to fight hard to take it. They killed seventy-four out of the one hundred and thirty defenders. Here they found eleven English prisoners in the dungeons and released them.

The second fort, called La Gloria, was still more strongly defended, and Morgan no longer had the advantage of surprise. The battle was fierce, and according to Exquemelin the buccaneers only succeeded by using captured monks and nuns as living shields as they climbed their scaling-ladders. The third fort surrendered easily.

The buccaneers looted the town, raped the women, and tortured prisoners until they confessed where they had hidden their treasures. After they had been there for fifteen days a force of three thousand men under the President of Panama came to drive them out. Morgan and his men went to meet the relief expedition and put it to flight. After thirty-one days the buccaneers left the town, having lost eighteen men killed and thirty-two wounded out of a force of about four hundred. Their plunder was considerable.

Returning to Jamaica, Morgan wrote his account of the expedition. He said nothing about the atrocities, and made a big point of the release of the eleven Englishmen from the dungeons. In forwarding this report Sir Thomas Modyford told the Government that he had " reproved " Morgan, who, he said, was authorized only to attack Spanish shipping. He did not withdraw Morgan's commission, however, and a few months later the buccaneers prepared to set out on another expedition.

There was very little else that Sir Thomas could have done. Morgan was the popularly elected leader of the buccaneers, and enjoyed their complete confidence. It would have been useless to try to persuade the buccaneers to stay at Jamaica to defend the island against a possible Spanish attack. Sir Thomas could not have paid them wages, and if he had tried to immobilize them they would merely have gone to Tortuga. Moreover, in attacking Spanish towns they were greatly reducing the threat of invasion. The troops the Spanish could put into an attack were now needed to defend their own towns against future raids.

Morgan's next plan was to attack Cartagena, but this was altered to a raid on Maracaibo and Gibraltar, which had once been sacked by Lolonois. It was another remarkable expedition, in which a small force of buccaneers routed a much larger force of Spaniards, who fought with great bravery. Again it was Morgan's better tactics that decided the issue.

The plunder was large, and the news of the attack was received enthusiastically in Jamaica. The buccaneers had a great reception when they got back to Port Royal. They were bringing wealth to the island, and they had further reduced the danger of invasion. Wealthy planters and members of the Council were as pleased as the innkeepers and brothel-keepers. The only person who had misgivings was Sir Thomas Modyford, who had just received another letter from London. This told him that the King was displeased about the raid on Puerto Bello and repudiated it, holding Modyford to answer for it. The King does not seem to have repudiated his share of the plunder.

Expecting that the King would be still more displeased when he heard about the raid on Maracaibo and Gibraltar, Sir Thomas told the Government that he had again reproved Morgan for attacking Spanish towns when he was only supposed to privateer against shipping. Sir Thomas went farther, and temporarily withdrew Morgan's commission. Morgan had now bought plantations, and retired to the country for a while. He seems to have made some arrangement with the buccaneers,

for they did not desert to Tortuga. Most of them had enough
money to be able to live at ease in Port Royal, and those who
got rid of it too quickly went out and did some buccaneering
on their own. Now, of course, it was technically piracy, but
no one in Jamaica bothered about that. They were still the
island's only defence, and it would have been suicide to drive
them away. It was lucky for Jamaica that the buccaneers
had so much faith in Morgan that they remained 'on call'
even when privateering was suspended.

As a result of the buccaneers' raids the Spanish plan for the
invasion of Jamaica had been spoiled, and at the end of 1669
Sir Thomas was able to write to London with the news that all
was quiet and peaceful. There was a virtual truce in the
Caribbean. But it was only a breathing space, and in January
1670 the Spanish resumed their attacks on British shipping.
Sir Thomas wrote to London reporting the matter, but still
hesitated to act. Then a Spanish man-of-war attacked and
burnt some villages on the coast of Jamaica, and a fresh
invasion scare was raised. The Governor called the Council,
and, without any fresh authorization from London, Morgan,
as " Admiral and Commander-in-Chief of all the ships of war
belonging to this harbour," was ordered to " attain, seize and
destroy all the enemy's vessels that come within his reach."
This time his commission went even farther. In order to
destroy ammunition dumps and disperse Spanish troop con-
centrations he was empowered " to land in the enemy's country
as many of his men as he shall think needful." The buccaneers
were on the usual terms. " In regard as there is no pay for
the encouragement of the said fleet, they shall have all the
goods and merchandise that shall be got in the expedition, to
be divided among them according to their usual rules."

Previously Morgan had exceeded the terms of his commissions
by attacking towns instead of only shipping. His excesses had
always been condoned afterwards, and probably they had
been privately connived at in advance. Now he was being
given authority to do almost what he liked.

In giving Morgan these wide powers Modyford was deliberately flouting the wishes of the King and the orders of the
Government in London, but with the full approval of his

Council. It is not difficult to understand why. The attack by the Spanish man-of-war brought the threat of invasion closer than it had ever been, and it was realized that only prompt action could save the island. If Modyford had sought authority from London, Jamaica could have been lost before a reply was received. Moreover, he and his Council could not rely on the Government at home to look after their interests. They feared—with good reason—that the Spanish Ambassador in London might persuade the King to sacrifice the British West Indies for a general settlement with Spain. Their only safe course was to act as they thought necessary and hope for approval afterwards.

Morgan was instructed to attack Santiago, in Cuba, " or any other place belonging to the enemies where you shall be informed that magazines and stores for this war are laid up." He was told to seize such stores, and " to take, kill, and disperse the said forces." Having given these instructions, Modyford wrote and told the Government what he had done, and pleaded for the King's understanding.

Morgan was so widely trusted as a commander that when he began to prepare for the expedition French buccaneers from Tortuga and Hispaniola came to Port Royal to join him. He had already fitted out eleven ships and embarked six hundred men when a fresh despatch from London arrived. It had, of course, crossed Modyford's last report, and it could not have been more untimely. Modyford was ordered to keep the buccaneers quiet, and especially to " oblige them to forbear all hostilities at land."

On receiving these instructions Modyford sent for Morgan. Nothing is known of what was said at this interview, but afterwards Modyford wrote to the Government saying that Morgan had promised not to land on Spanish territory except for wood, water, and provisions; otherwise," unless he were assured of the enemy's embodying or laying up stores in their towns for the destruction of this island, he would not attempt any of them." Modyford could hardly have believed this in view of the size of the expedition that Morgan was preparing. He got together a fleet of thirty-six ships—eight of them French—manned by nearly two thousand men. At a council of war

on his flagship, attended by all his captains, Morgan asked a
simple question : Panama or Cartagena ?   It was decided to
attack Panama.

Exquemelin, who took part in this expedition, says that
special articles were drawn up.   Under these Morgan was to get
one per cent. of the total plunder, while each captain was
allowed eight shares for the expenses of his ship.   Surgeons
were to have an allowance of two hundred pieces of eight for
medical supplies, and carpenters were to get a bonus of one
hundred pieces of eight over their salaries.   The rates for
disability pensions were as follows :

Loss of both hands	.	.	. 1,800 pieces of eight (or 18 slaves)
Loss of both legs	.	.	. 1,500 pieces of eight (or 15 slaves)
Loss of one leg	.	.	. 600 pieces of eight (or 6 slaves)
Loss of one hand	.	.	. 600 pieces of eight (or 6 slaves)
Loss of one eye	.	.	. 100 pieces of eight (or 1 slave)

Morgan's fleet sailed in December 1670.   First they retook
the island of Old Providence, which the Spanish had held for
the last four years.   Morgan used the island as an advanced
base, and sent a force of four hundred men with three ships
to try to take the town of Chagres, on the American mainland.
This was the gateway to Panama, and was strongly defended.
It was protected by the castle of San Lorenzo on the top of a
cliff, and the garrison had been warned and reinforced.   The
Spanish opened fire on the buccaneers before they reached the
shore.   However, under a brave leader, Captain Bradley,
Morgan's force at last managed to breach the walls of the
castle, and after hard fighting they won the town.   The
Spanish lost three hundred men, including the Governor and
all the other officers.   Morgan reported that he lost thirty
men killed and seventy-six wounded.   Exquemelin estimated
the buccaneers' losses at over a hundred killed and seventy
wounded.   Captain Bradley was among the wounded and
died soon afterwards.

Meanwhile Morgan had received a letter from Modyford,
whom he had now told of his plan to take Panama.   The
Governor did not recall Morgan or try to dissuade him.

Morgan landed his main force and went up the river Chagres
in seven small sloops and thirty-six river-boats and canoes.   The

buccaneers took some light cannon as well as small arms. They reckoned that it would take six days to reach Panama, but it was not until the ninth day that they saw the Pacific. They had now had to leave their boats and march through jungle, harassed by heat, insects, and some hostile Indians. The Spanish commander of Panama, Don Juan Perez de Guzman, was warned of the attack, and mustered a force of over two thousand, including cavalry. Expecting a frontal attack, and wanting to save the town from destruction, Guzman led his army out three miles. Morgan caught him by surprise with a skilfully planned turning movement, and after a short but fierce battle the buccaneers took the town.

Panama was the richest town in Spanish America, and enormous loot was taken. Hiding-places of treasure were discovered by the usual methods of torture, and there is no reason to disbelieve Exquemelin's statement that there was much murder and rape. The Dutchman's assertion that Morgan deliberately set fire to the town is less credible, as this spoiled his prospects of holding Panama to ransom. Possibly the Spaniards started the fire, possibly it broke out by accident; certainly most of the city was burnt to the ground.

The buccaneers captured several ships in the Bay of Panama, including a vessel that was very suitable for conversion into a private man-of-war. This gave some of the men the idea of going a-pirating in the Pacific. Morgan heard of the plan and, worried about the possible loss in strength of his force, had the masts of the ship cut away, and destroyed several other vessels that might have been used for the same purpose.

At length Morgan and his men withdrew with their plunder and marched back to Chagres. Exquemelin says that Morgan swindled his men in the share-out, and that the French especially were poorly rewarded. There is other evidence that there was dissatisfaction over the smallness of the individual shares in view of the great loot taken. This may have been due to the inability of the buccaneers to understand the mathematical consequences of dividing even a large sum by two thousand; or it may be true that Morgan cheated.

At Port Royal the returning buccaneers were given a great reception. Morgan was hailed as a conqueror, and received a special vote of thanks from the Council for having saved Jamaica. This was not an exaggeration. The buccaneers had severely crippled the Spaniards' military and naval power and forced them to abandon their invasion plans.

After Morgan the most popular man in Jamaica was Sir Thomas Modyford, who had had the courage and vision to use the buccaneers to defend the island in defiance of the instructions he had got from London. But Modyford himself was now in serious trouble.

Before Morgan had sailed with the Panama expedition, a new treaty had been signed between Britain and Spain. It had been made expressly to end the buccaneering war, and it was known as the " Treaty of America." For the first time Spain had admitted British rights to trade and settle in the New World. This radical change in Spanish policy was the result of the earlier victories of Morgan's buccaneers.

A copy of the treaty did not reach Jamaica until after Morgan had sailed. It may be that Modyford could have recalled Morgan before he landed at Chagres. Possibly his previous experience had made him sceptical about Spanish treaties; certainly he knew that an order from him would have been insufficient to persuade the buccaneers to return home without drawing their pay. Either Morgan would have ignored it, or the buccaneers would have gone on without Morgan, and probably sought the protection of the French Governor of Tortuga. It seems reasonable to think that Modyford regarded the buccaneers as a better defence for Jamaica than a scrap of paper signed in Madrid. He may also have known that the destruction of Panama was unlikely to cause the Spanish to denounce the new treaty, as it removed most of their power to break it.

Unfortunately for Modyford, the British Government had just decided on a policy of appeasement towards Spain. There was the prospect of a third war with the Dutch, and the King wanted Spain to remain neutral. The " Treaty of America " was a British diplomatic victory, and from the point of view of the Government the raid on Panama was ill timed. When the news reached London, the Spanish Ambassador protested and threatened and demanded that Modyford should be punished.

The King yielded to the demand and sent out a new Governor with orders to send Modyford home under arrest.

The leading citizens of Jamaica had expected something like this, and had already sent a petition to the King asking him to keep Modyford as their Governor. The petition was signed by all the members of the Council and other Jamaican notables. The first signatory was Henry Morgan.

But Modyford had to go home, and the new Governor made it clear that he was not going to support buccaneering. Morgan retired to his plantations. Six months later he, too, was summoned to London " to answer for his offences against the King, his crown and dignity."

Morgan spent three years in London, " awaiting the King's pleasure." He was not under arrest, and was treated as something of a hero. The diarist Evelyn described the sack of Panama as " very brave," and added admiringly that " such an action had not been done since the famous Drake." Modyford, the official scapegoat, was kept in the Tower, but in complete comfort. No charges were ever brought against him, but he was evidently questioned several times. He did not try to escape blame by accusing Morgan of going beyond the terms of his commissions. The two men remained loyal friends. Modyford admitted that he had acted contrary to instructions, but argued that Jamaica would have been lost otherwise. He denied the suggestion that he had received bribes from Morgan. The Calendar of State Papers contains a curiously candid statement on this point written by Modyford's son :

" The country gave him [Sir Thomas] £1000 per annum out of an imposition on liquors, which for the five years made not above £600 per annum. The privateers gave him £20 for every commission, which in all may amount to about £400, and all their presents and his gains by them directly or indirectly never exceeded £500."

The gains of the King and his brother the Duke of York greatly exceeded this sum.

Eventually political events enabled Britain to take a firmer attitude towards Spain, and it was considered unnecessary to sacrifice Modyford and Morgan. Indeed, the King's attitude hardened so much that he decided to send them both back to Jamaica. Modyford was appointed Chief Justice of the island, Morgan was knighted and made Lieutenant-Governor. A knighthood normally went with this appointment, and it was not conferred on him in recognition of his exploits as a buccaneer.

Although Morgan was technically less of a pirate than Drake, it cannot be claimed that he was as honourable or humane. He had none of Drake's religious fervour, and his morals were shocking. More important, I think, is the fact that his men committed some barbarous atrocities. At the same time Morgan himself has probably received a good deal more censure than he deserved.

Most eighteenth-century biographies of Morgan were simply embellishments of Exquemelin, and repeated all the atrocities with a few extra details. In the nineteenth century more emphasis was laid on Morgan's private life. There is no need to reconsider this here. Like the other buccaneers, Morgan was evidently fond of wining and wenching, and his sex-life may even have been as disreputable as that of his King. Exquemelin, who surely knew his market, did not go into this in much detail, and saved his efforts for the torture scenes. His book is full of this sort of thing:

" They put him on the rack, and inhumanly disjointed his arms, then they twisted a cord about his forehead, which they wrung so hard that his eyes appeared as big as eggs, and were ready to fall out. But with these torments not obtaining any positive answer, they hung him up by the testicles, giving him many blows and stripes under that intolerable pain and posture of body. Afterwards they cut off his nose and ears, and singed his face with burning straws."

But perhaps that is enough.

Exquemelin probably exaggerated, but there is other evidence that the buccaneers tortured their prisoners. An Englishman named John Style, who served with Morgan and seems to have had no axe to grind, wrote:

" It is a common thing among the privateers, besides burning with matches and such-like slight torments, to cut a man to pieces, first some flesh, then a hand, an arm, a leg, sometimes tying a cord about his head and with a stick twisting it till his eyes shoot out, which is called a ' woolding.' "

These tortures were barbarous, but not original. ' Woolding ' was not invented by the buccaneers. It was a recognized part of the torture called *cordeles* by the Spanish. It was used both in the secular courts and by the Inquisition as a means of extorting confessions. The buccaneers used this and other tortures for a similar purpose—to make their victims confess where they had hidden their treasure. It may be said that their motives were less worthy, but it seems absurd to single them out for a charge of brutality. They copied their methods not from animals but from the Spanish Church and State.

It is difficult to discover how far Morgan was responsible for the atrocities of the buccaneers whom he led. There is no evidence that he was personally sadistic, and there is much evidence that his authority over his men was very limited. He might be called " Colonel " or " Admiral," but he had little power. He was not appointed, but elected; his command was derived from his men, who could depose him when they wished. He was certainly a popular commander, but that was only because he brought them victory and great plunder. These men, who included French as well as English, were not fighting for the defence of Jamaica; they were fighting for loot and nothing else—except, perhaps, revenge. They hated the Spanish.

When Morgan planned an expedition he had to get the consent of his men before it could be carried out. When some of them wanted to desert at Panama, the only way he could stop them was by destroying all the suitable vessels in the bay. They fought on the understanding that when the battle was over they would be free to loot. There was no means of stopping them from committing atrocities against civilians. Morgan had no military police.

I am not trying to suggest that Morgan deplored the atrocities and only allowed them because he was powerless to prevent them. It seems more likely that he did not care one way or the other. It is true that he is reported to have stopped his men from getting drunk in Panama by falsely telling them that the

Spanish had poisoned all the wine, but this was probably for reasons of military security rather than out of compassion for the inhabitants of the town. There is no evidence that he ever tried to discourage his men from cruelty. There was no reason why he should. Torture, murder, and rape were normal sequels to military action in the New World in the seventeenth century. Sir Thomas Modyford, who was by contemporary standards a humane Governor, told Morgan, in his Santiago commission, that if he had to withdraw from Spanish territory without being able to subdue the inhabitants he was to " destroy and burn all habitations, and leave it a wilderness, putting the men-slaves to the sword and making the women-slaves prisoners to be brought hither and sold for the account of your fleet and army."

There are fashions in barbarism, and neither Morgan nor his fellow buccaneers seem to have been unfashionable. They can only be condemned together with the society in which they lived. There was no Geneva Convention then, and in wartime civilians were commonly killed and maimed. Perhaps we should not be too squeamish. For all we know, future historians may be squeamish about our own civilian massacres at Hiroshima and Nagasaki.

A BUCCANEER OF HISPANIOLA

The pictures at the bottom show three typical episodes in a buccaneer's life.

CAPTAIN WILLIAM DAMPIER

Dampier described his piracies frankly in his book *A New Voyage Round the World*, published in 1697. The book was well received, and in 1698 the author was appointed commander of H.M.S. *Roebuck*.

CHAPTER SEVEN

The Last of the Buccaneers

WHEN Sir Thomas Modyford and Sir Henry Morgan returned to Jamaica the great days of the buccaneers were over. No fresh commissions had been issued to them, and they were forbidden to enter Port Royal.

This was not due to the change of Governors. Modyford's successor, Sir Thomas Lynch, was a resolute man, but all the resolution in the world would not have availed if he had been opposed by the Council and other leading citizens of Jamaica. As it happened, the same Council that had passed a vote of thanks to Morgan after Panama now gave Lynch full support in his drive against the men whom Morgan had led.

The reason was simply that the buccaneers had worked themselves out of a job. They had removed the threat of a Spanish invasion of Jamaica so completely that they were no longer needed to defend the island. It was their exploits that had at last forced Spain to admit the rights of other nations in the New World; and in spite of Panama—perhaps because of it—Spain made it clear that she was going to observe the " Treaty of America " of 1670. Jamaica was for the first time recognized as a British possession, and British merchant shipping was allowed a free passage in the Caribbean.

The principal industry of Jamaica was the cultivation of sugar, and the most influential citizens of the island were planters. They had accepted the need to use the buccaneers as a defence of their plantations, but they had not made any money out of buccaneering. Most of the wealth brought in by the buccaneers had gone into the hands of keepers of taverns and brothels in Port Royal. Indeed, the planters had suffered from a continual drain on their labour force, as bondsmen and slaves were regularly running away to join the buccaneers. Further, the planters had to export their sugar to make a profit. They welcomed the " Treaty of America " because it meant that for the first time there was to be a chance of trading-ships sailing from Jamaica without being molested and robbed. They did not want that chance to be spoiled by the buccaneers. If they were allowed to continue unchecked, the Spanish would be certain to take reprisals.

There was a further reason for the people of Jamaica to want to keep peace with Spain now, although I think there is a danger of attaching too much importance to this. It was simply that Spanish power was declining generally, and Britain's chief rival in the world was France. This is obvious to us now, and, rather belatedly, it had become obvious to the Government in London; but it could not have been so easy for the citizens of Jamaica to understand. Spain had always been the enemy in the West Indies, even when Britain was technically at war with France and Holland and at peace with Spain. Yet it seems that the Jamaican planters realized something of the new danger when they heard of French plans to seize San Domingo, the capital of the Spanish part of Hispaniola.

While it was generally agreed in Jamaica that the buccaneers should no longer be encouraged, it was clear that something would have to be done about them. If they were turned loose they would carry on plundering the Spanish as free-lances, evoking reprisals; they might also attack British shipping; and there was the added danger that they would seek the protection of the French Governor of Tortuga. They had to be disbanded somehow. So Lynch began his term of office by proclaiming a general pardon and amnesty from prosecution for all piratical offences committed up to that time, and offered a grant of thirty-five acres to every buccaneer who would come in. The pardon was rather hypocritical, and the few buccaneers who responded found that the offer of land was not so good as it seemed. The British Government, in authorizing Lynch to make this offer, had reminded him that there were still many outstanding dues of the Crown to be paid—the King's tenths and the Lord High Admiral's fifteenths of the proceeds from privateering expeditions. Morgan and his men had often shared out their plunder before returning to Port Royal, and Mody-ford had not been over-energetic in collecting these royal perquisites. Lynch had the unhappy task of trying to get the buccaneers to settle their over-due accounts.

The result was that the buccaneers mostly carried on buccaneering. Some went to French or Danish islands to get commissions as privateers, while others simply turned pirates. There is no point in trying to make any distinction between them, as the British now shared the Spanish opinion that they were all pirates. This opinion changed again when Britain and France were allies in a brief war with Holland, and some of the buccaneers received commissions from Lynch against the Dutch. But Dutch plunder was never of much value, and the buccaneers continued to prefer to attack the Spanish. If they could get commissions they accepted them; if not, they plundered without. The French made good use of them in their own war with Spain, in which Britain was neutral.

But buccaneering was now on a much smaller scale. There was no successor to Morgan, and generally each ship sailed independently. Operations were confined to the sea, and the buccaneers' difficulties increased as the Spanish took more effective measures to protect their treasure-ships.

As the Jamaican planters had feared, their own shipping suffered too. Ships carrying sugar out of the island were often seized, and there was no means of protecting them. The Governor asked for naval assistance, and on one occasion he nearly got a strong force. Britain and Spain agreed to share the task of stamping out the buccaneers—Britain to provide the men and ships, and Spain to pay the bill. King Charles II agreed to fit out five or seven frigates, all well armed, and he granted a commission to Sir Robert Holmes to lead the expedition. In the end, however, the King of Spain could not find the money, and the plan fell through.

Sir Thomas Lynch did his best. " This cursed trade," he grumbled, " has been so long followed, and there is so many of it that like weeds or hydras they spring up as fast as we can cut them down." He became more ruthless, and the people of Port Royal were soon familiar with the spectacle of British buccaneers being publicly hanged.

When Lynch returned home Morgan became acting Governor, and he was even more ruthless. He never did things by

halves. He was a rich planter now, and described the buccaneers as " a dangerous pestilence " and " ravenous vermin."
He reported to the Government: " I have put to death, imprisoned, or transported to the Spaniard for execution all
English and foreign pirates I could get within the power of this
Government." He added, rather unconvincingly: " I abhor
bloodshed and I am greatly dissatisfied that in my short
Governorate I have been so often compelled to punish criminals
with death."

In 1679 three buccaneer ships—two English and one French—
made the first big land raid since the days of Morgan. They
attacked Puerto Bello with two hundred men, held the town
for two days, and got away again without suffering any casualties. A year later a more daring adventure was planned in
Port Royal. The plan was to march across the Isthmus of
Darien to Panama, sack the town, and then go on a piratical
cruise in the Pacific, returning home via Cape Horn. The
first part of the plan meant leaving their ships off Chagres,
and for the second part the buccaneers relied on being able to
take suitable prizes in the Bay of Panama.

Several famous buccaneer captains took part in this venture,
and the company included William Dampier and several men
of good birth. The standard of education may be judged from
the fact that no fewer than five of them wrote journals of the
expedition. These have fortunately all been preserved, so this
expedition is one of the best documented as well as one of the
most remarkable in buccaneering history.

Captain John Coxon was in command of the fleet of seven
ships that sailed for Darien. Thirty men were left to guard the
ships; the remainder, numbering three hundred and thirty-
one, began their march across the isthmus. Guided by friendly
Indians, they ended their journey in native canoes and rowing-
boats. Reaching the Pacific, they took the town of Santa
Maria and strengthened their little fleet with the capture of
two small sailing craft. Then, most of them paddling or
rowing, they set off for Panama by sea.

News of their approach reached the town, and the Spanish
got ready what one of the diarists described as " five great ships
and three pretty big barks." The five great ships remained at

anchor, and their crews were put on board the three barks, which weighed anchor and bore down on the buccaneers. Over two hundred men were on board the barks. The buccaneers, meanwhile, had divided their boat fleet, and had only sixty-eight men, in canoes and rowing-boats, to face the assault. The battle began about half an hour after sunrise, and went on till just before noon. Fighting with great courage, the buccaneers won the battle and captured the ships. They then boarded the largest of the three galleons lying at anchor, and fired the other two. It was a remarkable victory. Almost equally remarkable was the subsequent goodwill between the two sides. Casualties had been heavy, but there were no atrocities. " To give our enemies their due, no men in the world ever did act more bravely than these Spaniards," wrote one of the buccaneers.

Captain Peter Harris was killed in this battle, and shortly afterwards the buccaneers lost their leader, Captain Coxon. He left the main expedition and with about seventy men marched back across the isthmus. Coxon eventually returned to Jamaica, where Morgan had issued a warrant for his arrest for his part in the Puerto Bello raid. However, instead of being hanged, Coxon was commissioned to hunt down a French pirate named Jean Hamlin.

The new commander of the buccaneers was Captain Richard Sawkins, who had greatly distinguished himself in the sea-battle. According to Basil Ringrose, who wrote the best journal of the voyage, Coxon's defection was due to his jealousy of Sawkins, " a man who was as valiant and courageous as any man could be, and the best beloved of all our company."

While waiting for the rest of the buccaneers to join the battle force, Sawkins received a message from the Governor of Panama asking " from whom we had our commission and to whom he ought to complain for the damage we had already done them." Sawkins, in reply, offered to visit the Governor " and bring our commissions on the muzzles of our guns, at which time he should read them as plain as the flame of gunpowder could make them " (Ringrose). But Sawkins did not attack the town, which was considered too strongly defended. The buccaneers cruised in the bay for a while, robbing ships coming in, until they were joined by the rest of their party, under Captain Bartholomew Sharp. Then they sailed south along the coast.

Sawkins was killed in an assault on a strongly defended town, and Sharp—" a sea-artist and valiant commander," according to Ringrose—was elected in his place. Sharp suggested going farther south, and promised that " each bold seaman should have booty worth one thousand pounds in gold and valuable goods." But Sharp was unlucky, for they found few prizes, and after a while the men became restless. The prize-money taken so far had been shared out, but some of the men had lost the whole of their shares at dice. Sharp and those who were still in pocket now wanted to sail round Cape Horn and return, taking whatever prizes they should meet; but others, especially the unsuccessful gamblers, wanted to resume cruising in the Pacific in the hope of better luck. This led to a difference of opinion, which seems to have been aggravated by some feeling against Sharp on account of his negligence over Sabbath observance. A vote was taken, and Sharp was deposed. The new commander was John Watling, after whom Columbus's first windfall in the New World is still named. The change seems to have pleased Ringrose, who wrote in his journal: " January the ninth was the first Sunday that we ever kept by command and common consent since the loss and death of our valiant commander Captain Sawkins. This generous-spirited man threw the dice overboard, finding them in use on the said day."

If Watling was more pious, he seems to have been less humane than Sharp. In preparation for a raid on Arica, in Chile, some Indians were captured and questioned. Among them was an old man whose answers sounded false. " Finding him in many lies, as we thought, concerning Arica," wrote Ringrose, " our commander ordered him to be shot to death." Sharp, who opposed the attack on Arica on strategic grounds, tried to dissuade Watling from killing the old man, and when he failed he solemnly took a vase of water and washed his hands in front of the company. " Gentlemen," he said, " I am clear of the blood of this old man; and I will warrant you a hot day for this piece of cruelty, whenever we come to fight at Arica."

As Ringrose said, this was " a true and certain prophecy."

The raid on Arica was a disastrous failure, and when Watling was killed the rest of the company begged Sharp to resume command. At first he refused, but finally agreed. The appointment was not approved unanimously, however, and before long there was another split in this very quarrelsome band of pirates. When a poll was taken it was found that Sharp's supporters were in the majority; so the dissenters, numbering forty-four, left the ship and put out in the long-boat. They reached the isthmus and marched back to the Caribbean. Among this party were William Dampier and a surgeon named Lionel Wafer, both of whom wrote accounts of their adventures. Wafer was, an outspoken critic of Sharp, whom he described as " a captain in whom we experienced neither courage nor conduct."

The main party continued their cruise, and at last took some valuable prizes. On one ship they found seven hundred pigs of a metal that they took to be tin. They let six hundred and ninety-nine go to the bottom of the sea, saving one for casting into bullets. Later they found it was not tin but silver, and that they had thrown away plunder then worth over £150,000.

Farther south the buccaneers ran into bad weather and gales, and they missed the Magellan Straits. But they managed to round Cape Horn, and finally sighted the West Indies for the first time for two years. The beauty of the scene was spoiled by the sight of a British naval frigate lying at anchor off Barbados. They sailed on to Antigua, but were refused permission to go into port. At last they found a landing-place at Nevis, where the company broke up. Captain Sharp and some of his supporters sailed to England, where they were arrested on the complaint of the Spanish Ambassador. The evidence against them was poor and they escaped hanging—although, as Sharp wrote in his own journal, they were " very near to it."

Sawkins's piety was not unique among buccaneers, and Père Labat tells an amusing story, possibly apocryphal, about a French filibuster named Daniel. Stopping at an island to take in provisions, Daniel seized some of the inhabitants and forced them to supply food and drink. Among his prisoners

was the local priest, and Daniel asked him to say Mass on board
the ship. The priest was in no position to refuse, so he sent
for his church ornaments, and an altar was erected. Captain
Daniel arranged for cannon to be fired at appropriate places
in the service, and all went well until one of the crew began
misbehaving. Daniel reprimanded him, whereupon the man
uttered a blasphemous oath. Daniel promptly drew his
pistol and shot the man through the head, swearing that he would
do the same to anyone else who showed disrespect to the Holy
Sacrifice. The man had been standing near the priest, who
was very startled; but Daniel reassured him, saying: " Do not
trouble yourself, Father. It is only a villain who has been
punished for disrespect. He will not forget his duty in future."
As Père Labat drily observed, there was little danger of that,
as the man was dead. Daniel had him thrown overboard
without a burial service, and recompensed the priest with the
gift of some goods and a negro slave.

A more curious connection between the Church and piracy
lies in the story of Lancelot Blackburne, a graduate of Christ
Church, Oxford, who is said to have sailed as a buccaneer
shortly after his ordination as a clergyman. The story rests
mainly on the word of Horace Walpole, so it cannot be taken
too seriously. However, it is certain that Blackburne went to
the West Indies in 1681 and on returning to England was paid
£20 " for secret services." He also brought back a sword.
What makes the story especially interesting is the fact that
Blackburne became Archbishop of York.

While the English buccaneers were active in the Pacific the
French continued their depredations in the Caribbean. In 1683
a new round of war started between France and Spain, and
commissions were granted freely. A large expedition was fitted
out under the joint command of three notorious filibusters—
Granmont, Laurens de Graaf, and Nicholas van Horn. The
last-named was a Dutchman, and the company of twelve
hundred that took part was made up of French, English, Dutch,
and other Europeans. They sailed in six ships to Vera Cruz,
in the Gulf of Mexico. Learning that the Spanish were
expecting two of their own ships from the Caraccas, the

buccaneers put eight hundred men on two ships, and sailed into port flying Spanish colours. The inhabitants lit a bonfire to welcome them, and the town was easily taken. The Governor was found hiding in a loft, and was ransomed for seventy thousand pieces of eight. The other spoils were large, but van Horn and de Graaf quarrelled over the division, and van Horn received a wound that turned gangrenous and caused his death.

Meanwhile another band of English buccaneers was preparing a fresh assault on the Pacific coast of South America. This time, instead of trying to cross the isthmus, the buccaneers decided to sail round Cape Horn from east to west.

Only one ship was fitted out, the *Revenge*. The elected captain, John Cook, had been on the Sawkins–Sharp expedition, and had been one of the men who had left Sharp and returned across the isthmus. Since then he had served under a Dutch captain carrying a French commission and been elected captain of a Spanish prize. He had lost this to some French buccaneers and had been marooned. Another French buccaneer, Captain Tristian, had taken him to Petit Guaves, where Cook had seized Tristian's ship and sailed away. He had taken two French prizes, and renamed one the *Revenge*. She mounted eighteen guns, and a crew of about seventy was engaged for the Pacific expedition. Among these were Dampier and Lionel Wafer. The sailing-master was Ambrose Cowley, and the quartermaster was Edward Davis.

The *Revenge* sailed in August 1683. Sailing first to the Guinea coast, the buccaneers took a Danish ship of thirty-six guns, which was much more suitable for the voyage they had planned. They transferred to the new ship, renaming her *Bachelor's Delight*, and burnt the *Revenge*. After putting the Danish crew ashore they sailed south-west, and rounded Cape Horn in February 1684. They now fell in with another English ship on a similar mission which had sailed direct from England. The commander was Captain Eaton. Joining forces, the buccaneers took three Spanish pirates, and then Cook died. Edward Davis was elected captain in his place.

After taking some more prizes, Davis and Eaton fell out over the division of the plunder and parted company. Davis cruised off Chile and Peru, taking more small prizes, and then fell in with another buccaneer, the *Cygnet*, under Captain Swan. They joined forces and sailed towards Panama. Reaching the bay, they were surprised by the approach of a large number of canoes, which they found to be carrying a party of nearly three hundred buccaneers, mostly French, who had marched across the isthmus. Their leader was a Frenchman named Gronet, and the English buccaneers gave them one of their Spanish prizes. Gronet said that another party, numbering nearly two hundred, was following across the isthmus under an English buccaneer named Townley. Davis and Swan decided to join forces with Gronet and wait for Townley as well. Davis was elected supreme commander of the combined force.

Dampier, who wrote an account of this expedition, tells that Gronet offered Davis and Swan privateering commissions signed by the French Governor of Petit Guaves. Gronet explained that for some years it had been the Governor's custom to give blank commissions to captains to take to sea with them and dispose of as they thought fit. Davis accepted the offer, for all he had, according to Dampier, was an old commission which " fell to him by inheritance at the decease of Captain Cook, who took it from Captain Tristian together with his bark." Swan declined, saying that he had " an order from the Duke of York neither to give offence to the Spaniards nor to receive an affront from them "—and since the Spaniards had killed some of his men when he was robbing them, he felt he had been sufficiently affronted and so " thought he had a lawful commission of his own to right himself."

Townley and his party arrived and joined the fleet, and the buccaneers' strength was further increased by the arrival of another French party led by a veteran who had served under both Lolonois and Morgan. The buccaneers were now nearly a thousand strong and had a fleet of ten ships. Their immediate objective was the Spanish treasure fleet from Lima.

The Spanish fleet came, and was found to be stronger than was expected. It consisted of fourteen ships, most of them well armed, carrying two thousand five hundred men. Outgunned, the buccaneers tried to get in close in order to board the enemy; but the Spanish manœuvred skilfully, and Davis was held to a running fight. He was reluctant to disengage, for if the buccaneers could win this battle they would gain mastery of the Pacific; but his other captains failed to give him the support he needed, and in the end Davis had to let the Spanish get away.

This failure led to quarrels among the buccaneers, and the fleet broke up. Gronet and most of the French went one way, and Swan in the *Cygnet* sailed for the East Indies. Cowley and Dampier accompanied him on a voyage that is still famous. They discovered the north coast of Australia, and on their return home each wrote an account of the expedition. Dampier's story, *A New Voyage Round the World*, earned him immediate fame and is now a classic. Dampier related his piracies candidly, but instead of being arrested he was rewarded with the command of H.M.S. *Roebuck* and sent on a voyage of exploration.

Townley went with Swan for a time, and Davis continued alone. Lionel Wafer remained with him, and left a disappointingly short account of the rest of the voyage. Many more prizes were taken before the *Bachelor's Delight* put in at Juan Fernandez ("Robinson Crusoe island") for the final share-out before sailing back to the West Indies. Each man got five thousand pieces of eight, but by the time they were ready to put to sea again some of the men had lost all their money at dice, and were reluctant to return empty-handed. So eighty of the buccaneers, including Davis, went back to Peru. They found the parties of Townley and Gronet—both these captains were now dead—besieging the town of Guayaquil, and joined in the attack. The town was taken and considerable plunder was shared. The buccaneers had to head off a determined attack by two Spanish men-of-war, and then decided to sail home. Only Davis's ship was strong enough for the Cape Horn passage, so the others went back to the isthmus to return to the Caribbean by land. Davis put in again at Juan Fernandez. By that time five of his men had again lost all their money in gambling, and decided to stay on the island for a while. The remainder rounded Cape Horn and arrived back in the spring of 1688. They returned at a good time, for the

King had just issued a proclamation offering a pardon to all pirates who surrendered. The buccaneers took advantage of this and landed at Port Royal. Davis later went to Virginia and then to England, and nothing more is heard of him until fourteen years later, when he took part in an attack on Tolu and Puerto Bello.

In some ways Davis was the most remarkable of all the buccaneers. He managed to command his crew throughout an expedition lasting four years, which was an unparalleled achievement. Dampier wrote of him with great respect. He had no more power than any other pirate captain, and yet discipline was good. He does not seem to have ever been challenged for the leadership. He was prudent as well as brave, and there is no evidence that his men committed any atrocities. Indeed, treatment of captives was one of the matters about which the English and French buccaneers disagreed strongly. Gronet was more ruthless. On one occasion, after taking some prisoners in the Bay of Panama, he demanded a ransom from the President and was refused. De Lussan, the French chronicler who sailed with him, states that "the President's refusal obliged us, though with some reluctance, to take the resolution to send him twenty heads of his people in a canoe. This method was indeed a little violent, but it was the only way to bring the Spaniards to reason." De Lussan admits also that prisoners were frequently tortured to make them give information.

While Davis had been in the Pacific, buccaneering had continued in the West Indies, but on a reduced scale. Prizes were becoming more difficult to take, and for a time French Governors were instructed to be more conservative in the way they issued commissions. Jamaica, once the headquarters of the English buccaneers, was now completely closed. However, there was an alternative haven in the Bahamas, whose Governor, Robert Clarke, was usually accommodating. When Captain Coxon tired of chasing Jean Hamlin he went to Clarke and bought a fresh commission against the Spanish. Clarke was recalled under arrest in 1682, but the Bahamas remained a favourite pirate resort. Commissions of a kind could also be bought from the Governor of the Danish island of St. Thomas, who was an ex-pirate himself.

When genuine commissions could not be obtained the buccaneers made the best use of whatever documents they had. Dampier says that French commissions on inspection often turned out to be no more than licences granting hunting and fishing rights in Hispaniola. Another English buccaneer recorded: " We met a French private ship of war mounting eight guns who kept in our company some days. Her commission was only for three months. We showed them our commission, which was for three years to come. This we had purchased at a cheap rate, having given for it only ten pieces of eight; but the truth of the thing was that our commission was made out at first only for three months, the same date as the Frenchman's, whereas among ourselves we contrived to make it that it should serve for three years, for with this we were resolved to seek our fortunes."

Holding commissions, genuine or otherwise, rarely helped the buccaneers if they fell into the hands of the Spanish. Indeed, some Spanish Governors had a habit of executing buccaneers with their commissions hanging round their necks. But a commission was useful in friendly and neutral ports, and also to some extent at sea. The lack of a commission did not deter buccaneers, but they carried one when they could get it.

When Davis returned to the West Indies the situation had changed again. War was brewing, and the French especially were getting concerned about the exodus of able fighting men to the Pacific. They wanted to put them under some sort of discipline, and began to take their leaders into the King's service, giving them commissions of advanced rank in the army of marines. De Graaf, for example, was enlisted as a major in 1687.

British Governors were less enthusiastic, but the general pardon of 1688 showed a similar trend. In that year war broke out between France and Spain, and in 1689 Britain came in on the side of Spain. This marked the end of Anglo-French partnership in the Caribbean, and, indeed, the end of buccaneering. The English buccaneers were commissioned against the French, and the French buccaneers against the English and

Spanish.   The next attack on Jamaica was made by a French
expedition led by de Graaf.

So the buccaneers became *bona fide* privateers, and the confederation of the Brethren of the Coast was broken for ever.
Those who were dissatisfied with the rather meagre plunder—
and there were many—left the West Indies for good and
sought new bases and new hunting grounds.   They found the
former in North America and the latter in the Eastern Seas,
and a new era in the history of piracy began.

CHAPTER EIGHT

Who Would be a Pirate ?

AFEW years after the end of buccaneering Père Labat wrote: " The pirates are, as a rule, filibusters who have grown so accustomed to this free life in times of war, when they generally hold commissions, that they cannot make up their minds to return to work when peace is made, and therefore continue their roving."

It was not just indecision that prevented them from returning to work, for when peace was made the work did not exist; but otherwise Labat's diagnosis was shrewd. There was continuity in the profession of robbing at sea. Buccaneers and privateers did not ' turn pirates.' Their status was changed by external circumstances. Fenimore Cooper has said that " the transition from fighting for plunder to plundering unlawfully was very trifling." It was hardly a transition at all.

During the Second World War, when knowledge of the somewhat ungentlemanly methods of fighting used by Commandos began to leak out, doubts were expressed about the place of these men in peacetime society. It was suggested that after the war they might start a wave of violent crime.

Happily, these fears proved unfounded. The war was followed by some increase in violent crime, which was widely advertised in some newspapers; but the new criminals, instead of being Commandos, turned out to be mainly deserters and column-dodgers. This is not difficult to understand. Knowledge of how to kill does not make murderers. The mainspring of crime is not method, but motive.

Men who joined the Commandos—and they were all volunteers—did not stand to gain anything. On the contrary, they increased their chances of losing their lives or limbs without any compensating increase in reward. The envious might take refuge in cynicism and put it down to a desire for relief from boredom, but no one could call it selfishness. As

nearly all crime is for selfish gain, it was unreasonable to expect
ex-Commandos to be criminals.

Men who served on privateers had different motives. They
risked their lives not to defend their country but to gain loot.
They were not expected to have any higher motive.

The buccaneers were closer to piracy than to privateering
in that they elected their own captains, but not otherwise.
Privateers were not usually held to the letter of the law. In
theory there were safeguards against the abuse of commissions
by privateers. In practice these were ineffective.

On the outbreak of war the normal procedure was for the
King to authorize the Lord High Admiral to grant privateering
commissions to men of integrity and repute. As the Empire
extended, the Lord High Admiral was empowered to delegate
his authority to colonial Governors. Most colonial Governors
accepted bribes, and they did not get them from men of
integrity and repute. The result was that anyone could get a
commission if he was willing to pay for it.

The commonest abuse of a privateering commission was the
robbing of neutrals. This was an obvious temptation, as
vessels owned by non-belligerents were often richer prizes and
less well protected than enemy-owned merchantmen. Moreover, ' mistakes ' of this kind were easily covered up.

A typical privateering commission empowered the captain
" to set upon by force of arms and to subdue and take the
men-of-war, ships and other vessels whatsoever, as also the
goods, moneys, and merchandizes belonging to the King of
Spain, his vassals and subjects, and others inhabiting within
any of his countries, territories, or dominions, and such other
ships, vessels, and goods as are, or shall be, liable to confiscation,
pursuant to the treaties between us and other princes, states,
and potentates." This was the standard wording for commissions during the Age of Piracy. It made abuse easy.

In the Caribbean the nationality of the owner of a ship could
usually be deduced from the appearance of the vessel, the
nationality of the crew, and, to some extent, the nature of the
cargo and the ports of origin and destination. Deduction was
not so easy in other waters. It was especially difficult in the
Eastern Seas, where the prizes were richest and the crews

usually Moors. Here the nationality and domicile of the owner had to be inferred from an examination of the ship's papers.

It was only inference, for belligerent ship-owners were not so silly as to advertise their nationality, and it was easy to get false papers. To offset this, Admiralty Passes or safe-conducts were issued to *bona fide* neutrals. The prevalence of bribery made it easy for anyone to get these too. So almost every merchant ship stopped by a privateer was able to produce the right papers and the right Pass. If these had been accepted at their face value hardly any prizes would have been taken.

An interesting example of the technical difficulty of privateering is the case of the *Amsterdam Post*, which was stopped by a British privateer in the Atlantic. Her captain and her crew were British. Her papers showed her to be British owned, and she carried a British Admiralty Mercantile Pass. But a search brought to light a second set of ship's papers, which made her out to be Dutch. Britain was at war with Spain, not Holland; however, the circumstances were suspicious, and the ship was taken to Boston to be tried by a Vice-Admiralty Court. Further investigation showed that her owner, although a Dutchman, lived in the Canary Islands, and the Court quite properly adjudged her a lawful prize.

As merchant ships changed their apparent nationality to suit the circumstances, privateers began to do the same. They flew false colours in order to trick merchantmen into producing the wrong papers. This was hard on neutrals, who usually carried the Passes of all the belligerent nations. The fact that their ship's papers were in order did not save them from seizure if they had produced the wrong Pass. On the high seas the onus was not on the privateer to establish the guilt of his victim; the victim had to prove his innocence to a highly prejudiced judge. The slightest element of doubt was enough to warrant a seizure, and then the victim could only hope for acquittal at the Vice-Admiralty Court—if he ever reached one.

The Vice-Admiralty Courts had two purposes. One was to keep a check on the amount of plunder taken so that the King and the Lord High Admiral would be sure of getting their tenths and fifteenths. The other was to prevent the robbing of ships not owned by enemy nationals or residents in enemy territory.

Until 1689 all prizes taken by British privateers had to be brought back to England for adjudication. The growth of the Empire made this system unworkable, so in wartime colonial Governors were empowered to set up local Vice-Admiralty Courts. These were the same Governors who were authorized to grant privateering commissions, and they used their powers in the same way. It thus became easy for privateers to take neutral prizes back to the colonies where they had bought their commissions and pay an additional bribe to have the prizes legally condemned.

This formality was often waived in the case of seizures in the Eastern Seas, as the distance to the nearest Vice-Admiralty Court was considerable. Sometimes the Admiralty made it easier for privateers to keep within the law by allowing them to take prizes " into the ports of such princes or states as are in alliance or amity with us." There was never much trouble in getting a prize condemned provided a little thought was given to the choice of the prince or state.

In general it seems that the British Government did not care greatly about the abuse of privateering commissions. Privateering was a cheap way of carrying on a war. It was perhaps regrettable that neutrals should have to help pay for it, but the alternative was worse. To encourage privateering the Government steadily reduced its own claims on the plunder, and on at least one occasion privateers were authorized to keep the whole of their loot " without making account in any court or place of this realm." From 1708 the Crown claimed no part of the plunder at all, and thenceforth encouraged privateering solely for the injury it inflicted on the enemy.

The captain of a privateer was not usually the owner. As a rule the promoters of the expeditions were ordinary investors who were ready to risk their capital for the possible gain of a larger profit than they could get elsewhere. Like the directors of the big Elizabethan combines, these speculators stayed on shore; and to get their profit they had to rely on the energy of their captains and crews in taking prizes.

Contrary to popular belief, the seamen of the seventeenth

and eighteenth centuries had the normal instinct of self-pre-
servation. They did not like exposing themselves to the danger
of death or disablement just for the fun of a fight. Before they
would attack another ship they needed a good reason—what
we call an incentive.

The privateering capitalists were strong believers in incentives, and they organized their expeditions on a profit-sharing
basis. Not having to pay so much in bribes, they were able to
offer more generous terms than the Killigrews could. They
rarely claimed more than fifty per cent. of the plunder, and
sometimes were content with as little as one-third. When the
rest of the spoils were divided, each man got one basic share,
the captain and other officers getting additional shares. There
were special bonuses for exceptional service; there was one for
the first man to spy a sail that led to the taking of a prize, and
another for the first man boarding a ship that offered resistance.
There was also some sort of social security scheme, pensions
being paid for loss of limbs and other disabilities due to enemy
action, according to a fixed scale. All these arrangements
were agreed upon in advance and written down in formal
articles. These, of course, were the model for the famous
articles of the pirates.

For an incentive to be effective, the economists tell us, there
must be some sort of economic threat as well as a promise.
This was obviously necessary in an enterprise involving physical
danger. So the crews of privateers were further stimulated into
action by not being paid any wages at all. The first article
they had to agree to was always " No purchase, no pay."
(The word ' purchase ' was the conventional euphemism for
plunder.) They got their rations, and nothing more unless
they earned it. Even the captain came under these conditions.

There was never any difficulty about finding crews for
privateers. They were vastly more attractive to seamen
than ordinary merchantmen. Apart from the prospects of
bigger rewards, the conditions were much better. Discipline
was relaxed, and there was a spirit of partnership between
officers and men. The food too was better, as the nature
of the undertaking made it easy to supplement rations without
expense.

Most seamen preferred privateering to piracy. Individual shares of the plunder were not so high, but prizes were usually bigger and there was security from the law. But when the end of a war stopped privateering, the men generally preferred to carry on the same way of life without authorization to seeking less lucrative and less pleasant occupations.

Not all the pirates served their apprenticeship on privateers. Many were recruited from ordinary merchantmen and from the Royal Navy. Captain John Smith of Virginia explained the main reason for this as early as 1630:

" I could wish merchants, gentlemen, and all setters forth of ships not to be sparing of a competent pay nor true payment; for neither soldiers nor seamen can live without means, but necessity will force them to steal; and when they are once entered into that trade, they are hardly reclaimed."

The pirate Captain Bartholomew Roberts, whose story will be told later, is credited by Johnson with having said the same thing from the other side of the fence:

" In an honest service there is thin commons, low wages and hard labour; but in a pirate life there is plenty and satiety, pleasure and ease, liberty and power. And who would not balance creditor on this side when all hazard that is run for it, at worst, is only a fore-lock or two at choking?"

A condemned pirate, standing under the gallows, was more explicit about the hard labour. His last words on earth were:

" I do wish that masters of vessels would not use their men with such severity as many of them do, for it exposes us to great temptations."

I think it would be hard to over-estimate the stimulus that was given to piracy by the institution of flogging. It is sometimes pretended that in the Age of Piracy men were not so ' soft ' as we are, and the sea-dogs did not mind being flogged. From the diaries that some of them wrote it is clear that they minded very much.

Corporal punishment still has many advocates, most of whom also favour capital punishment. Similarly contradictory arguments are advanced in support of both. Capital punishment, it is said, is a more powerful deterrent than life imprisonment; it is also said to be more humane to end a man's life than to condemn him to spend the rest of it in gaol. In the same way corporal punishment is said to be both a deterrent and, because it is over quickly, less cruel than incarceration. In each case the two arguments seem irreconcilable. Presumably the humaneness of such punishments could be measured by offering prisoners the choice. The deterrent effect is discussible, but it can hardly be doubted that flogging on ships greatly deterred seamen from remaining honest and encouraged them to desert and join pirate vessels.

There were two common ways in which merchant seamen became pirates. One was by mutiny, usually involving the murder of the captain. The other, more usual way was to join the pirates who took their ship as a prize.

Recruits to piracy from the Royal Navy were mostly deserters. It is interesting to note that in wartime there was so much desertion from the Navy to privateers that ratings were often not allowed any shore leave at all, but were kept on board literally for years. When they were in port the authorities obligingly allowed amenities, including boatloads of prostitutes, to be rowed out to them. The main reasons for the common tendency to desert seem to have been the harshness of discipline and the inadequacy of the prize money. In the reign of Queen Anne the normal division of naval prize money was one-eighth to the Admiralty, three-eighths to the captain, one-eighth to the other officers, and three-eighths to the petty officers and crew. Seamen rarely got their rightful share, and plunder was inconsiderable because they had to undertake such unprofitable work as fighting enemy men-of-war.

Most pirates, then, were recruited from privateers, merchant ships, and the Royal Navy. I have already mentioned that recruitment was greatly stimulated by post-war unemployment, while in the colonies the numbers were swollen by escaped bondsmen and transported criminals. At home as well as abroad there was a constant pressure of poverty and hardly any moral restraint.

According to our standards the seventeenth and eighteenth centuries were periods of great inequality of wealth and social injustice. They were also periods of widespread corruption and dishonesty at all social levels. There was one law for the poor and very little law for the rich. There is no reason to think that the poor were ignorant of this. Johnson relates that a pirate named Captain Bellamy made this little speech to the captain of a merchantman he had taken as a prize. The captain had just declined an invitation to join the pirates:

" Damn ye, you are a sneaking puppy, and so are all those who submit to be governed by laws which rich men have made for their own security, for the cowardly whelps have not the courage otherwise to defend what they get by their knavery. Damn them for a pack of crafty rascals, and you who serve them for a parcel of hen-hearted numbskulls. They vilify us, the scoundrels do, when there is only this difference: they rob the poor under the cover of the law, forsooth, and we plunder the rich under the protection of our own courage. Had you not better make one of us, than sneak after the arses of those villains for employment? "

As his invitation was still declined, Captain Bellamy went on:

"You are a devilish conscious rascal, damn ye! I am a free prince and have as much authority to make war on the whole world as he who has a hundred sail of ships and an army of a hundred thousand men in the field. And this my conscience tells me; but there is no arguing with such snivelling puppies who allow superiors to kick them about deck at pleasure, and pin their faith upon a pimp of a parson, a squab who neither practises or believes what he puts upon the chuckle-headed fools he preaches to."

This reference to the clergy is interesting, for pirates are often portrayed as having been easily converted by parsons—at least, when they stood on the scaffold. They are often recorded as having professed deep repentance for their sins in lengthy speeches to the crowds. Here is an extract from a typical " dying confession " :

" I greatly bewail my profanations of the Lord's Day, and my disobedience to my parents, my cursing and swearing, and my blaspheming the name of the glorious God. Unto which I have added the sins of unchastity. And I have provoked the Holy One at length to leave me unto the crimes of piracy and robbery, wherein at last I have brought myself under the guilt of murder also. But one wickedness that has led me as much as any has been my brutish drunkenness. By strong drink I have been heated and hardened into the crimes that are now more bitter than death to me."

This speech, attributed to a pirate named Archer, was published by the clergyman who saw him off, the Rev. Cotton Mather of Boston. The wording of the confessions of other pirates attended by the same clergyman is strikingly similar, and the authenticity of the speech becomes still more doubtful when the style is compared with that of Mather's own sermons. Similarly abject confessions were put into the mouths of pirates after they were beyond speech by a succession of holders of the office of Ordinary of Newgate.

Accounts of executions written by non-clerical witnesses tell a different story. In general, pirates do not seem to have had much time for religion, even at the gallows. There are a few authenticated cases of death-bed repentance, but probably the penitents shared the view of the Roman Emperor who regarded Christianity as a possibly valid passport to Heaven—there was no other passport on offer, so he might as well take it—but delayed his conversion until his death-bed because he did not want to give up sinning until he had lost the physical power to sin. Death-bed repentance may well have been considered a cheap insurance policy for the next world, just as a privateering commission was in this. I have not been able to discover a single case of a pirate being reclaimed by the clergy until he was awaiting execution. There is no apparent reason why the clergy should not have been able to persuade people that the Defender of the Faith was fulfilling his responsibilities in supporting privateering and slave-trading, and yet condemning piracy, for similar moral anomalies are accepted from the Church to-day; but it looks as if sermons against piracy fell on deaf ears simply because it was generally believed that the purpose of religion was to preserve inequality of wealth. From the choice of phrase attributed to Captain Bellamy it seems that Karl Marx was not original in his discovery that religion was distributed to the masses as an opiate.

There was, then, very little moral deterrent to piracy. It seems doubtful whether this made a great deal of difference.

Moral deterrents are rarely a match for the incentive of hunger. As Carlyle said, " Many a man thinks that it is his goodness that keeps him from crime when it is only his full stomach. On half allowance he would be as ugly and as knavish as anybody. Don't mistake potatoes for principles."

The other possible deterrents were not very strong. The physical risk was little greater than in any other kind of employment at sea. Pirates rarely had to fight, and the number of pirates killed in action was probably less in proportion than the number of seamen who were done to death by flogging or other means by honest captains. All service at sea was hazardous, for in the Age of Piracy there were few regulations for the safety of life at sea. There was no compulsory load-line. Thus William Richardson reports that on one ship he served on, of three hundred tons, after loading, the crew could wash their hands over the gunwale in the sea. Richardson also tells of a man who fell overboard and had to be left to drown because it was impossible to launch the jolly-boat. " Everyone knows," Richardson explained innocently, " that this is not easily done in a merchantman, for the skiff is stowed inside the longboat, and the jolly-boat on her is sometimes bottom up and lumbered with other ropes."

The penalty for piracy was execution, but as a deterrent this was about as effective as a man in a bath-chair shaking his fist at an Olympic runner. During the peak periods of piracy the number of men caught was probably less than one in a thousand. Johnson's history is misleading because it deals mainly with the few pirates who stood trial. The great majority remained anonymous and died in bed.

The Navy was responsible for catching pirates. During the periods of peace in the Age of Piracy it was under-manned, inefficient, and corrupt. It was hopelessly inadequate to police even the black spots; and corruption among colonial Governors and other officials secured the pirates' bases.

The positive incentives to piracy were prospect of gain, easy conditions, and freedom from the harsh discipline of honest service. Pirates called themselves free-booters, just as smugglers called themselves free-traders, and they were jealous of their freedom even from one another. They did not take to piracy for love of it, but in the hope of getting rich quickly. With little extra risk, a pirate could gain far more from a single successful voyage than he could hope to earn during a lifetime of honest service. While such conditions lasted, who would not be a pirate?

CHAPTER NINE

On the Account

"GOING on the account" was the contemporary expression for embarking on a piratical voyage. The phrase has been overworked by historians and credited with more significance than it really had. It has been regarded as a kind of frontier between honest service and lawlessness. In fact it meant merely that no wages were paid and service was not accounted for until plunder was taken. All men who served on privateers went on this kind of account when they agreed to the condition of " No purchase, no pay." The pirates' version of this was " No prey, no pay," which was more honest, but superfluous. They could not draw pay without prey because there was no one to pay them.

A pirate ship was a sea-going stock company. In this, as in many other respects, it resembled a privateer. There was only one important constitutional difference between the two.

A privateer was fitted out by capitalists, and the crew, although sharing in the profits, still had the status of employees. They were on piece-work. The captain was appointed by the owners and had the same powers of discipline as any other ship's captain, although he did not normally use them to the same extent.

A pirate ship was owned by the crew, and the captain was elected by a popular vote. A pirate company was, in fact, a property-owning democracy, and it was democratic to the point of anarchy.

Romantic novelists have usually portrayed the pirate captain as a tyrannical despot. Nothing could be farther from the truth. He was the only kind of sea-captain of his age who was neither tyrannical nor despotic. He was not allowed to be. Johnson summed up his status in the remark, " They only permit him to be captain on condition that they may be captain over him."

The captain's tenure of office was precarious. He could be

deposed at any time. This was not done by mutiny—there were no mutinies on pirate ships—but simply by popular vote. A simple majority was sufficient for election or deposition, but usually the choice was unanimous. If there was a substantial minority in opposition the company divided itself. An example of this followed the re-election of Bartholomew Sharp. The usual reason for deposition of the captain was incompetence in action or general failure to get plunder. Some captains, such as Edward Davis, retained office for a long time. On the other hand, Defoe reports that on one pirate ship there were thirteen changes of command in a few months.

The extent of the captain's authority was defined clearly by a pirate named Walter Kennedy, who was hanged at Wapping in 1721. In his trial at the Old Bailey, Kennedy said, " They chose a captain from amongst themselves, who in effect held little more than that title, excepting in an engagement, when he commanded absolutely and without control." Johnson elaborated this: " The captain's power is uncontrollable in chase or in battle, drubbing, cutting, or even shooting anyone who does deny his command." When the ship was not in action, however, he could not even give an order. Thus, says Johnson, the appointment " falls on one superior for knowledge and boldness—pistol proof, they call it."

The captain was nominally in charge of prisoners, but he was not allowed to decide on their treatment. A merchant captain named George Roberts, who was taken prisoner by Captain Edward Low—described by Johnson as a " ferocious brute " and " of unequalled cruelty "—wrote that Low told him he hoped he would be treated civilly, but added that " it did not lie in his particular power, for he was but one man, and all business of this nature must be done in public and by a majority of votes by the whole company." Captain Bellamy, who has already been quoted, is said to have told the master of a merchantman, " Damn my blood, I am sorry they won't let you have your sloop again, for I scorn to do anyone a mischief when it is not to my advantage."

The captain received a larger share in the plunder than anyone else, but otherwise he had no privileges. He had a cabin, but he could not call it his own. According to Johnson,

" Every man may at his pleasure intrude into the captain's cabin, swear at him, or take what part of his victuals or drink that may please them without his offering to deny them." He had the same rations as everyone else. According to Exquemelin, among the buccaneers—who gave their captains rather more authority than the later pirates—" nor does the steward of the vessel give any more flesh, or anything else, to the captain than to the meanest mariner." Johnson confirmed this: " There is no certain allowance of victuals or drink, unless there is a prospect of a shortage, in which case all is placed under charge of the quartermaster, who discharges to all with the same equality, be they captain or ship's boy."

Walter Kennedy explained the reason for the limitation of the captain's powers:

" Most of them having suffered formerly from the ill-treatment of their officers, provided carefully against any such evil now they had the choice in themselves. By their orders they provided especially against any quarrels which might happen among themselves, and appointed certain punishments for anything that tended that way; for the due execution thereof they constituted other officers besides the captain, so very industrious were they to avoid putting too much power into the hands of one man."

The most important of the other officers was the quartermaster, whom Johnson described as " the trustee for the whole ship's company . . . like the Grand Mufti amongst the Turks to their Sultan, for the captain can do nothing which the quartermaster does not approve of. The quartermaster is an humble imitation of the Roman tribune, for he speaks for and looks after the interest of the company." Captain Snelgrave, a reliable observer, mainly confirmed this: " The captain of a pirate ship is chiefly chosen to fight the vessels they may meet with. Besides him they choose another principal officer, whom they called quartermaster, who has the general inspection of all affairs and often controls the captain's orders. This person is also to be the first man in boarding any ship they shall attack, or go in the boat on any desperate enterprize."

Methods of making up boarding parties varied, but I have not found a case of a company relying on volunteers. Basil

Ringrose says that on his ship men were chosen by ballot. Under Bartholomew Roberts the rule was " every man to be called fairly in turn, by list, to board a prize, and on such occasions to be allowed a shift of clothes."

It was the quartermaster's job to decide what loot should be taken from a prize. He was compelled to take all gold, silver, and jewels, as these were declared " not returnable " under the pirate articles. He took silks and other merchandise at his discretion, according to storage space and the accessibility of the nearest market. He kept charge of the plunder until the share-out was made. This also was under his supervision, as was the sale by auction of individual articles at the mast-head. The share-out was usually made very soon after the prize was taken.

As Johnson indicated, the quartermaster was also a kind of civil magistrate. He was allowed to order punishments for minor offences such as quarrelling, misuse of prisoners, and neglect of arms. More serious offences were tried by jury. The quartermaster was the only man allowed to administer a flogging, and he could not do this without the support of the majority of the crew. His power was limited by the fact that, like the captain, he could be deposed at any time by popular vote. When the ship was not in action the captain came under the quartermaster like the rest of the crew, but in battle or chase the quartermaster had no power of any kind. By this shrewd division of authority the pirates, as Walter Kennedy said, avoided " putting too much power into the hands of one man."

If any of the pirates started to fight among themselves it was the quartermaster's duty to try to effect a reconciliation. If he failed, he took the disputants ashore to settle the issue " at sword and pistol " (Johnson). The duellists were placed back to back at a prescribed distance from each other, and the quartermaster gave the order to fire. If either man failed to obey immediately, the pistol was knocked out of his hand—presumably to prevent him from shortening the range. If both missed with their pistols they set to with cutlasses. The first man to draw blood was the winner. Basil Ringrose reports interestingly that on one occasion " our quartermaster,

James Chappel, and myself fought a duel together on shore," but he does not state the result.

"Besides the captain and quartermaster," says Snelgrave, "the pirates had all other officers as is usual on board men-of-war." These were sometimes elected, but more commonly appointed by the captain and quartermaster. Sometimes the captain had a second-in-command, or lieutenant; but he had no duties unless the captain was killed in battle or chase, when he had to assume command at once. A more important officer was the master, or sailing master, who was responsible for navigation and trimming the sails. He was chosen solely for his ability as a "sea artist," as they called it. Then there was the bosun, who looked after the maintenance of the vessel, the movement afloat, and the ground tackle. He was in charge of naval stores such as cordage, pitch, tallow, and spare sails. The gunner was in charge of the ordnance and responsible for exercising the company in using it. Other technical officers included the carpenter, sailmaker, and surgeon. In theory all officers were liable to dismissal from office at any time, but in practice technicians were hardly ever deposed. Very few pirate ships were lucky enough to have a full establishment of specialist officers, for the obvious reason that such men could find good employment in honest service.

Before each voyage the pirates drew up articles. These were usually sworn on the Bible over bowls of punch, and the ceremony was a curious mixture of solemnity and jollity. Like the articles of the buccaneers, they were based on the articles normally in force on privateers, with which many of the pirates were familiar. The idea that the pirates invented their own laws and customs is erroneous.

Here is a copy of the earliest pirate articles I have been able to find. The ship was originally a slaver of the Royal African Company whose crew mutinied off Nevis. In this case I have preserved the original spelling.

"June the 30th day, 1683. Articles of Agreement between us abord of the Camillion, Nich. Clough Commander, that wee are to dispose of all the goods thatt are abord amongst us, every man are to have his full due and right share only the Commander is to have two shares and a half a share for the

Ship and home [whom?] the Captain please to take for the Master under him is to have a share and a half. Now Gentlemen these are to satisfy you, as for the Doctor a share and a half, and these are our Articles that wee do all stand to us well as on [one?] and all.

" These are to satisfy you thatt our intent is to trade with the Spaniards, medling nor make no resistances with no nation that wee do fall with all upon the Sea. Now Gentlemen these are to give you notice that if any one do make any Resistances against us one any factery [on any occasion?] hereafter shall bee severely punish according to the fact that hee hath comitted and as you are all here at present you have taken your corporall oath upon the holy Evangelists to stand one by the other as long as life shall last."

The document bears fourteen signatures and the marks of eight illiterates.

It is difficult to understand why pirates' articles were written down at all, when so many of the crew were illiterate and the contract obviously could not be legally enforced. The only occasions when such documents were produced in a court of law were when they were used as evidence for the prosecution in trials of the signatories. I can only imagine that it was due to the natural imitativeness of man. Just as the first motor-car, or " horseless carriage," was built with the engine at the front, and even a place for the whip, so the first pirates drew up articles because they had always sailed under articles on privateers. The existence of such articles seems to prove more than anything else that pirates were not very original thinkers.

Captain George Lowther's articles (1721) are typical of his period :

" 1. The captain shall have two full shares, the quartermaster one and a half, and the doctor, gunner, boatswain and master one and a quarter.

" 2. He that shall be found guilty of unlawfully taking up a weapon aboard the privateer, or any prize taken by us with intent to abuse or strike another of the company, shall suffer whatever punishment the captain and the majority of the company shall think fit.

" 3. He that shall be found guilty of cowardice in the time

of the engagement shall suffer such punishment as the captain and the majority of the company shall think fit.

" 4. If any gold, jewels, silver or other valuables be found aboard the prize to the value of even one piece of eight, and the finder do not deliver it to the quartermaster within the space of twenty-four hours, he shall suffer such punishment as the captain and the majority of the company shall think fit.

" 5. He that shall be found guilty of defrauding another in gaming even to the extent of one shilling only shall suffer such punishment as the captain and the majority of the company shall think fit.

" 6. He that shall have the misfortune to lose a limb in the time of engagement shall have the sum of £150 sterling, and shall remain with the company as he may choose.

" 7. Good quarter shall be given to all when called for.

" 8. He that first sights a sail that may prove a prize shall have the best pistol or other small arm aboard her as he may choose."

These articles were closely adapted from typical privateering articles of the period. It is noteworthy that the pirates even called their ship a privateer. Two of the articles are of special interest. Compared with the conditions in honest service the pension clause (article 6) was unusually generous, and the provision of employment for disabled ex-servicemen was unique. The other point of interest is article 7, which was scrupulously observed by nearly all pirates.

It has often been written that pirates commonly killed their prisoners, usually by the picturesque method of making them ' walk the plank.' This is untrue. I have ransacked official records, reports of trials, and much other documentary evidence without being able to discover a single case of walking the plank. I do not mean merely that I have not found an authenticated case. In all the contemporary literature on pirates I could not find even an accusation or suggestion that the practice was ever used. The very expression seems to have been invented many years after the Age of Piracy.

Pirates very rarely killed their prisoners, and from the many depositions of men who were captured by them it is clear that their behaviour generally was far more civilized than the

Captain Condent

Original
Jolly Roger

Modified
Jolly Roger

French Jolly Roger

Captain
Emanuel Wynne

Captain
Edward England

Captain
Christopher Moody

Captain Bartholomew Roberts

PIRATE FLAGS

PIRATES ASHORE FOR CAREENING

Careening, or bottom-cleaning, had to be done frequently in the tropics, owing to the prevalence of marine growths and the teredo worm. Pirates were most vulnerable during this operation, but little advantage was taken of their enforced immobility.

treatment given to prisoners of war by most civilized nations to-day. This was not because the pirates were humanitarians. It was simply a matter of policy.

Pirates did not like fighting. They never engaged in battle if they could possibly avoid it. Their aim was plunder, not bloodshed; and their whole policy was directed towards taking prizes without having to fight for them.

Novelists seem to have assumed that pirates would have killed their prisoners in order to destroy the only witnesses of their crimes. This assumption is false simply because the danger to the pirates of being arrested and brought to trial was far less than the danger of being killed in an engagement. It was sound policy to let the prisoners go, taking the risk of seeing them again one day, for the sake of discouraging resistance at sea.

I have said that the pirates rarely killed their prisoners, and there is a rider to this. They gave quarter only if no resistance was offered. If they were opposed they killed without mercy. They deliberately publicized this policy, which was so effective that they hardly ever needed to kill. This is not surprising. The captain of a merchant ship had little incentive to risk his life in defence of the owner's cargo. The crew had no incentive at all.

This explains why pirates found it so easy to take bigger and better-armed ships than their own.

Living men tell tales, and the pirates did their best to see that their victims told the right ones. Usually they did not steal the personal possessions of the officers or men, and took only what they wanted from a ship's cargo. According to Governor Spotswood of Virginia, " It is a common practice with these rovers, upon the pillaging of a ship, to make presents of other commodities to such masters as they take a fancy to, in lieu of that they have plundered them of." If the prize was suitable for conversion into a pirate vessel, they either gave their prisoners their old ship or, if they wanted to keep both, put the men ashore at a place where they would be able to get picked up. As a general rule the only man likely to suffer punishment was the captain; for if his crew said that he had treated them cruelly the pirates usually gave him a public flogging. This greatly encouraged seamen to join them.

When a prize was taken the crew of the captured vessel were usually given the opportunity of joining the pirates. The response to this invitation often depended on the conditions under which they had been serving, and especially on the treatment they had received from their captain. The crew of a bullying captain usually deserted *en masse*. The average seaman who had been living in daily fear of a flogging found something irresistible in the sight of pirates slapping their captain on the back with impunity. Those who volunteered were interviewed by the quartermaster, who explained the articles to them and rejected or accepted them as he thought fit.

Romantic novelists sometimes draw lurid pictures of the sufferings of honest seamen forced to serve on pirate ships. This picture is as false as that of the despotic pirate captain. In fact the pirates rarely imitated the naval practice of ' pressing.' There were usually enough volunteers to make it unnecessary. They resorted to it only when in need of making up their establishment, especially in skilled trades. Sailing masters, carpenters, and surgeons were in the greatest danger of being conscribed. Peter Scudmore, who joined the pirate Bartholomew Roberts in 1721, claimed that he was the first surgeon ever to sign pirate articles voluntarily. Some pirates made it a rule only to force single men. Thus the much-maligned Edward Low told his prisoner, Captain George Roberts, " we have an article which we are sworn to not to force any married man against his will," and privately advised Roberts to claim a wife.

Once taken, conscripts were treated in the same way as the rest of the crew. This paralleled the lack of discrimination by the Navy in its treatment of volunteers and victims of press-gangs. The Services to-day also make no difference in duties and privileges between volunteers and conscripts. Thus a forced man on a pirate ship was not a slave, but enjoyed the same freedom, and even the same rights of franchise, as the rest of the crew, and he shared in the plunder according to his rank. If he attempted to desert he was, of course, subject to the usual punishment for this offence, which was death. Similarly, if he refused to fight for the ship he was liable to be shot out of hand, as were voluntary pirates who proved recalcitrant in action. This meant that he had to fight for an ignoble cause, but that was the way of the world with conscripts, and still is. Twentieth-century conscripts also have to fight for ignoble causes unless, through an accident of birth, they happen to be used only in defence against aggression.

The common misunderstanding about the numbers and status of forced men probably derives from evidence given at trials of pirates. Even Johnson sometimes expresses surprise at men who ' proved ' they were forced being found guilty of piracy and executed. I doubt if many innocent men suffered in this way. Probably many more guilty men gained the benefit of the doubt. The explanation is quite simple. When a captured seaman was invited to join the pirates he often asked to be ' forced.' If the pirates needed men, the quartermaster usually offered to ' force ' them. The men were given certificates to this effect, which they carried as insurance policies and, if they were caught, offered as evidence in their defence. The commonest plea heard at any trial of pirates was that the accused had been forced. The plea was rarely allowed, for the courts knew that pirates rarely forced men unless they were technicians. Most acquittals on these grounds were, in fact, of technical officers like carpenters and surgeons.

Sometimes seamen had enough foresight to manufacture stronger evidence. This usually happened when a number of men on a merchant ship decided among themselves that if they were boarded by pirates they would join them. When the time came a spokesman of the little band told the pirate quartermaster which of the men were in the plot, and asked for them to be forced. Their request was granted with much waving of cutlasses and brandishing of pistols and shouting in the hearing of the officers and men on the merchant ship who were not going to join the pirates. Then, if the ' forced ' men were caught, they had the chance of calling witnesses who honestly believed them innocent. This ruse often worked.

There are further points of interest in the articles of Captain Phillips (1723). They are reprinted by Johnson, who says that

the pirates " swore to 'em upon a hatchet for want of a Bible."
When they were drawn up the pirate company numbered
only five, of whom four were elected officers: Phillips as
captain, a master (or navigator), a carpenter, and a gunner.
The articles seem to have assumed that the company would
expand, as it did:

" 1. Every man shall obey civil command; the captain
shall have one full share and a half in all prizes; the master,
carpenter, boatswain, and gunner shall have one share and a
quarter.

" 2. If any man shall offer to run away, or keep any secret
from the company, he shall be marooned, with one bottle of
powder, one bottle of water, one small arm and shot.

" 3. If any man shall steal any thing in the company, or game
to the value of a piece of eight, he shall be marooned or shot.

" 4. If at any time we should meet another marooner [i.e.
pirate] that man that shall sign his articles without the consent
of our company shall suffer such punishment as the captain
and company shall think fit.

" 5. That man that shall strike another whilst these articles
are in force shall receive Moses's Law (that is, forty stripes lack-
ing one) on the bare back.

" 6. That man that shall snap his arms, or smoke tobacco
in the hold without a cap to his pipe, or carry a candle lighted
without a lanthorn, shall suffer the same punishment as in the
former article.

" 7. That man that shall not keep his arms clean, fit for an
engagement, or neglect his business, shall be cut off from his
share, and suffer such other punishment as the captain and the
carpenter shall think fit.

" 8. If any man shall lose a joint in time of an engagement,
he shall have four hundred pieces of eight; if a limb, eight
hundred.

" 9. If at any time we meet with a prudent woman, that
man that offers to meddle with her, without her consent, shall
suffer present death."

Article 7 suggests that the carpenter was temporarily carrying
out the duties of quartermaster, and presumably he would
have administered the punishment prescribed in article 5.

Article 6 was an ordinary fire precaution.

Articles 2 and 4 were strictly observed on all pirate ships. One of the pirates' biggest fears was that one of their company should desert and turn informer, selling information that might lead to the capture of the others. For this reason every man had to sign on for the duration of the expedition, and no man was allowed to leave without the consent of the others, even if he offered to sacrifice his share of the plunder. This was more clearly laid down in the articles of Captain Low, who graduated under Lowther : " If any of the company shall adjure or speak anything tending to the separation or breaking up of the company, or shall by any means offer or endeavour to desert or quit the company, that person shall be shot to death by the quartermaster's order without the sentence of a court-martial."

The punishment of marooning, prescribed in Phillips's article 3, was even more severe. The word derives from the Maroons, a West Indian community founded by escaped Negro slaves who mated with Amerindian women. The word is a corruption of Cimaroons, meaning " dwellers in the mountains," and thus by extension fugitives or lost people. The pirates were often called marooners because of their use of this punishment. It amounted to casting the offender ashore on a desert island—usually one of the innumerable little sand-spits in the Caribbean—and leaving him to die. Sometimes the pirates chose an island that was submerged at high tide, but in any case the man had almost no chance of survival. He was given a pistol and powder and shot so that he could kill himself when his hunger and thirst became unendurable. A more brutal punishment could hardly have been devised. Walking the plank would have been merciful by comparison. It is noteworthy that the pirates applied it only to their own backsliders. The articles attributed to Bartholomew Roberts prescribed marooning as the punishment for desertion of quarters in battle as well as desertion of the ship and stealing from the company; but " if one man robs another, then the ears and nose of the guilty one are to be slit, and he is to be set ashore where he is sure to encounter hardships, but not in some uninhabited island."

Phillips's article 9 was another inheritance from the articles of the privateers. Johnson gives a reason for it and also notes the difficulty of enforcing it:

"When any [woman] fell into their hands, they put a sentinel immediately over her to prevent ill consequences from so dangerous an instrument of division and quarrel; but then—here lies the roguery—they contend who shall be sentinel, which happens generally to be one of the greatest bullies, who, to secure the lady's virtue, will let none lie with her but himself."

Johnson cites a case where this happened, but it is unconfirmed, and I doubt if it occurred very often. There was little privacy on an overcrowded pirate sloop, and it is more likely that when the article was not observed the pirates applied their general principle of fair shares for all. Snelgrave is more plausible: "It is a rule among pirates not to allow women to be on board their ships when in the harbour. And if they should take a prize at sea, that has any women on board, no one dares, on pain of death, to force them against their inclinations. This being a good political rule to prevent disturbances amongst them, it is strictly observed."

There may have been an additional reason for the article. If the pirates gained a reputation for treating women decently they were more likely to be asked for quarter when they challenged a ship with women on board. But evidence on this point is slight, for women travelled by sea rarely and carefully.

This article appears to have been generally waived in the case of coloured women, whom the pirates treated in the way they had been taught on His Majesty's slavers.

A little more of the pirates' sexual behaviour may be inferred from Bartholomew Roberts's extension of this article: "No boy or woman allowed among us."

Captain Phillips's articles were typical, although of course there were variations and extensions. Some articles included the penalty for the murder of one pirate by another, which was usually tying the murderer and the corpse together, attaching weights, and throwing them overboard. This has been cited as an example of the brutality of pirates, but they should not be credited with originality here. It was the normal way of punishing murderers in the Royal Navy.

The pirates' articles survived the Age of Piracy, and some of their provisions reappear in the articles of Mrs. Ching, the widow of a nineteenth-century Chinese pirate admiral, who carried on the family business after her husband's death. Mrs. Ching's articles, which are reprinted by Philip Gosse, include the following echoes from Phillips and company, with some Oriental refinements:

" 1. If any man goes privately on shore, or what is called transgressing the bars, he shall be taken and his ears perforated in the presence of the whole fleet; repeating the same, he shall suffer death.

" 2. Not the least thing shall be taken privately from the stolen and plundered goods. All shall be registered, and the pirate receive for himself out of ten parts, only two: eight parts belong to the storehouse, called the general fund; taking anything out of this general fund without permission shall be death.

" 3. No person shall debauch at his pleasure captive women taken in the villages and open spaces, and brought on board a ship, he must first request the ship's purser for permission and then go aside in the ship's hold. To use violence against any woman without permission of the purser shall be punished with death."

Such, then, was the pirate constitution, and on the whole the articles seem to have been observed fairly well. They were enforced not so much by magisterial awards—quartermasters hardly ever used their power of flogging—as by public opinion. There is not a great deal of evidence of cheating and trickery over the share-out of plunder. There was some, of course, but not more than among honest merchants and traders of the period. There was probably as much honour among pirates as there was among honest people. I have not been able to find a single case of a physical dispute during the share-out or of murders being committed to reduce the number of share-holders.

The pirates' biggest weakness was drink. There does not appear to have been a single case of a ' dry ' pirate ship, and of the pirates who were caught many were surprised while too drunk to be able to defend themselves. Dampier, in his account of the comparatively sober company commanded by Edward Davis, reports: "We weighed before day, and all got out of the road except Captain Swan's tender, which never budged; for the men were all asleep, when we went out, and, the tide of flood coming on before they awoke, we were forced to stay for them till the following tide." On another occasion during the same voyage Captain Swan complained that he was unable to take a prize because his crew were all drunk.

This makes it all the more difficult to understand why the pirates' articles were generally effective. Those seamen, mostly illiterate and uneducated, freed from moral and legal restraints, would to-day be regarded as unfit for self-government; yet they observed a constitution that was so liberal that it might be expected to have made excessive demands on their powers of self-discipline. The only inference I can draw is that where discipline is removed, self-discipline emerges in the most unlikely places. Discipline is not a synonym for morale. It is at best a necessary evil, and, as everyone who has been in the Forces knows, it plays havoc with self-discipline.

Most writers on pirates have said that it was lack of discipline that led to their undoing. I cannot understand this, because most pirates were never undone. And when they had to fight they usually fought bravely and well. There are several cases of small pirate ships successfully engaging men-of-war. Nobody could say that the Navy suffered from lack of discipline.

The pirate constitution was copied mainly from the articles of the privateers, modified by a hatred and distrust of authority; and thus, by accident, the pirates evolved a form of community life that bordered on anarchy. It worked. Anarchism on a small scale usually does, if it is left in peace. Anarchism on a large scale has not yet been tried.

CHAPTER TEN

Flags, Red and Black

PIRATES changed their ships as easily as they changed their captains.

In the early days of the Age of Piracy the changes were numerous and rapid. The buccaneers began with a canoe or rowing-boat, and used it to take a larger boat; with this they took a small ship, and with the small ship they took a big ship. They kept this ship until they happened to take a better one.

The first requirement of a pirate ship was speed. The size depended on the pirates' range. In the Caribbean sloops of thirty to fifty tons were favoured. A shallow draught was essential, as it enabled the pirates to escape pursuit by sailing among the many shoals and reefs of these waters. Thus when the West Indian pirates took a larger ship than their own they often turned it adrift after removing the plunder.

With a few exceptions pirate ships were not built as such, but were converted merchantmen. Experienced sea-captains could spot them by their raised gunwales, which gave the crew better protection in battle. All deck-houses were cut down, to leave the deck flush and unencumbered. Similar structural changes were made below deck, for different reasons. According to Johnson, " every man hath his own quarter where he may lie and eat and sleep, though all have the same equality in ranging the ship all over, the bulkheads being thrown down to make a clear ship throughout." Often, though, many of the crew had to sleep on deck in all weathers, for the ships were nearly always very overcrowded. There does not seem to have been a maximum establishment, and I have not found a case of a company refusing recruits on the grounds that the issue of shares was over-subscribed.

An additional advantage of small ships over large was that they were easier to careen.

The word 'careen' comes from the Latin for keel, and literally the verb means to turn (a ship) on one side; its extended meaning is to clean a ship's bottom. This was one of the jobs that made the pirates' life difficult. It was also a job they could not afford to neglect. An encrustation of marine growths on the ship's bottom greatly reduced her speed.

When the pirates were in haste they carried out a partial careening, or " boot-topping." The ship was anchored in still, shallow water, and all the cargo, guns, and other equipment were moved to one side to give her as big a list as possible. Then men scraped the other side as far down below the normal water-line as they could go. When they had finished, the cargo and guns were moved again and the process was repeated on the other side.

This was not a very satisfactory method, and it was only used when a proper careening could not be carried out. For this a secluded spot was needed, preferably with trees growing right down to the beach. The ship was run close in, guns and cargo were removed, and the topmast was taken down. Then blocks and tackles were fixed from the mast to the trees, and the hull was pulled over until the vessel was almost flat on her side. Sometimes another ship was used as a hulk by which to pull the vessel over.

After the encrustations had been removed, and any necessary repairs and caulking carried out, the ship's bottom was daubed with sulphur and tallow. Then she was turned over and done on the other side.

In the case of a larger ship sailing in tropical waters the process was much bigger. The teredo worm was prevalent in the tropics, and the ships of that age did not have metal sheathing. Their bottoms were protected instead by a double-timber sheathing coated with sulphur, which acted as a worm-deterrent. To avoid perforation this sheathing had to be renewed periodically, the new sheathing being sealed with a mixture of tar, tallow, and sulphur.

In the tropics careening had to be carried out at least three times a year, and the pirates' problem was to find a place where they could work without fear of being surprised. While the work was being done they camped ashore in tents, and also built an earthwork commanding the beach, in which they mounted the ship's guns.

One of the best-known features of pirate lore is the flag called the "Jolly Roger." Its antiquity is uncertain, but it seems to have been an eighteenth-century invention. The first reference to it in the *Oxford English Dictionary* is dated 1724, and the earliest mention of the name that I have been able to find is dated 1719. The matter is of some interest, because the evolution of piracy from buccaneering is seen clearly in the evolution of the pirate flag.

The buccaneers, like other privateers, sailed under their national flag or the flag of the nation from which they had drawn their commission. Sometimes, when calling a ship to surrender, they also flew a red flag. This was said to have been dipped in blood, but probably it had been dipped in paint; still, the colour was symbolical. The meaning was simply that no quarter would be given if resistance were offered.

The red or bloody flag survived buccaneering. Captain Every (1695) generally engaged under the cross of St. George and his own colours—four silver chevrons in a bloody field—and when this flag flew at the masthead it meant that he was willing to give good quarter; but if resistance was offered he hoisted a plain red flag, signifying that the offer of quarter was withdrawn.

The first record of the use of the black flag is dated 1700, when a French pirate named Emanuel Wynne flew it in an engagement with H.M.S. *Poole* off Santiago. The captain of the man-of-war described the flag as " a sable ensign with cross-bones, a death's head, and an hourglass." The hourglass may have been a symbolic intimation of the short period of time available for deliberation. The skull-and-bones was an old symbol of death, and not peculiar to piracy. It was used as a cap-badge by several European armies as early as the sixteenth century.

The tone of the report by the captain of H.M.S. *Poole* suggests that he had previous knowledge of the black flag by repute if not experience, so its origin remains uncertain. It was in general use for the next twenty or thirty years, although the design varied. In 1703 a pirate named John Quelch was reported to have been off Brazil flying the "Old Roger." Instead of the skull-and-bones, this showed "an anatomy with an hourglass in one hand and a dart in the heart with three drops of blood proceeding from it in the other." A similar flag was used by pirates who were executed at Boston in 1719. There are reports also of a black flag showing a skeleton holding a glass of punch in one hand and a sword in the other, while sometimes the flag took the form of a black skeleton on a white ground.

The black flag seems to have been used for the same purpose as the buccaneers' red flag. Johnson defines its object as to "strike terror upon all beholders." Captain Snelgrave reported that "Captain Howell Davis came in the river [Gambia] with a Black Flag showing, which said flag is intended to frighten honest merchantmen into surrender on penalty of being murdered if they do not" (1718). Captain Richard Hawkins, who was taken by pirates in the West Indies in 1724, reported that "when they fight under the Jolly Roger they give quarter, which they do not when they fight under the red or bloody flag." Other reports also suggest that the Jolly Roger was run up first, to signify an offer of quarter, and that if this was refused the red flag was flown to show that the offer had been withdrawn.

I have read two different explanations of the origin of the term "Jolly Roger." They are both so plausible that neither can be accepted as correct.

According to one version, the French buccaneers called the red flag the "*joli rouge*," pronouncing the final 'e.' This was easily corrupted to Jolly Roger by the English buccaneers, and the name was later transferred to the black flag.

The other theory is that the term originated in the Eastern Seas. The Chiefs of Cannonore, who were notorious pirates, had the Tamil title of Ali Raja, which meant "king of the sea." They also flew the red flag; and English pirates also sometimes claimed that they ruled the waves. The word "Raja" was frequently corrupted to "Roger" by seamen in the seventeenth century, and Ali Raja could have changed to

Ally Roger, Olly Roger, and then Old Roger or Jolly Roger.

But perhaps the name just came from the English word 'roger,' meaning a begging vagabond, and etymologically closely related to the word 'rogue'. The *New Canting Dictionary* (1725) defines Old Roger as a synonym for the devil.

A few words may be said here about pirate treasure. The subject has already been given far more words than it deserves, and if all the money that has been spent on treasure-hunting could be recovered this would be the richest treasure of all.

Presumably people believe in pirate treasure because they want to. There is no other reason for the belief. Pirates did not bury their treasure. They shared out their loot as they got it. This hardly needs to be explained. The pirates did not trust one another sufficiently to leave the plunder in a common hoard once they left their ship. Besides, each man wanted to use his share, either to invest in a business or, more generally, to spend.

Very rarely individual pirates, through force of circumstances, buried their own shares, and not all of them were able to recover the loot. Such hoards would not have been very large. Buried treasure is usually associated with pirate captains, who drew larger shares; but this idea seems to be wrapped up with the false conception of the despotic captain.

Some pirates who were captured tried to buy their acquittal with stories of hidden loot. They were not taken seriously by their contemporaries, and there is no reason why they should be to-day. The only pirate treasure that is almost certainly awaiting a finder is the consignment of six hundred and ninety-nine pigs of silver that Bartholomew Sharp and his crew mistook for tin and turned loose in the *San Rosario*. It is probably still at the bottom of the Pacific, somewhere off the west coast of South America.

CHAPTER ELEVEN

The Pirate Round

BETWEEN 1697, when the Treaty of Ryswick was signed, and 1701, when the War of the Spanish Succession began, England was at peace. During the same period English piracy flourished wonderfully.

It is tempting to assume that this was a simple case of cause and effect, but history is rarely as simple as that. Certainly the pirates gained many recruits from the privateers when the treaty was signed, and lost many when the war was resumed; but this particular and most remarkable era of piracy began before 1697 and ended before 1701.

It has been shown that the decline of the buccaneers began with the enforcement of the Anglo-Spanish Treaty of America in the early sixteen-seventies. For many years after the closing of Port Royal the buccaneers could still find alternative bases, in the Bahamas and in Danish and other isles in the West Indies. They could still get commissions of a sort, and harbour facilities for refitting and careening. But profits were diminishing and risks increasing; and while Sharp and Davis were adventuring on their tremendously hazardous expeditions in the Pacific, other buccaneers found new bases and more attractive hunting grounds.

The new bases were in the American colonies and plantations, most of which welcomed the buccaneers with open arms. The reason for this hospitality was a series of Acts of Trade and Navigation.

The main object of these Acts was to protect the English carrying trade from Dutch competition. The main provisions were that, with certain exceptions, no goods could be imported into England or her colonies in any other than English bottoms, and that the master and three-quarters of every ship's crew had to be Englishmen. This attempt at a ' closed shop ' seems to have been copied from the Spanish, and it met with no more success. It caused war between England and Holland, discontent in the American colonies, and piracy on the high seas.

The American colonies were regarded then simply as possessions—as sources of revenue for the mother country. " The only use of the American colonies," said Lord Sheffield, " is the monopoly of their consumption and the carriage of their produce." Under the Navigation Acts all colonial imports and exports had to be carried by English ships.

English merchants, being human, like to sell dearly and buy cheaply, and so long as England was not over-producing, the Navigation Acts favoured them both ways. Unable to trade with any other country, the colonists had to buy and sell at prices fixed by the English merchants. This meant that they could not afford to buy all the goods they needed, and they could not sell all their own produce, as the English market was not big enough to take it. Moreover, they had to pay whatever freight charges English shippers liked to impose, and whatever customs duties the Government in London chose to levy.

Thus mulcted, the colonies sought ways of evading the Navigation Acts. One obvious method was smuggling, and this was the only way the planters of Virginia and Maryland could export their surplus tobacco. For imports, however, the colonists preferred the pirates to the smugglers. Their prices were lower.

The position at this time has been aptly summed up by the American historian Shirley Carter Hughson:

" When the colonists found that they could neither buy nor sell save in an English market, at prices arbitrarily fixed by English merchants, they were quite willing to tolerate the lawless traders who could afford to sell them products of the world's markets at the lowest prices, since they cost them nothing more than a few hard blows. . . . It paid the colonists to incur the risk of losing their outward-bound cargoes, which were never during this period of any great value, when by this toleration they were enabled to buy in the cheapest market the world had ever known."

Carolina was one of the first of the colonies to open its doors to the buccaneers, and other colonies and plantations soon followed. Rhode Island offered excellent harbour facilities.

Pennsylvania was full of merchants ready to buy without asking questions. In Massachusetts pirates were always sure of a welcome, and in Boston they were almost given the freedom of the city. One popular figure in Boston was a notorious French pirate named Michel Andreson, alias Breha, who plundered Spanish and Jamaican shipping impartially. When, in 1684, Proclamations against pirates were put up in the streets, the citizens of Boston tore them down. When a public-minded Bostonian went and told the Governor that Andreson and his crew were in town, his fellow citizens nearly lynched him. But no harm was done, for the Governor had already come to a private arrangement with Andreson.

Nearly all the colonial Governors connived at piracy. The pirates' best friend of all was Colonel Fletcher, who became Governor of New York in 1682. They had to pay for his protection, of course, but he was reasonable in his demands. He could afford to be, for before long New York was swarming with pirates.

These Governors were not appointed by their Crown. They were nominated by the Lords Proprietors of the colonies, and although in theory the appointments had to be approved by the Government, in practice this regulation was usually evaded. As an official of the Crown pointed out, the Governors were " only stewards and overseers, always liable to be turned out at the pleasure of their employers." Their salaries were insufficient to meet their official expenses, and for their income they had to rely mainly on presents from the colonial elected Assemblies. In supporting piracy the Governors were not only lining their pockets, but were acting in accordance with the will of the majority of the people they were governing.

War usually caused a slump in piracy, but when war broke out in 1689 American piracy enjoyed a tremendous boom. Colonial Governors, now empowered to grant commissions to privateers, naturally did not forget their old friends; and they did not expect, or even want, the new ' privateers ' to seek plunder from the French in the dangerous West Indian or West African battle zones, when they could make " a more profitable and less hazardous voyage to the Red Sea."

This quotation is from a report dated 1695, entitled " A

EXECUTION DOCK, WAPPING

Pirates convicted in London were normally hanged at Wapping instead of Tyburn.

WALKING THE PLANK

A nineteenth-century picture of a nineteenth-century fiction. The picture is no more unrealistic than might be expected, for pirates never made their prisoners walk the plank.

HENRY EVERY, THE "ARCH-PIRATE"

Captain Every, sometimes called Avery, was one of the most successful of the Red Sea pirates. He and his crew enjoyed the protection of the Governors of the Bahamas, Pennsylvania, and New York.

Discourse about Pirates, with Proper Remedies to Suppress them." The author was Edward Randolph, Surveyor-General of Customs in the American colonies, who had for many years been waging an almost one-man war against smugglers and pirates.

Another pamphlet, entitled " Piracy Destroyed," written in 1701 by an officer of the East India Company, gives more information about the other end of the newly fashionable piratical voyage. Pirates from America began to appear in the Eastern Seas, it explains, " shortly after the late private war the East India Company had with the Moors "—that is, about 1690; " for the news of the rich booties, their ships seized, stirred up the old buccaneer gang (who found it more difficult to rob the Spaniards than formerly, and finding their prizes in the West Indies grow scarce) to direct their course to the East. And their success answering their expectation, their numbers daily increased by the news of the rich booties they had taken and reposed at Madagascar; and during the late war, this so successful and undisturbed pirating in the East rung so in the ears of those that with small success were privateering against the French, that whole companies both from England and our American colonies flocked thither."

Not many of these pirates came from England. The majority were ex-buccaneers from the American colonies, and for the first time in history the Governor of Jamaica found it hard to get men to serve on privateers. When the pirates reached the Eastern Seas they got fresh recruits from the crews of English ships belonging to the East India Company.

The Company itself was greatly alarmed by the sudden influx of pirates. Previously it had enjoyed a monopoly of piracy (" private war ") in the Eastern Seas, and had long since settled down to honest, respectable trade. This did not stop the Indians from holding the Company responsible; and as the pirates sailed under British colours, the Company suffered reprisals and often had to pay compensation.

The Company had the power to try pirates in the High Courts of Bombay and Madras, but very few pirates were brought to trial. One or two were hanged; others were branded with the letter P; and a few were sentenced to " run the gantlope." One of the biggest trials was of twenty English pirates caught by a Dutch man-of-war off Malacca and handed over to the Company officials (1690). They were found " equally guilty, but in consideration of the small execution they had done, and that justice is inclined to mercy, the Court thought fit to sentence two to death as well for example as terror's sake, taking the fortune of the dice."

Meeting a Dutch warship was the pirates' greatest danger, and most of them did not sail far enough eastward to run even this risk. There were no British men-of-war to disturb them, and they had not much to fear from the Company's own ships. Although these were well armed, the crews had little stomach for fighting, and their captains mostly gave the pirates a wide berth. The pirates returned the compliment, for there were richer and easier prizes to be taken. Their favourite victims were the ships sailing from Mocha to India. These were usually laden with treasure, and were easy to take. The pirates would lie in wait for them at the entrance to the Red Sea.

The only drawback to piracy in the Eastern Seas was the distance from America, and an advanced base was essential. At first the pirates used the isle of Perim, or Bab's Key, but they had to abandon this because of the lack of fresh water. They found an ideal alternative in Madagascar and the adjacent islands. Although these were much farther from the Red Sea, everything else was in their favour. Unclaimed by any European Power, and under no central native authority, Madagascar caused no political problems; and its many excellent harbours gave it ideal natural advantages. Security for careening was good, there was ample fresh water, and the provisions available included an abundance of anti-scorbutics. Scurvy always broke out during a long voyage, and although the seventeenth-century seamen had never heard of vitamins, they had learned empirically the value of oranges and limes in the treatment of this disease. There were plenty of both at Madagascar.

Trade follows flags of all colours, and it was not long before Madagascar attracted traders from America. Usually travelling in pirate ships, men went out not for piracy but to set up depots and stores to supply pirates with provisions and other goods. One ex-pirate, Adam Baldridge, set up a trading-post on St. Mary's Island, which had one of the best harbours of all. Baldridge provided not only amenities, but protection too, for he built a fort as well as warehouses. This saved his customers the trouble of having to put up an earthwork before they started the inevitable careening, and St. Mary's soon became the favourite base for operations in the Red Sea. It was also a refuge for shipwrecked seamen and deserters. Most of these waited for a berth on a pirate ship, but some settled down at St. Mary's, where life was more primitive but much easier than in England or the colonies. Some took native wives. Henry Watson, who was a prisoner of the pirates in 1696, suggests that the reason for such mating was not only biological:

" Their design in marrying the countrywomen is to ingratiate themselves with the inhabitants, with whom they go into war against the petty kings. If one Englishman goes with the Prince with whom he lives to war, he has half the slaves that are taken for his pains."

This is mainly confirmed by other evidence, although it is unlikely that marriage was a condition of military alliance. The native Madagascans welcomed Englishmen because they brought firearms. These natives, like the West African Negroes, waged almost continuous internecine wars with very primitive weapons. The aid of an armed Englishman was well worth half the prisoners of war. There were usually too many anyway, and most of those given to the pirates would otherwise have had to be killed.

The pirates used these slaves to supply them with their daily needs, and sold their surplus to ordinary European slavers that put in from time to time. The pirate settlers also claimed some of the cattle taken as tribute, and had quite an easy time. If they got bored they could always go home on the next ship returning from the Red Sea. Many did to after a few years and went back to their old trade of piracy; others retired for good, and spent the rest of their days in Madagascar.

Adam Baldridge, who stayed at his trading-post from 1690 to 1697, kept a journal in which he recorded all the shipping news. Here is a typical entry:

"October 1691. Arrived the *Bachelor's Delight*, Captain George Raynor, 180 tons or thereabouts, 14 guns, 70 or 80 men, that had made a voyage into the Red Sea and taken a ship belonging to the Moors. . . . They took so much money as made the whole share run about £1100 per man. They careened at St. Mary's and while they careened I supplied them with cattle for their present spending, and they gave me for my cattle a quantity of beads, five great guns for a fortification, some powder and shot, and six barrels of flour, about 70 bars of iron. The ship belonged to Jamaica and set sail from St. Mary's November 4th, 1691, bound for Port Dauphin on Madagascar to take in their provision, and December 9 they set sail from Port Dauphin bound for America, where they arrived at Carolina and complied with the owners, giving them for the ruin of the ship £3000, as I have heard since."

This ship, incidentally, was the same *Bachelor's Delight* in which Edward Davis had cruised in the Pacific for four years. Davis had sold it to a pirate syndicate in Carolina, where it had been refitted for the voyage to the Red Sea. The Governor of Carolina, who was notoriously accommodating, had sold the owners a privateering commission, and he received a further bribe when the ship returned home.

The share-out recorded by Baldridge was not exceptional, and it gives some idea of the value of the prizes taken in the Red Sea. Although these pirate ships often carried more than a hundred men, each of them usually received over £1,000 at the end of a single cruise—sometimes from a single prize. Occasionally the individual share was as high as £3,000. Many pirates retired after a single voyage. With such sums at stake it is not surprising that seamen preferred piracy to privateering even in wartime—especially when commissions and harbour facilities at their base were so easily obtained.

Indeed, in the eyes of the pirates it was almost as legal as privateering. They sailed with a commission signed by a Governor, the highest official in the colony. It was true that the commission authorized them only to attack French shipping and shore installations, usually on the Guinea coast. But when they returned to their base they were not blamed for having attacked Moorish ships in the Red Sea instead. On the contrary, the people were delighted with the wealth they brought into the colonies, and the Governor was only too ready to sell them a fresh commission as soon as they felt like going out again on the " pirate round." Everyone was happy —except, of course, the Moors, who were only heathens anyway, and the East India Company, which was the biggest piratical concern of all. The only person in the colonies who seemed to worry about it was Edward Randolph, the Surveyor-General of the Customs, who was above bribery and tireless in trying to carry out his impossible duties. All he could do was to collect evidence and send it with his recommendations to the Council for Trade and Plantations in London. He had been doing this for years without any effect.

Randolph's recommendations were quite simple. He remarked that " the Governors of plantations permitting pirates of all nations to be masters and owners of vessels was a great encouragement to the illegal trade." He recommended that commissions should only be granted to *bona fide* privateers, and that strict safeguards should be taken to ensure this was done. He said that the only way to prevent piracy was to destroy the pirates' bases, and asked for a man-of-war " under the command of a sober person " to be sent out to carry out this work. Finally, and most important of all, he asked the Council to be more careful in approving the appointments of colonial Governors.

Randolph gave the Council detailed evidence of connivance by the Governors in nearly all the American colonies. In Pennsylvania, he said, several pirates came in " and were, upon an acknowledgement of the Governor's favour, permitted to settle and trade there. A sloop of ten guns was launched there, being built for the trade to the Red Sea. Several pirates were concerned in her, I saw her upon the stocks."

The building of ships for piratical purposes was one of the most startling features of this startling era of piracy. Normally pirates did not spend any money on capital equipment. They stole their ship, and sank or burnt it as soon as they captured a better one. Yet here they seem to have been investing money in their trade.

In fact very few of the pirates made such investments. Ships, whether newly built or refitted, were owned by syndicates, as the *Bachelor's Delight* was. The capital was provided by speculators, who invested in a piratical cruise just as they invested in a privateering venture. The whole arrangement was similar to the combines of the Elizabethans like the Killigrews, except that the pirates had a greater share of the loot.

There is no better proof of the extent of official connivance than the fact that investors thought their investment a good risk. They had no guarantee that the pirates would bring the ship back to port. They could not have gone to law or appealed to the Government in London for help if they were let down. They could not get any real security. Often the pirate captain would buy a share in the ship, or leave a security; but there was no guarantee that he would stay captain. Although on these trips, so much akin to privateering voyages, the captain seems to have commanded a little more respect than was normal on a pirate ship, he could still be deposed at any time by a popular vote.

One colonial official, a rare supporter of Edward Randolph, reported that " several vessels, suspected to be bound on this design, sailed from one province or another of the continent, leaving some of their wives and families as pledges of their return behind them." Such pledges had small value. Seventeenth-century seamen do not appear to have felt very strongly about the permanence of marriage or the institution of the family. This official added in his report: " The people make so much advantage from the currency of their money that they will not be very forward to suppress it." That seems to be the true explanation of the investors' confidence in the pirates' return. The pirates would come back because they were sure of security and support, and did not consider the price too heavy even if it meant handing over a substantial part of their huge booty.

The shipyards in Boston were kept especially busy, according to Randolph, and he hints even at competition among the colonies for the services of the pirates. " There is every year one or two more vessels fitted to the Red Sea, under pretence of going to the West India plantations. Sir William Phips, the late Governor, invited the privateers [sic] to come from Pennsylvania to Boston, assuring them their liberty to trade. Tew had £2000 in the hands of one merchant in Boston, others have money in Rhode Island, and some of the Governors have enriched themselves by the pirates."

Thomas Tew was one of the most notorious captains of this period. He was also fairly typical, and his story may perhaps serve as an example of the normal " pirate round."

A man of a good Rhode Island family, Tew went to Bermuda and bought a share in the ship *Amity*, then owned jointly by a number of merchants and officials, including a member of the Governor's Council. In December 1692 the accommodating Governor of Bermuda, Isaac Richier, sold them a privateering commission authorizing Tew to help the Royal African Company in an expedition against a French factory on the Guinea coast.

Johnson tells us that while at sea Tew called his crew together and made a little speech. He told them that he had only accepted the commission because he wanted some employment, and that " he thought it a most injudicious expedition, for, if they succeeded, they would do no good to the public, advantaging only a private company of men, from which they could expect no proper reward for their bravery "— which was true enough. He went on that " he personally could see nothing but danger in the undertaking without the least prospect of booty, that he could not suppose any man so fond of fighting as to do it for its own sake," and " few ventured their lives but for some particular view of public gain or private interest." Finally he proposed making " one bold push " by which they could gain enough to retire on, to which the company responded in unison, " One and all, a gold chain or a wooden leg, we'll stand by you."

Probably nothing of the kind was said on the *Amity*, for there was no reason why Tew should have needed to deceive his crew in this way. Bermuda was swarming with willing pirates. But Tew's speech seemed to me to be worth quoting because it epitomizes the outlook of pirates at this period. Johnson made mistakes and pandered to his readers' bloodlusts, but he had a wonderful knack of bringing his characters to life. Tew's speech shows not only why, for once, seamen preferred piracy to privateering even when there was a war on, but also the ordinary seaman's attitude to privateering. However men may have felt about serving their country in the Royal Navy, patriotism was neither invoked nor evoked on a private man-of-war. Each privateering expedition was financed by capitalists seeking profits, and manned by seamen seeking loot, and any help it might give to the war effort was incidental.

Tew's expedition was very successful. With a crew of only seventy the *Amity* engaged a Moorish ship in the Red Sea, well armed and with five hundred soldiers on board. There was hardly a fight, and the pirates suffered no casualties. The booty was large. Johnson estimates it at £3,000 per man, but the more reliable Baldridge says that the share-out at St. Mary's yielded £1,200 per man.

Baldridge checked in the *Amity* in October 1693. "They bought cattle from me for their present spending, and careened at St. Mary's." According to Johnson, Tew now fell in with a French pirate named Misson, who eventually settled down and founded an anarchist Utopia in Madagascar, called Libertatia. Regrettably there is no other evidence even of Misson's existence, so his colourful story must be omitted. It deserves a few words of comment, however, for this invention of Johnson's probably expresses a typical pirates' dream-world. Writing over sixty years before the French Revolution, Johnson credited Misson with establishing a republic based on the principles of Liberty, Equality, and Fraternity. An example of Misson's 'advanced' views is found in his condemnation of the slave trade:

"The trading for those of our own species could never be agreeable to the eyes of divine justice. No man had power of the liberty of another, and while those who profess a more enlightened knowledge of the deity sold men like beasts, they proved that their religion was no more than grimace and that they differed from the barbarians in name only, since their practice was in nothing more humane."

This was virtually an insult to the Royal Family, which owned shares in the slave-trade monopoly; and it may be that Johnson invented Misson simply as a mouthpiece for his own advanced views, which if declared openly might have involved him in a charge of seditious libel. At any rate, Libertatia almost certainly never existed. Although it seems that Tew's quartermaster and twenty-three other members of his crew decided to settle on Madagascar, Tew was not elected Admiral of Misson's Fleet, as Johnson says, but left St. Mary's in December 1693 (Baldridge) and arrived at Rhode Island in the following April (Edward Randolph) bearing " £100,000 in gold and silver and a good parcel of elephants' teeth, bought up by the merchants of Boston."

I have been unable to find any Articles of Agreement or other reliable information on the financial arrangements made between the Red Sea pirates and their American promoters. However, if the figures given by Baldridge and Randolph are correct, it seems that out of a total booty of about £130,000 the pirates shared amongst them about £85,000 to £90,000 (allowing for extra shares for officers, bonuses and pensions), or between sixty-five and seventy per cent. The usual privateering terms at this period gave the crew sixty per cent., but of course the average gross profits from expeditions against the French were not comparable with the plunder gained from the Moors. The promoters did very well out of the business, and the fact that the pirates meekly paid over such a large sum as £40,000 to £45,000 without any legal compulsion is striking evidence of the value they placed on having a good base and of how good that base was.

One other thing that is shown very clearly from Baldridge's journal, read in conjunction with Randolph's reports and other documents printed in the Calendar of State Papers, is that the pirates always took their loot with them. They shared out as soon as they made a landfall, and they did not bury their treasure.

Another point of interest is that the pirates were no longer regarded by the American colonists only as free-traders running the blockade of the Navigation Acts. Originally they had been encouraged because they brought in necessary goods that the colonists could not obtain legally. Now, although they brought some ivory and Eastern merchandise, the bulk of their plunder was usually gold and silver and jewels, and they were encouraged mainly because they brought wealth into the colonies. They were especially popular in the seaports, for most pirates were good spenders.

On his return Tew spent the summer at Newport, while the *Amity* was refitted. Then he bought a fresh commission from Colonel Fletcher for £300, and sailed again in November 1694. " Upon such great encouragement," says Randolph, " three other vessels were fitted out to join with him. They were all expected to return this last spring. . . . 'Tis supposed Tew will go to the Bahama Islands."

Tew did not go to the Bahamas. On December 11, 1695, Baldridge wrote in his journal:

" Arrived the ship *Amity* having no captain, Thomas Tew having been killed by a great shot from a Moor's ship in the Red Sea."

Johnson's account of Tew's death is more picturesque but less accurate:

" In the engagement a shot carried away the rim of Tew's belly, who held his bowels with his hands some small space; when he dropped, it struck such a terror in his men that they suffered themselves to be taken without making resistance."

A good curtain for Johnson's bloody-minded readers, but the anatomical details are of doubtful authenticity and the statement that the *Amity* was taken is disproved by Baldridge. This particular engagement is of special interest because the *Amity* was part of a pirate fleet commanded by one of the most famous pirates in history, who needs a chapter to himself.

CHAPTER TWELVE

The Arch-pirate

IN 1700 a little book was published in London with the intriguing title *The Life and Adventures of Captain John Avery, now in possession of Madagascar.* The author was anonymous, signing himself merely " a person who made his escape from thence." His story was that Captain Avery, a notorious English pirate, had established himself as King of Madagascar and was living on the island in great state and luxury. He was said to be as wealthy as any Eastern potentate, having robbed a Moorish ship of priceless treasures, which included the beautiful daughter of the Great Mogul of India. Many of the women on board had been killed, but the Princess had suffered a fate worse than death and was now also living in luxury in Madagascar as Avery's consort. Other versions of the same story appeared, and in his own lifetime Avery achieved a fame that was never gained by any other pirate. He was widely spoken of as the " Arch-Pirate." The legend persisted for many years, and in 1712 a play about him was put on at Drury Lane. It was called *The Successful Pirate*, and seems to have been a successful play.

If it does nothing else, the story of Avery at least shows how unwise it is to accept contemporary evidence about pirates unless it can be confirmed. It happens that the story of Avery also reveals a good deal about piracy in general during this period, and that is why it is getting a chapter in this book.

Captain Johnson was the first to expose the Avery myth, but his biography is not altogether reliable. Fortunately the career of the " Arch-Pirate " is adequately documented, and it is unnecessary to rely on Johnson.

This pirate's real name was Henry Every. The *Dictionary of National Biography* follows Johnson in calling him John Avery, but does not cite any authority for this. Certainly he signed himself Henry Every, and this is the name that appears in the Calendar of State Papers. He seems to have been known by his intimates as Long Ben, but the reason for this is a mystery. He was said to be " middle-sized, inclinable to be fat, and of a jolly complexion."

Little is known about Every's origin. A Dutchman who sailed with him said that he was once an honest seaman, serving first in the Navy and then in the merchant service, and that he was driven to piracy by the infidelity of his wife. He seems to have been captain of an unlicensed slaver, for in 1693 Captain Phillips of the *Hannibal* was complaining that on the Guinea coast he had " never found the negroes so shy and scarce," which he attributed to " kidnapping tricks having been played on them by Long Ben, alias Every, and others of his kidney who had seized them off without any payment." Henry Bruce, a West Indian merchant, wrote in his memoirs that from 1690 to 1692 Every was under the protection of Governor Jones of the Bahamas.

The authenticated story of Every begins in 1694, when he was sailing master on the privateer *Charles the Second*, which sailed from Bristol to Corunna to join a Spanish expedition against the French. There was a bloodless mutiny on the *Charles*, caused by the lack of plunder taken and the poor prospects. The crew had not received any pay for eight months, and did not expect to get any loot from the French. They invited the captain to retain his command if he would agree to turn pirate; he refused, and was put ashore with a few other dissenters. Every was elected captain and the ship was renamed the *Fancy*.

Sailing to the Cape Verde Islands, the pirates took some provisions off three English ships without paying for them. Then they took two Danish ships. They were not valuable prizes, and the first share-out yielded only eight or nine ounces of gold per man. After some more rather desultory piracy the *Fancy* sailed round the Cape of Good Hope to Madagascar. After the inevitable careening the pirates sailed to the isle of Johanna, in the Comoro Gulf. A French pirate ship came in soon after, loaded with booty taken from the Moors in the Red Sea. Every showed that he had not forgotten there was a war on by seizing the ship and her contents. Then he forgot all about the war and signed on the entire French crew.

Before leaving Johanna, Every wrote an open letter to his compatriots, which he asked the native chief to deliver to the next English ship that called. The letter read:

"To all English Commanders.

"Let this satisfy that I was riding here at this instant in the ship *Fancy*, man-of-war, formerly the *Charles* of the Spanish Expedition who departed from Croniae [Corunna] the 7th May 1694, being then and now a ship of 46 guns, 150 men and bound to seek our fortunes. I have never as yet wronged any English or Dutch, or ever intend whilst I am commander. Wherefore as I commonly speak with all ships I desire whoever comes to the perusal of this to take this signal, that if you or any whom you may inform are desirous to know what we are at a distance, then make your ancient [ensign] up in a ball or bundle and hoist him at the mizen peak, the mizen being furled. I shall answer with the same, and never molest you, for my men are hungry, stout and resolute, and should they exceed my desire I cannot help myself. As yet an Englishman's friend,

"At Johanna, 18th February 1695
"Henry Every.

[Postscript] "Here is 160 odd French armed men at Mohilla who waits for opportunity of getting any ship, take care of yourselves."

This mixture of threats and assurances was picked up by an East Indiaman and sent to London in May with a request for stronger measures against the pirates.

Meanwhile the *Fancy* had been joined by two other pirate ships from the American colonies, and the combined force sailed to the Red Sea to lie in wait for the Mocha fleet. While waiting they were joined by two more ships, which had come up from St. Mary's. One was the *Amity*, commanded by Captain Tew. Captain Every was given temporary supreme command of the whole formidable pirate fleet.

One of the ships became unseaworthy, and it was decided to destroy her and distribute her crew among the other four. They cruised independently for a while, each keeping within range of the flagship. The Mocha fleet came down, but most of it managed to get past the pirates during the night. Two ships, however, did not escape.

The smaller of these, called the *Fateh Mahomed*, was engaged first by the *Amity*. The Moors resisted, and one of their shots killed Tew; and the *Amity* disengaged. The *Fancy* pursued the Moors, who surrendered without offering much more resistance. Captain Every then went after the larger ship, the *Gang-i-sawai* (*Gunsway*).

According to the Indian historian Khafi Khan this was " the greatest in all the Mogul dominions." He says that she had sixty-two great guns, and that there were four hundred musketeers and other soldiers on board. The *Fancy* engaged her with only one other ship in support (the *Pearl*), as the *Amity* and the fourth ship had fallen behind. The battle lasted for two hours, and both sides suffered fairly heavy casualties. Then the pirates succeeded in boarding the *Gang-i-sawai*.

Khafi Khan blames the Moorish captain, Ibrahim Khan, for not putting up a better fight. " The English are not bold in the use of the sword," he says, " and there were so many weapons aboard that, if any determined resistance had been made, they had been defeated." He relates that when the pirates boarded, Ibrahim Khan ran down into the hold, where there were some Turkish girls whom he was bringing from Mecca to be his concubines. " He put turbans on their heads and then incited them to fight. But these girls quickly fell into the hands of the Englishmen, who had made themselves masters of the ship." Finally, the pirates " busied themselves stripping the men and killing them, and dishonouring the women both young and old. They then left the ship to go free, but took with them most of the women. Several of the ladies threw themselves into the sea, and others killed themselves with the swords and daggers of the Englishmen."

There is plenty of reliable evidence confirming the statement about the treatment of the women. A letter from the East India Company at Bombay, reporting the affair, states that the pirates " did do very barbarously by the people . . . to make them confess where their money was, and there happened to be a great umbraw's wife, related to the King, returning from her pilgrimage to Mecca in her old age. She they abused very much, and forced several other women, which caused one person of quality, his wife and nurse to kill themselves to prevent the husband's seeing them (and their being) ravished. All this will raise a black cloud at court, which we wish may not produce a severe storm."

An umbraw was a grandee of the Great Mogul's court. Perhaps it was this ill-treatment of the Mogul's aged relative that inspired the story of the abduction of a beautiful princess. Anyway, the Mogul could hardly have been more displeased, and the writer's forebodings were quickly justified.

Members of the crew of the *Fancy* also admitted both torture and rape. One, who later turned King's evidence, said: "The treasure was very great, but little in comparison with what was on board; for though they put several to the torture, they would not confess where the rest of their treasure lay. They took great quantities of jewels and a saddle and bridle set with rubies designed as a present for the Great Mogul. The men lay with the women aboard, and there were several that, from their jewels and habits, seemed to be of better quality than the rest." This is confirmed by the evidence of another informer, who added that many of the women jumped into the sea to escape being raped, while others died from the treatment they received.

The pirates shared out their loot at the French island of Réunion, each man receiving about £1,000 and some jewels. The *Fancy* appears not to have touched again at Madagascar, where Every was supposed to have established his kingdom. There was some disagreement among the crew about which part of America to sail for, which was understandable, as they had no colonial base. However, Every succeeded in persuading the men to make for the Bahamas, where he had good reason to expect a cordial welcome. To be on the safe side he called first at the island of St. Thomas, where he learnt that the Bahamas had a new Governor. Every wrote him a letter in the hope that he would prove as amiable as so many of his predecessors had been. He asked for permission to take the ship in, and an assurance of protection and liberty to leave at will; for these privileges he offered twenty pieces of eight and two pieces of gold from each member of the crew, and also the ship and her contents, excluding the plunder.

The new Governor, Nicholas Trott, accepted the offer

without argument, and the *Fancy* put in. Before the ship could be handed over she was driven ashore by a gale and became a total loss except for her guns. At the Governor's request these were salved by the pirates and mounted in an earthwork commanding the entrance to the harbour.

Knowing that the East India Company would by now have asked the Government to take action against them, the pirates thought of ways of getting a Royal Pardon. As the Governor of the Bahamas was not empowered to issue pardons, they applied to the Governor of Jamaica, who later wrote to the Council for Trade and Plantations:

" 15th June 1696. The pirates that ran away with one of Don Oburri's ships [i.e. the *Charles*] from Corunna have been in the Red Sea and gotten great wealth, up to £300,000 it is reported. They are arrived at Providence and have sent privately to me, to try if they could prevail with me to pardon them and let them come hither; and in order to it I was told that it should be worth to me a great gun (£20,000), but that could not tempt me from my duty."

Meanwhile the promised " black cloud " had been raised at the Great Mogul's court, and the East India Company was paying heavily for the depredations of the *Fancy*. The Company's establishments at Surat, Agra, and other places were seized, and merchants and agents were put in prison and treated so severely that some died. The others were held for six months. The Company begged the Government to take some sort of action. The Government replied by issuing a proclamation offering a reward of £500 per head for each of Every's crew. The East India Company doubled the reward.

Having been refused a pardon by the Governor of Jamaica, the crew of the *Fancy* broke up and scattered. Some went to New England, others to the Carolinas, at least one to Pennsylvania, and a few stayed in the West Indies. Two other parties bought sloops and sailed for England. The captain of one now called himself Bridgeman, but he was really Henry Every.

Every and about twenty others reached County Mayo in June 1696. In landing their booty they aroused the sheriff's suspicions, and one man, Philip Middleton, was caught. He

"THEIR EXCELLENCIES THE LORDS JUSTICES OF ENGLAND FOR THE ADMINI-
STRATION OF THE GOVERNMENT IN HIS MAJESTY'S ABSENCE" (1697)

Three of their Excellencies—Lord Somers (top centre), the Earl of
Romney (bottom left), and the Earl of Orford (bottom right)—were
secret shareholders in Captain Kidd's privateering expedition (1696–99).

Articles of Agreement made & concluded
upon this Tenth Day of September Anno 1696.
Between Cap.t William Kidd Comander of the good Ship
Adventure Golly on the one part. And John Walker
Quarter Master to the said ships Company on the
other part as followeth Vizt.

Imp.r
That the above said Cap.t William Kidd shall receive for the
above said ship (he finding the said Ship in wear & Tear) Thirty five
Shares. As also five full shares for himself & his Commission
of such Treasure Wares and Merchandizes as shall from time
to time be taken by the said Ship and Company by Sea or Land.

2.
That the Master for his care shall receive Two
Shares of all such Treasures, and the Cap.t shall allow all
the other Officers a gratification above their own Shares
out of the ship Shares as the said Cap.t or other in his place
shall deem reasonable.

3.
That the above Ships Company do oblige themselves
to pay out of the first money or Merchandize taken for all
such Provisions as were received on board the said Ships
in the River of Thames according to the Tradesmens Bills.
And for what Provisions the said William Kidd shall from
time to time purchase for Victualling the said Ship &
Company in America or else where, the said Ships
Company do oblige themselves to pay for the said Pro=
visions such advance as shall be demanded by the In=
habitants of the places where the said Provisions shall
be purchased

4.
That the said Ships Company shall out of the first pur=
chase taken after the Victualling of the said Ship is paid pay for
the Chirurgeons Chest & all Ships Debts by the said Voyage
contracted.

5.
That if any Man shall loose an Eye, Legg or Arme or
the

Ext   215

CAPTAIN KIDD'S ARTICLES
A copy of part of the articles drawn up between Captain Kidd and his
crew in New York (1696). These were conventional privateering articles.

turned King's evidence, making a long deposition in Ireland in August, and repeating the substance of this three months later in London.

Another of the pirates, John Dann, reached London safely and went on to Rochester. On his first day there he was arrested—" a maid having found my gold quilted up in my jacket," he said later. The discovery was not surprising, for his jacket was found to contain over £1,000, all in sequins (half-sovereigns). There is evidence here that not all pirates were profligate—although John Dann perhaps wished he had been less thrifty. Dann also turned informer, and his evidence agreed closely with that of Middleton. My account of the cruise of the *Fancy* is based partly on the depositions of these two informers.

Some other members of the crew were arrested and tried before the end of the year. Again, their evidence mainly confirmed what Middleton and Dann had said. The atrocities were freely admitted, and the allegations of Nicholas Trott's connivance were repeated. There were also some startling revelations about official support of piracy in the American colonies. Of the twenty-four men on trial, six were hanged at Wapping and most of the others sentenced to transportation to Virginia; but the real importance of the trial was the evidence against colonial Governors who were still in office. Some of the results of this evidence will be shown in a later chapter.

Henry Every was never caught. According to Dann, he went from Ireland to Scotland, but " had spoken of going to Exeter, being a Plymouth man." Dann himself picked up a clue near London. The quartermaster of the *Fancy*, a man named Adams, had brought his wife back from the Bahamas, and Dann saw her again at St. Albans, getting into a stage-coach. He stopped and talked to her, and she told him she was " going to Captain Bridgeman's," but gave no hint of where that was.

Johnson's story is picturesque. He says that Every went to Bideford and negotiated with some Bristol merchants for the sale of his own share of the plunder, which was all in diamonds. The merchants visited him, paid a small deposit, and took the diamonds away, and he never saw them again.

When he asked for the money they threatened to expose him; and in the end he died " not being worth as much as would buy him a coffin." This account contains too many implausibilities to be taken seriously.

So the story of the " Arch Pirate " ends in mystery. As Every would hardly have kept the name of Bridgeman after the arrest of his fellow pirates, the mystery will probably never be solved. I like to think that he may have lived to go to the Theatre Royal, Drury Lane, to watch a performance of *The Successful Pirate*.

CHAPTER THIRTEEN

The Mystery of Captain Kidd

THE story of Henry Every ends with a question mark. With a little more evidence the mystery might be solved. The story of Captain Kidd is punctuated with question marks. With a little less evidence the mystery has been solved —several times, in several ways.

" Historic facts," said Froude, " are like a child's box of letters. You have only to pick out such letters as you want and spell any word you like. . . . Select such facts as suit you, and leave alone those which do not suit you, and let your theory of history be what it may, you can find no difficulty in providing facts to prove it."

It is easy to draw a convincing picture of Kidd as either a villain or a martyr simply by ignoring the facts that do not fit your particular theory. What makes him so baffling and fascinating is that all the known facts together do not seem to fit any theory.

Few pirates' case-histories are better documented than that of Captain Kidd. His dossier contains a great mass of contemporary evidence besides the verbatim report of his trial. The Calendar of State Papers is full of fascinatingly contradictory information, and there is a lot more in quite unlikely bundles in the Public Record Office. Much of the evidence has been sifted and analysed by eminent jurists and historians, and enough time has passed for his case to be reviewed objectively and dispassionately. Indeed, most of the legal and historical analysts have given their findings in an objective and dispassionate style. But their verdicts do not agree. They range from Sir Cornelius Neale Dalton's view that Kidd was " a worthy, honest-hearted, steadfast, much-enduring sailor " to Lord Birkenhead's " he thoroughly deserved the hangman's rope."

Encyclopædia Britannica (1950 edition) seems to be on both sides. The article on Kidd bluntly calls him a pirate, but the article on piracy (by Philip Gosse) says " the famous Captain Kidd was no pirate at all." I can think of a reasonable editorial explanation for this inconsistency, but it is typical of the prevailing contradictions of opinion.

Whether Kidd was a pirate or not is wrapped up—too closely, in my opinion—with the question of whether or not he had a fair trial. The *Dictionary of National Biography* states that " it is clear that he had not a fair trial, and was found guilty on insufficient evidence." Legal opinion seems to be divided, although it is mostly against Kidd. Lord Birkenhead, in his *Famous Trials of History* (1926), considers that the trial was fair and that " there can be no doubt of his guilt." Graham Brooks, in his introduction to the *Trial of Captain Kidd* (published in 1930 in William Hodge's notable series of " Notable British Trials "), declares emphatically that there was " no miscarriage of justice " and that " it was abundantly clear that Kidd was guilty of all the charges preferred against him." But another barrister, Charles Wye Kendall, in his *Private Men-of-War* (1931) without producing any fresh evidence says: " Kidd was the victim of a very ugly perversion of justice."

It will be seen that the verdicts quoted, although contradictory, have one point in common: they are all very emphatic. Each writer ' solved ' the Kidd mystery in his own way, and seems to have been left without any doubts. A study of each analysis shows also that each verdict was thoroughly substantiated by the evidence. The lawyers' arguments in particular are brilliantly convincing. But a comparison of the arguments reveals that in each case the evidence was incomplete. Each of these writers seems to have selected the most suitable facts, drawn inferences from them—usually reasonable, but usually contradicted by the facts that were omitted—and produced a definite and apparently just verdict.

On one point, at least, all writers on Kidd seem to be agreed. He does not deserve his popular reputation. Yet in spite of the agreement, there is an unsolved mystery here too.

Captain Kidd is probably the best-known pirate of all. In popular esteem he is almost the apotheosis of the pirate captain

—bold and dashing, ruthless and bloodthirsty, a tyrant over his crew and the terror of the high seas. His place in pirate literature is unique. More ink has been spilt about him than about anyone else in the trade. Yet few pirates spilt less blood. The legend of Captain Kidd, ace pirate, is only a legend. If he was a pirate of any sort, he was certainly not an ace. As Philip Gosse has said:

" If Kidd's reputation was in just proportion to his actual deeds, he would have been forgotten as soon as he had been ' turned off ' at Wapping Old Stairs. His fame in piracy was as undeserved as the glory of Dick Turpin, the reputed king of the ' gentlemen of the road,' who was in life a mere pickpocket but after death stole the famous ride to York from Nevison, a genuine and daring highwayman." As a matter of fact Turpin was just as genuine a highwayman as Nevison, and neither of them made the ride to York; but the comparison is apt.

There were good reasons for Kidd's notoriety in his lifetime, but these were more political than piratical. It was no wonder that his trial was sensational. Two Ministers of the Crown were impeached on his account, the whole Government was under suspicion, and there were even whispers that the King was involved in the scandal. Kidd's name was bandied about freely during brawls in and out of the Houses of Parliament. He was as much a political issue then as the meat ration is now, probably with as little reason.

But this was over two and a half centuries ago, and the political squabble has long since gone the way of all political squabbles. The mystery is why Kidd's fame has survived. He was neither good enough nor bad enough to deserve a place in the first hundred notable pirates. The only unusual thing about him is that he was unlucky. Most ' doubtful ' pirates got the benefit of the doubt; Kidd got the rope—and even that broke twice.

Yet Kidd is remembered while far bigger men are forgotten, and it is unlikely that he will ever be displaced as the Great Pirate. Scores of books and articles have been written to kill the myth—but the myth lives on. Doubtless interest has been stimulated by the stories of his non-existent treasure—but other pirates have been credited with buried treasure. The only answer to this mystery seems to be that you cannot destroy a popular belief merely by proving that it is false.

The story of Kidd began in 1695, when the British Government was at last persuaded to take some action against the " pirate round." In that year Randolph's charges against colonial Governors were supplemented by a private report from Peter Delanoy, a member of the New York Assembly. He wrote: " We have a parcel of pirates, called the Red Sea men, in these parts, who got great booty of Arabian gold. The Governor encourages them since they make due acknowledgment. One captain gave him a ship which he sold for £800, and every man of the crew a present of Arabian gold. Another was openly caressed in the coach and six and presented with a gold watch to encourage him to make New York his port at his return; and he retaliated the kindness with a present of jewels." The pirate whom Colonel Fletcher " openly caressed " was Thomas Tew.

Instead of ordering the Lords Proprietors to replace Fletcher, the Government took the sensible course of appointing a servant of the Crown as Governor of New York, Massachusetts, and New Hampshire, making him also Captain-General of all forces in Connecticut, Rhode Island, and the Jerseys. The appointment was offered to the Earl of Bellomont, an Irish peer, who agreed to accept it only on condition that he was given a salary large enough to enable him to live without taking bribes. After some grumbling the Government eventually agreed to this unheard-of demand. Bellomont then proposed that a warship should be sent to the Red Sea to seek out the pirates, and a prominent New Yorker, Colonel Livingston, recommended that the command should be given to Captain William Kidd.

Kidd was then about fifty. He was a successful and respected sea-captain, with a fine record of privateering against the French. He owned property in New York, where he lived with his wife and children, and had never been involved with pirates.

The proposal for a naval expedition fell through because the Admiralty said that no warship could be spared while the war with France continued. Bellomont then organized a straight-forward privateering expedition. The King approved, promising to take ten per cent. of the proceeds, " chiefly to show that he was a partner in the undertaking." The King's share was a private venture, not to be confused with the " King's tenth " that he would get anyway. The King said also that he would put up £3,000 of the capital, but he never did. As things turned out, this was probably just as well for the monarchy.

In October 1695 " Rules of Agreement " were drawn up between Bellomont, Kidd, and Livingston. Under these Bellomont promised to put up four-fifths of the money (£6,000) on condition that Kidd and Livingston together supplied the balance. Bellomont did not provide his share of the money by himself. He had a private—and secret—agreement with some prominent Whig politicians, including Sir John Somers, Keeper of the Great Seal; Edward Russell (later the Earl of Orford), First Lord of the Admiralty; the Earl of Romney, Master of the Ordnance; and the Duke of Shrewsbury, a Secretary of State. These Whig nobles took shares in the enterprise but kept their names out of it.

The King granted two commissions to " our trusty and well-beloved Captain William Kidd." One was an ordinary privateering commission against all French shipping; the other was to seize four named pirates—including Thomas Tew —and any others he might find, together with their ships and contents. The pirate ships were expected to be the main source of plunder.

The " Rules of Agreement " also laid down the division of the profit. After the King had taken his ten per cent., it was to be shared as follows: sixty per cent. to Bellomont, fifteen per cent. to Kidd and Livingston, and a maximum of twenty-five per cent. to the crew. Kidd was instructed to try to persuade the crew to accept less. The crew would, of course, be on a " no purchase, no pay " basis, and Kidd and Livingston had to promise that if the plunder was insufficient they would recompense Bellomont for the whole of his outlay. As security Kidd had to enter into a bond in £20,000, and Livingston entered into a bond of £10,000 as guarantor of Kidd's integrity.

The crew was hand-picked. It consisted mainly of married men, who, the promoters thought, were most likely to remain honest. The ship, the *Adventure Galley* (thirty guns), was fitted out, and sailed from England in May 1696. She was held up at the Nore, where about seventy of the best seamen were impressed by the Navy. Crossing the Atlantic, Kidd took a small French vessel, and on reaching New York he handed her over to the Vice-Admiralty Court. She was condemned as a prize, and the proceeds of the sale were used to buy provisions for the *Adventure Galley*. To make up his crew Kidd had to sign on another seventy men in New York. Bellomont had not yet arrived to take up his appointment, and Colonel Fletcher was still Governor. The town was at its piratical worst. To persuade men to join the ship Kidd posted up new articles, raising the crew's share in the plunder to the usual sixty per cent.

Up to this point the facts, although puzzling, are fully authenticated. There is less certainty about what happened when the *Adventure Galley* reached the Red Sea, but certain facts are undisputed. Over a year had passed since the ship left England, and the crew was restless. The ship was leaking, provisions were low, and in a single week one-third of the men died of cholera. Kidd had to make up his crew at the island of Johanna, a popular pirate resort.

The remaining evidence about the voyage is conflicting. Kidd's own version is that he spent his time trying to restrain the piratical desires of his crew. According to Kidd's opponents, he led his men into piracy. It seems certain that there was some kind of mutiny, and shortly after this Kidd struck one of the mutineers, William Moore, with a bucket. Moore died on the following day. It is certain also that five ships were plundered. Three were small vessels, and were robbed only of provisions. The other two—the *Maiden* and the *Quedagh Merchant*—were taken as prizes. Both were owned by Armenians. The loot was shared out at St. Mary's, according to the terms of the articles signed in New York. When news of these facts reached London, Kidd was proscribed a pirate. A Royal Proclamation was published offering a free pardon to all pirates east of the Cape of Good Hope except Kidd and

Every. At the same time a naval squadron was sent out to take Kidd.

The squadron reached the Eastern Seas too late, and in April 1699 Kidd reappeared in the West Indies in the *Quedagh Merchant*, which was loaded with his share of the plunder. There he learnt—" with great consternation," he said afterwards—that he had been declared a pirate.

Leaving the ship, Kidd went to Boston, hid some of his plunder, and made a cautious approach to Lord Bellomont. A letter he sent to him referred to two enclosures—French passes taken from the *Maiden* and *Quedagh Merchant*—which Kidd claimed would prove his innocence. Bellomont then " wheedled " (his own word) Kidd into going ashore, and then arrested him and sent him back to England in chains.

The arrest of Kidd caused a sensation in London, where political feeling was running high. The names of the Whig sponsors of the expedition were known, and the Tories accused them of having sent Kidd a-pirating. Somers, now Lord Chancellor, was their special target, a resolution being moved in the House of Commons to ask the King to remove him " from his presence and counsels for ever." The House demanded to see the documents in the case, and the Admiralty sent over a pile of papers that were in such a mess that a special Parliamentary Committee had to be appointed to sort them out. This took three weeks. Then the House examined Kidd as well as the papers. He was a disappointment to the Tories, for instead of incriminating the Whigs he persisted in declaring that he was innocent. He was sent back to Newgate to await his trial.

Altogether Kidd had to wait nearly two years from the time of his arrest. Then he had four separate trials, on six indictments. Under the rules of procedure at that time Kidd was not allowed to be represented by counsel (except at the preliminary hearing), and had to conduct his own defence.

The first indictment was unexpected. Kidd was charged with the murder of William Moore, whom he was said to have injured fatally with a bucket worth eightpence. The only witnesses for the prosecution were Robert Bradinham and Joseph Palmer, both former members of the crew who had deserted at St. Mary's, joined a pirate ship, and later appealed for pardon under the terms of the proclamation. Palmer said that he had seen Kidd strike Moore and had heard the exchange of words before the blow, while Bradinham was the surgeon who had attended Moore. Kidd said that Moore had been mutinous, but Palmer denied this. Kidd also said that Moore had been sick and that the blow had not caused his death, but Bradinham denied this. Kidd was found guilty.

The other five indictments related to piracy. Three concerned the minor looting incidents; the other two charged Kidd with unlawfully seizing the *Maiden* and the *Quedagh Merchant*.

Again the only witnesses for the prosecution were Bradinham and Palmer.

Kidd admitted that the five incidents had taken place, but denied that he had committed any act of piracy. He claimed that throughout the voyage he had been struggling to control the piratical desires of his crew, and that he had not always succeeded. He disclaimed responsibility for the three minor incidents. He admitted taking the two prizes, but said that each had been sailing under a French pass, and was therefore legitimate prey. He said that mutiny had made it impossible for him to take them back to New York for adjudication by the Vice-Admiralty Court of Prize, and the share-out at St. Mary's was forced on him.

Kidd was unable to produce the two French passes. He told the court he had given them to Lord Bellomont, who had since died. The court decided that the passes had never existed, and Kidd was found guilty on all counts and sentenced to death. When sentence was passed he protested: "I am the innocentest person of them all, only I have been sworn against by perjured persons." He was executed at Wapping on May 23, 1701, and his body was hung in chains farther down the river.

Over two hundred years later an American named Ralph D. Paine found the French passes in the Public Record Office in London, and the great Kidd controversy began.

Was Kidd a pirate? Did he have a fair trial? These two questions have usually been treated together, as if both had to have the same answer. Most legal writers seem to have treated the issue as a straightforward case of William Kidd versus what Graham Brooks calls " the fair name of British justice." This seems to be over-simplification.

It may be impertinent for a layman to argue with lawyers over matters of law, even when the jurists disagree among themselves. Both Lord Birkenhead and Graham Brooks put Kidd back in the dock and found him guilty on all counts, and the arguments of Graham Brooks seem to have persuaded such a distinguished historian as Philip Gosse to reverse his opinion of Kidd. Yet so much evidence was omitted, and so many inferences are refuted by that evidence, that perhaps a layman may be permitted to dissent.

No one has disputed that the French passes were deliberately suppressed. Bellomont had sent them to England, and they had been among the documents examined by the House of Commons; indeed, copies were printed in the Journal of the House, although Kidd was evidently unaware of this, and no one bothered to tell him. He thought they were still in New York. The House ordered that the passes should be made available as evidence at Kidd's trial, and this order was flouted by the Admiralty. Graham Brooks admits that this was " a blot on the fair name of British justice," but argues that the trial was still fair and the verdict just. He says: " The passes could only have provided Kidd with a defence to the indictments if in fact the ships were (or were reasonably believed by Kidd to be) the property of French subjects or of persons domiciled in French dominions. It was not sufficient for Kidd merely to prove that he found a French pass on board the ship."

That is the view of a twentieth-century lawyer—but it was not the view of Kidd's contemporaries. When Bellomont received the passes he wrote to Kidd: " I am apt they will be a good article to justify you." At the preliminary hearing Kidd's counsel said: " If those ships that he took had French passes, there was just cause of seizure, and it would excuse him from piracy." No one denied this. Indeed, the presiding judge told Kidd in court that " if there was a French pass on the ship, you ought to have condemned her as a prize "; and in his summing up he told the jury that the question of whether the passes existed was "the great case that is before you, and on which the indictment turns." He also made it pretty clear that he did not believe in their existence.

If the French passes had been as unimportant as Graham Brooks suggests, they would hardly have been suppressed. In fact there is abundant external evidence that the possession of a French pass was sufficient for a ship to be seized as a prize. Indeed, the history of privateering reveals many cases during this period of ships being seized and subsequently condemned as prizes on much slighter evidence. Kidd's only fault here was allowing the crew to take their share of the plunder before the prize had been condemned by a Vice-Admiralty Court.

Another important issue is the reliability of the evidence for the prosecution. Only two witnesses were called—Bradinham and Palmer. Both had deserted from Kidd, joined a pirate ship, and later appealed for a pardon. Kidd said they were perjured, but Graham Brooks says that the jury was entitled to believe their evidence. He does not mention that Palmer's evidence conflicted with the deposition he had made when he was examined by an Admiralty Judge in New England. The reason for the change is made clear in a letter written by Bellomont to the Secretary of State in March 1700. The wording is guarded, but the meaning is plain enough:

"'Twas lucky, I find, that I secured Kidd. Joseph Palmer's last evidence now sent out is pretty home against Kidd. He was one of Kidd's men and is now sent home a prisoner. His friends are said to be substantial people, and if he confesses all he knows at Kidd's trial, he may, I hope, deserve the King's pardon. In order to his making a confession, it were not amiss perhaps if you suffered his sister, Mrs. Byer, who goes over in the sloop to solicit the King's pardon for him, to speak with you. She could easily persuade him to tell the whole truth, and a frown from you will make her endeavour it."

In another letter Bellomont urged that the King should be asked to pardon Palmer if his evidence convicted Kidd. Yet Graham Brooks says of Palmer and Bradinham that "there was no inducement for them—either of fear or reward—to give evidence which was not true." He goes on: "It is material to note that the men had not turned King's evidence to save their own skins; their pardon was not on account of, or conditional upon, their appearance in the witness-box against Kidd; they had already been pardoned before any question of evidence arose." They had not. The fact is that Bradinham and Palmer were pardoned on May 26, 1701—three days after Kidd was hanged; and their pardon was given specifically as a reward for the evidence they had given to send Kidd to the gallows.

Both Lord Birkenhead and Graham Brooks accept all the evidence against Kidd on the murder charge. The most important part of this was Palmer's ' eye-witness ' account of the quarrel between Kidd and Moore. Yet in his deposition in New England Palmer had said that " he was not upon ye deck when ye blow was struck." The jurist Charles Wye Kendall contradicts Lord Birkenhead and Graham Brooks by saying that " there does not appear to have been a shred of evidence to support a charge other than manslaughter." Certainly the murder charge was a very unusual one in a period when merchant captains held and often exercised powers of life and death over their crews. Graham Brooks suggests: " It may well be that Kidd felt that by this act of murder he had burnt his boats. He could no longer sail the seas a guiltless captain; he had definitely sunk into crime, and he might now just as well be hung for a sheep as for a lamb." It is inconceivable that a seventeenth-century captain would have regarded the accidental killing of one of his crew as sinking into crime.

Captain Kidd does not seem to have had a very fair trial.

Whether or not Kidd was a pirate is a different matter; and, indeed, much of his behaviour seems to defy explanation. The jurists who upheld the justice of his trial do not seem to have met this difficulty. Lord Birkenhead suggests that " the Heaven-sent opportunity of a good ship, well armed, and manned with an adventurous and manageable crew was a temptation too strong for him." The opportunity was not sent by Heaven, the ship leaked badly, and the crew was anything but manageable.

It is perhaps worth noting also that lawyers seem always to

have had a down on Kidd. Lord Campbell, the nineteenth-century Lord Chief Justice and Lord Chancellor, in a weighty book on his predecessors in the latter office, wrote of Kidd that " after a sharp engagement with an English frigate in which several fell on both sides, he was captured and brought home in irons." This is pure fiction.

The story of Kidd seems to be to me a succession of unsolved mysteries. The first of these is in the " Rules of Agreement " drawn up between Bellomont and Livingston and Kidd, which made piracy at least highly probable if not inevitable. I am not being wise after the event. Although none of the historians or jurists seems to have noticed it, the terms laid down in these Rules were probably unique in the history of privateering. I cannot find a single case since the beginning of the seventeenth century of any crew of a privateer being offered less than fifty per cent. of the plunder, and the usual allotment at this period was sixty per cent. The offer of twenty-five per cent.—or less if they would take it—was unprecedented. And it was becoming increasingly difficult to man privateers, for piracy was both more profitable and less dangerous to the seaman. The crews of privateers commonly mutinied and turned pirates when they had failed to get much plunder. The case of Every and the *Charles* was typical. The Red Sea was not likely to contain many French prizes, and pirate ships would be hard to take; Moorish ships, on the other hand, were known to be numerous, valuable, and poorly defended.

All these facts were well known in London, and I cannot imagine why such terms were ever proposed—still less agreed upon. Bellomont and the other Whig nobles could scarcely have been ignorant of the dangers, and it is hard to understand why they should have deliberately ignored them. Kidd's agreement to the terms is even more surprising. He lived in New York, the chief base for the " pirate round." He had served on privateers. He was wealthy, settled, and happily married. If, tempted by the prospect of gain, he had wanted to go a-pirating, he knew that the simplest course would be to buy a commission in New York from Colonel Fletcher. It is hard to believe that he was contemplating piracy when he signed these Rules of Agreement.

It is known that Kidd was advised by his friends against accepting the commission. He himself suggested later that Bellomont put pressure on him, but his accusation was vague and unsubstantiated. Even if Bellomont could have forced him to accept, it is difficult to find any reason why he should have done so.

The next mystery is how the crew was found. There was no shortage of berths during the French wars, especially when so many peacetime pirates were carrying on their illegal trade instead of making the usual transition to privateering. Yet not only were the men found, but according to the promoters they were hand-picked.

Another mystery is why the ship was held up by the Navy and many of the best of these hand-picked seamen taken out. One of the promoters of the expedition was the First Lord of the Admiralty. It is equally surprising that Kidd did not put back to port when this happened, instead of sailing to New York with the intention of making up his crew there. No one could have known better than he that the only seamen he would be able to sign on in New York would be pirates. Colonel Fletcher's word is rarely to be trusted, but he said no less than the obvious truth when he wrote to the Lords of Trade, shortly after Kidd left New York: " It is generally believed here they [Kidd's crew] will have money *pr. fas aut nefas* [by hook or by crook], that if he miss of the design intended, for which he had commission, 'twill not be in Kidd's power to govern such a horde of men under no pay." This was in spite of the fact that Kidd had raised the crew's share of the plunder to sixty per cent. Had it still been twenty-five per cent., piracy would have been inevitable.

Kidd's action in offering this increase is another utter mystery. He had signed an Agreement under which Bellomont was to receive sixty per cent.; now, without any authority, he signed articles promising his crew sixty per cent. Whatever plunder might be taken now, and however lawfully, Kidd, far from being able to claim a share, had made himself liable to make up a deficit that would increase in proportion with the plunder. Admittedly he had little option—but he must have foreseen this at the Nore. He could have put back then; or he could have waited at New York and sought fresh instructions from Bellomont. At least he could have gone to see Livingston, who was in New York when he arrived. This he does not seem to have done. Two weeks after Kidd sailed again, Livingston wrote to the Duke of Shrewsbury:

" I am just now informed that Captain Kidd was constrained to make new conditions with his men, and to allow them the usual shares of privateers, and hath only reserved forty shares for the ship; but this wants confirmation, the captain not having acquainted me therewith."

This is an extraordinary statement. Possibly a hint of reproach may be read into the last few words, but this is only an inference. Livingston shows a knowledge of the usual privateering terms, and an understanding that Kidd should have been constrained to offer them. He does not seem to have been alarmed or even uneasy. The extract quoted is from quite a long letter, the rest of which has nothing to do with Kidd. Yet Livingston had signed the Rules of Agreement, and thus knew that Kidd was breaking the contract with Bellomont; and Livingston and Kidd were virtually partners, having jointly guaranteed Bellomont's share of the capital. If Bellomont and the crew each claimed their promised sixty per cent., Livingston would be liable to stand with Kidd in making up the deficit.

Although Kidd did not tell Livingston of the new arrangement, he did not make any secret of it; and it is surprising that Livingston did not hear of it earlier. Kidd had posted up the new articles in New York as an advertisement for additional hands.

After New York the mystery deepens still further, for hardly any of the later evidence is reliable. It seems definite that after rounding the Cape of Good Hope the *Adventure Galley* passed several merchantmen and had piratical opportunities without trying to take advantage of them. There is no evidence of any sort that Kidd suggested piracy to his crew until over a year after they had left London. By then the men were certainly discontented and probably mutinous.

According to one account, after taking the *Quedagh Merchant* Kidd discovered that she was not French, after all, and wanted

CAPTAIN KIDD HANGING IN CHAINS

After execution the bodies of pirates were usually hung in chains by the side of the river. This was supposed to deter seamen from piracy.

RECORD OF SALE OF A PIRATE SHIP

Abraham Samuel, self-styled King of Port Dolphin (Dauphin), was one of several pirates who set up kingdoms in Madagascar after retirement from active service.

to restore her to her captain, but his crew stopped him. This is plausible. Kidd denied responsibility for the three looting incidents; but he was in command of his ship when they occurred, and they were undoubted, if minor, acts of piracy. The share-out of the plunder at St. Mary's was illegal, and it is impossible to know how far Kidd was to blame for this. It is noteworthy that this was not a piratical share-out. If it had been, Kidd would have received only two shares instead of forty per cent. of the plunder. The fact that the privateering articles signed in New York were observed makes it clear that neither Kidd nor his crew regarded themselves as pirates. Kidd's surprise at learning of his proscription at the West Indies was genuine, and he would not have gone to Boston if he had not been confident of proving his innocence. There is nothing remarkable in his hiding part of his plunder for use in bargaining for his freedom with Bellomont. This was normal colonial practice.

Such, briefly, is the mystery of Captain Kidd, which has been solved so many times, and in so many ways, and yet remains as baffling as ever. I have had to condense the evidence, which is voluminous; in doing so I have selected not to prove a theory, but rather to try to bring out the basic contradictions. I cannot offer a new solution. I have tried to clear up some misconceptions about the fairness of Kidd's trial, but otherwise I have not been able to suggest any new answers to the old questions. Instead I have had to cast doubts on old answers, and put some new questions.

There is, however, one aspect of the affair that may make the contradictions more understandable. All the arguments for and against Kidd have been based on the assumption that there was a clear line between piracy and privateering. This frontier was never clear, and nowhere was it more blurred than in New York while Colonel Fletcher was Governor. At the time when Kidd was living in New York there was perhaps even less distinction between the two terms than in England under Elizabeth I. Writing from New York shortly before Kidd's return, Bellomont told the Government: " They say I have ruined the town by hindering the *privateers (for so they call pirates*) from bringing in a £100,000 since my coming " (my italics).

Bearing this in mind, I think it may be that Kidd did not mean to be a pirate, but realized that he might not be able to keep strictly to the law on privateering; and, moreover, that his transgressions would be condoned provided he brought back sufficient plunder. The conduct of Livingston may perhaps be explained by the same assumption, which was quite reasonable. Indeed, if Colonel Fletcher had still been Governor when Kidd returned, the assumption would probably have been proved correct—and Fletcher was a typical Governor. Kidd was not to know that Bellomont would be an exceptional Governor, or that his cruise would become a political issue in London.

My suggestion, then—and it is no more than that—is that Kidd was a privateer who, like most other privateers, was a bit piratical.

There remains a last mystery about Kidd, although it hardly deserves the name. Had it not been for the literary skill of Robert Louis Stevenson, Edgar Allan Poe, and Washington Irving, it might have been forgotten long ago. Yet it is not long since the Press reported an expedition going out " in search of the £1,000,000 pirate's treasure of Captain William Kidd " (*News Chronicle*, 5th November, 1951).

Nearly all Kidd's treasure came from the *Quedagh Merchant*. She was valued by her owners at £45,000. The East India Company's estimate was £22,500. The owners were claiming compensation, and the East India Company expected to have to pay it. If the total plunder from the voyage was £45,000— it could hardly have been more—the share-out at St. Mary's would have yielded Kidd only £18,000. Some of this was in silks and other perishables, which had to be sold cheaply in the West Indies. It is doubtful if he arrived in New England with more than £15,000. He distributed this in various places, leaving some with his wife, some with friends, and some on Gardiner's Island. Bellomont and other officials recovered £14,000. So much for Kidd's £1,000,000 treasure.

When negotiating for a pardon, Kidd told Bellomont that he

had left £30,000 on the *Quedagh Merchant*. Bellomont reported that he "bad the gaoler to try if he could prevail with Captain Kidd to discover where his treasure was hid . . . but he said nobody could find it but himself and would not tell any further." Livingston said later that Kidd told him that "forty pound weight in gold would be hid and secured in some place between this [Boston] and New York, not naming any particular place, which nobody could find but himself." After another interview Livingston said that "Kidd did yesterday acknowledge to this narrator that ye gold aforementioned was hid upon Gardiner's Island. He believed there was some fifty pound weight of it." While in prison in London Kidd wrote to Bellomont suggesting that he should be sent, while still a prisoner, to Hispaniola, where he could "bring off fifty or three score thousand pounds which would otherwise be lost." Less than a fortnight before his execution Kidd wrote to the Speaker of the House of Commons with a similar proposal, raising the offer to £100,000. The Speaker did not believe him. Posterity has been more credulous.

CHAPTER FOURTEEN

Piracy Destroyed

THE execution of Captain Kidd had no deterrent effect on other pirates, for by the time of his trial (1701) piracy had almost disappeared. How sudden was its decline may be judged from this comment by the Editor of the Calendar of State Papers (Colonial Series, America and the West Indies) on the state of trade in the American colonies a few years earlier:

" Where the merchants embarked their capital, the population of the sea-board cheerfully embarked its labour; and piracy, thriving on the commerce of all nations, developed a commerce of its own, which bade fair to extinguish all other. Even the King's ships were drawn insensibly into the vortex. Their crews, collected by the press-gang and subjected often to brutal officers, deserted as soon as they reached a colonial port, and were easily persuaded to take part in some piratical venture which, at comparatively small risk, might bring them a dividend of one hundred pounds or more apiece. The present volume [1696, 1697] brings us face to face with a fact that is absolutely unknown to the vast majority of Englishmen,[1] namely that towards the close of the war which ended at the peace of Ryswick British pirates, fitted out from British colonies, practically swept British trade with the East Indies off the seas."

In August 1696, when Captain Kidd was making up the crew of the *Adventure Galley* in New York, Edward Randolph sent another long report to the Council for Trade and Plantations in London. It contained comments on nearly all the colonies in America and the West Indies. Here are some samples:

" Bahama Islands. Mr. Nicholas Trott is Governor. The islands have long been and are still a common retreat for pirates and illegal traders.

[1] Written in 1904, but, I think, still valid.

" Carolina. Mr. John Archdale, a Quaker, is deputed Governor. . . . About three years ago seventy pirates, who ran away with a vessel from Jamaica, came to Charleston with a vast quantity of gold from the Red Sea. They were entertained and had liberty to stay or go to any place. . . . The present Governor favours illegal trade.

" Pennsylvania. William Markham, a very infirm man, is Governor. . . . Several known pirates are allowed to live and trade there.

" Rhode Island. Caleb Carr, an illiterate person, was lately Governor. It is now a free port for pirates. . . ."

So the catalogue went on. The Surveyor-General reported pirate bases in one colony after another; and in each case, he said, piracy was connived at by the Governor.

The Council for Trade and Plantations had heard all this before several times, apparently without taking it very seriously. Perhaps the Council thought that Randolph exaggerated.

But before the year was over the Council learned very clearly that Randolph's reports told the simple truth. For in October some of the men who had sailed with Henry Every on the *Fancy* were brought to trial; and the evidence of these pirates impressed the authorities as Randolph had never been able to do.

In the following January the Council was writing to the Governor of Massachusetts to tell him that the King had ordered that " all Governors shall do their utmost to repress piracy. In the trial of Every's crew there is too frequent mention of New England as the place from which pirates are fitted out and where they are entertained."

In February, to Colonel Fletcher:

"The King has given orders to the Governors of the Colonies to prevent the sheltering of pirates under the severest penalties. By information given lately at the trial of several of Every's crew, your Government is named as a place of protection to such villains, and your favour to Captain Tew given as an instance of it."

In the same month a letter was sent to the Attorney-General in the Bahamas ordering him to " enquire particularly into the late scandalous reception of Every and his associates, and endeavour to discover any of the villains, or others involved in the like guilt, lurking about the islands."

Colonel Fletcher, of course, had nothing to say, except that his association with Tew had been purely social and he had no idea the man was a pirate. He described Tew as " what is called a very pleasant man, that sometimes after the day's labour was done it was divertisement as well as information to me to hear him talk. I wished in mind to make him a sober man, and in particular to cure him of a vile habit of swearing. I gave him a book for that purpose, and to gain the more upon him I gave him a gun of some value. In return he made me a present which was a curiosity, though in value not much."

Governor Markham of Pennsylvania gave sanctuary to Every's crew for £100 per head, and one of these pirates married his daughter. Markham was nominated by William Penn himself, and the Editor of the Calendar of State Papers severely censures the Quakers for their support of piracy. I think he is too harsh; for, as he admits, if the colonists had been allowed the same freedom of trade as the mother country, piracy would have been just as undesirable to them. Had it not been for the unjust Navigation Acts, the " pirate round " would never have existed.

If pirates are to be considered in their contemporary context, it is only fair that colonial Governors should be too. If the pirates lived in a brutal age, the Governors lived in a corrupt age: from a moral point of view bribery of officials then was regarded as lightly as income-tax evasion is to-day. And if the pirates were unable to find honest employment, the Governors were unable to live honestly on their salaries. Like most public officials, they were poorly paid, and it was understood that they would supplement their incomes by using their official positions for private advantage. This was especially true of officials overseas. It is unlikely that the Governors of the American colonies were any more susceptible to bribery than the officers of the East India Company.

Although appointed Governor of New England in 1695, the Earl of Bellomont did not reach New York until the beginning of 1698. By then the situation was rather worse than it had been when he was given his appointment. Two factors had stimulated piracy.

One was a new Navigation Act (1696). Having caused this wave of piracy by repressive Acts, the Government was following the traditional course of trying to prevent the crime by further repression. The new Act did not differ materially from the previous Acts, but it tidied them up, blocked all the loopholes, demanded stricter enforcement, and imposed severer penalties on evasion. It did not say how evasion was to be stopped, and as there was no one to enforce the Act, it merely made piracy more profitable and no more hazardous.

The second fillip to piracy was the signing of the Treaty of Ryswick in 1697. Although this meant that colonial Governors were no longer able to issue privateering commissions, it brought the usual post-war influx of recruits to the trade.

Such was the position when Bellomont was greeted in New York by a hostile Council and a hostile Assembly. His appointment was unpopular, and he quickly made this unpopularity personal. Bellomont has naturally been accused of many sins by the defenders of Kidd, but none of the charges made against him seems to be substantiated. As Governor of New England he was apparently incorruptible. As he said himself, he was able to take a firm stand only because he was not the steward or overseer of any Lords Proprietors, but the nominee and paid servant of the Crown. He did not have to seek favours from any General Assembly, but drew an exceptionally substantial salary and legal perquisites. All the same, he quickly found that even this unusually large income was insufficient for his office, and his comments made it easy to understand why less-favoured Governors were so easily bribed.

"No man of quality who is honest can live on the profits of this government, and I do not see yet how I can make £800 per annum of the salary and perquisites; though it is true that if I would make New York the mart of piracy, confederate with the merchants, wink at unlawful trade, pocket the off-reckonings, make £300 a year out from the victualling of the poor soldiers, muster half-companies, pick an Assembly which would give me what money I pleased, and pocket a great part of the public moneys, I could make this government more valuable than that of Ireland, which I believe is reckoned the best in the King's gift."

In spite of all his difficulties, Bellomont made a vigorous attempt to stop the piracy. Trott had already been removed from the Bahamas and charged with helping Every. Fletcher was deposed—and Bellomont sent him back to England under arrest. Markham, Walter Clarke, and other " pirate-brokers," as Bellomont called them, were also dismissed. But this in itself was no solution. New Governors were again nominated by the Proprietors, and a change in personnel made little difference so long as public opinion was on the side of the pirates and not the law. In November 1699, long after his first clean-up, Bellomont was writing to the Council for Trade to suggest that Samuel Cranston, the new Governor of Rhode Island, " be called to an account for connivance at the pirates making that island their sanctuary and suffering some to escape from justice." Meanwhile the Surveyor of the Customs in Pennsylvania wrote: " They walk the streets with their pockets full of gold and are the constant companion of the chief in the Government. They threaten my life and those who were active in apprehending them; carry their prohibited goods publicly in boats from one place to another for a market; threaten the lives of the King's collectors and with force and arms rescue the goods from them. All these parts swarm with pirates, so that if some speedy and effectual course be not taken the trade of America will be ruined."

The Government's course was neither speedy nor effectual. A new Act of Piracy was passed, authorizing colonial Governors to convene local courts for the trial and punishment of pirates on the spot. An official named George Larkin was sent out from England to instruct the colonials on judicial procedure. He wrote from Boston: " After reading His Majesty's Commission, I settled such forms of proceedings with some of the members of the Council as are to be observed in the trial of pirates . . . but truly I believe they would have been much better pleased if your Lordships had sent them an Act of Parliament for encouragement of so beneficial a trade." Acquittals were so common that in the following year the Government turned a somersault by ordering Governors to empty their prisons and send all pirates back to England for trial.

This era of piracy reached its peak in the first half of 1700; then, with dramatic suddenness, it began to decline. It has been said that the outbreak of the War of the Spanish Succession was responsible, but the evidence is clear that the era was over before the war began. Piracy was stopped by the only means possible, short of repealing the Navigation Acts: not by new Acts of Parliament or Orders in Council, not by threats of severer punishment, but by the effective enforcement of the law.

Much credit is due to the Earl of Bellomont, who closed New York to the pirates and with a small naval force strove tirelessly to clear them out of the rest of New England. Probably he could have done much more had he been given more men-of-war; but while there was a war on, the Government said the nation could not spare the ships, and as soon as it was peace the nation could not afford the ships, and they were laid up. This was the traditional excuse for Government inaction throughout the Age of Piracy: shortage of men and materials in wartime, shortage of money in peacetime.

Bellomont did his best, but he could not police the whole American seaboard. Luckily he had a few natural allies. One of these was Francis Nicholson, the energetic Governor of Virginia.

For those who like to divide historical characters into Good Men and Bad Men, Governor Nicholson can be shown as a shining hero in a world of gubernatorial villainy. This effect can be produced without deliberate exaggeration or falsification of the facts. There is no doubt that he was a relentless enemy of the pirates, and that he played an important part in clearing them out of American waters. Almost his only ally in his crusade was the Governor of neighbouring Maryland, although he could count also on the moral support of the Governors of the West Indian colonies of Jamaica and Barbados.

Throughout the era of American piracy—from the closing of Port Royal in 1670 to the virtual end of piracy in the seventeen twenties—Jamaica, Barbados, Virginia, and Maryland alone seem to have had Governors who gave active support to the British Government's attempts to destroy American piracy. Nicholson was one of many such incorruptibles. During this period of over fifty years there were many changes in colonial Governors; yet while in most colonies one pirate-broker was followed by another, in these four unbroken anti-piratical successions were maintained. This was not due to either climate or tradition, or even loyalty to the mother country. Nor was it a coincidence.

Jamaica and Barbados grew sugar, and Virginia and Maryland grew tobacco, and all four depended on their export trades. It was bad enough that they should only be allowed to export their produce in English ships; matters became much worse when the flow of shipping was interrupted by war or piracy. Both the Proprietors and General Assemblies of these colonies were bitterly opposed to piracy. The Governors were nominated by the Proprietors and paid by the Assemblies. All credit is due to Nicholson for his energy; but had he been Governor of, say, New York instead of Virginia, he could not have used it in the same way even if he would. Before dividing Governors into good and bad, it is worth remembering that so far as piracy was concerned it paid to be good in Virginia, while in New York there was greater profit in being bad.

In supporting the mother country against pirates the Governors of Virginia and Maryland were not showing their approval of the Acts of Trade and Navigation. These Acts were as unpopular in the south as in the north, and were just as widely defied and evaded. The tobacco-planters bitterly resented having to use only English ships to carry their produce away, and did not like paying taxes either. So while Surveyor-General Randolph could report favourably on the strong stand against piracy taken by the Governors of Virginia and Maryland, he had to state also that these colonies were the main centres of American smuggling. Smugglers do not seem to have enjoyed so much official backing as pirates, but the subject is outside the scope of this book.

If the New England pirates had stuck to robbing Moors, the Governors of Virginia and Maryland would not have been worried. They could not be expected to share the concern of the East India Company about the depredations of men like Tew and Every. But the Red Sea was a long way away, and with good bases to return to, many of the smaller pirates contented themselves with less lucrative but easier pickings off the North American mainland. No merchant shipping was safe from them. One result of this was an increase in investments in piracy. For the speculators in New England piracy became a better risk than honest trade, as well as being much more profitable.

Virginia's trade had suffered heavily from the French privateers during the war; and after the Treaty of Ryswick, as the Surveyor of the Customs said, the effects of the pirates were ten times worse. Ships had to sail in convoy, and even then were not always safe. Pirates lay in wait off the Virginian coast, and Governor Nicholson did not have sufficient naval strength to drive them off.

While all the American colonies were united in their dislike of the Acts of Trade and Navigation, piracy caused dissension among them that may have given rise to some satisfaction in London. In November 1697 Governor Nicholson actually sent an armed party over the border into Pennsylvania to capture pirates who were being sheltered there. This led him into considerable trouble with Governor Markham, and relations between the two colonies were strained.

Nicholson had no scruples about informing on his fellow Governors, and he collected and sent to London a lot of evidence against Markham which bore out the substance of Randolph's reports. When Bellomont arrived the Governors of Virginia and Maryland gave him all the help they could; but it was not until June 1700, when piracy had reached its peak, that Nicholson had the opportunity to take direct effective action.

A large pirate ship, well armed and with a crew of a hundred and forty, impudently cruised off the coast of Virginia while H.M.S. *Shoreham* was lying at anchor. As soon as Nicholson heard of this he left Government House and went on board the warship, which was manned by ill-trained and unenthusiastic seamen. The captain was not optimistic about the probable fighting efficiency of his crew, but at Nicholson's orders he engaged the pirate ship.

According to the Surveyor's report, " The fight continued from eight in the morning till five in the afternoon, in all which time he [Nicholson] never stirred off the quarter deck, but by his example, conduct, and plenty of gold, which he gave amongst the men, made them fight bravely, till they had taken the pirates' ship, with a hundred and odd prisoners, the rest being killed."

From the official report of the battle it seems clear that if it had not been for Nicholson—and his gold—the pirates would never have been captured. There can be little doubt either that the failure of warships to take pirates on numerous other occasions owed something to the Government's meanness in paying naval seamen. Most criminals only break the law if there is sufficient financial incentive; those who have to enforce the law are also human. You cannot expect crime to be stopped by an ill-paid police.

With the exception of the Editor of the Calendar of State Papers, no pirate historian seems to have even noticed this engagement, which in my opinion was of tremendous importance. I am trying hard not to read cause and effect into accidents of chronology, but I find it difficult to believe that it was merely coincidence that immediately after this battle American piracy began its sharp decline.

The history of piracy contains several examples of the very powerful deterrent effect of a single defeat of this kind. Pirates generally were much more prudent and less reckless than is commonly supposed. They did not like risking their lives. While there were outstanding exceptions, the rank and file pirated only so long as the dangers of capture remained slight.

" A few more such expeditious, brave and generous actions from other Governments would quickly clear our coasts of pirates," wrote the Surveyor of the Customs. I think he was probably right. This successful engagement was the first of its kind since the " pirate round " began.

Meanwhile other naval action was being taken thousands of miles away.

For many years the East India Company had been begging the Government to send warships against the pirates in the

Eastern Seas. During the war these requests had been ignored. The Company had asked for a squadron, and all they had got was Captain Kidd.

In 1698 all East India Company ships were authorized to take pirate vessels. This made their own sea-routes safer, but it did nothing to prevent piracy against Moors, and especially the Mocha treasure fleets. The East India Company could not be expected to send naval expeditions to the Red Sea and Madagascar.

Madagascar was still the pirates' base. Adam Baldridge had left St. Mary's at the end of 1697, when his trading post was seized by negroes. Within a short time it was retaken by pirates, and again became the main advanced base for ships from New England. So long as it was allowed to remain as such, all other measures taken in the Eastern Seas were bound to fail.

At last, after the depredations of Tew, Every, and Kidd, and with the French war in temporary abeyance, the British Government sent a naval squadron; and early in 1699 four men-of-war, under Commodore Warren, appeared off St. Mary's.

St. Mary's harbour, land-locked and bottle-necked, was magnificently defensible. That was why the pirates chose it for their base. Mention has already been made of the fortification erected by Baldridge. According to Warren, when he arrived the harbour was defended by forty guns and the pirate population of the island was fifteen hundred. But he did not have to fight. As soon as they saw the squadron the pirates sank some ships across the entrance to the harbour, bilged and burnt others, and destroyed most of their stores and merchandise. Many hid in the interior or fled across to the mainland of Madagascar. St. Mary's was surrendered without a shot being fired.

Commodore Warren continued to cruise off Madagascar for the best part of a year, and no further piracies occurred in the Eastern Seas. When Warren went home the policing was continued by two men-of-war. By then war had broken out, and most of the pirates of America and the West Indies were serving again on privateers.

Thus was piracy destroyed—temporarily, at least. Thus ended the " pirate round," the most profitable era in the Age of Piracy. It was brought to an end by the appointment of an honest Governor in New England, a single sharp action off Virginia, and the appearance of four men-of-war off Madagascar, which did not have to fire a shot.

It is easy to be wise after the event, but Edward Randolph and many others were wise beforehand. They had told the Government years earlier exactly how piracy could be destroyed. Probably they over-estimated the pirates' valour, and did not realize how easily the destruction could be accomplished. The curious thing is that the lesson was not learnt, and when piracy revived, another Government had to discover how costly it is to allow crime to flourish by refusing to spend the money needed to enforce the law.

On his arrival at St. Mary's, Commodore Warren sent his men to look for pirates, not to arrest them, but to offer them a pardon under the 1698 Act of Grace.

Acts of Grace were frequently issued during the Age of Piracy, and in theory each was a general amnesty. Sometimes one or two notorious pirates were excluded by name, and often rewards were offered to pirates who would surrender and inform against others.

Many pirates surrendered under the Acts of Grace, but few of them did so with the intention of giving up piracy for good. Most of them regarded an Act of Grace as a convenient breathing-space. They did not have to give up their past loot, and when pardoned they could prepare at leisure for a new piratical voyage. Most of them had little option, for while the Government gave them a pardon, it did not offer alternative employment.

Sometimes Acts of Grace actually acted as incentives to piracy. There are several cases of wavering seamen being converted to piracy by the knowledge that they would be able to leave it again when the next Act of Grace was issued.

Yet the Acts of Grace were not entirely useless, for in practice pardon did not follow surrender as a matter of course. Under each Act of Grace surrender had to be made to one of a number of stated officials; and there were other conditions, which were cunningly enmeshed in legal phraseology. Most pirates who surrendered never saw an Act of Grace, and they would not have understood it even if they were able to read it. They usually gave themselves up to the wrong person or at the wrong time, or failed to observe one of the other conditions of which they were ignorant. Some of Kidd's men gave themselves up under the Act of Grace, and found that the only pardon they got was forgiveness of their sins by the chaplain who saw them off at Wapping Old Stairs.

Although the Government succeeded in tricking a number of pirates into surrender in this way, it had the effect of making pirates more wary. Thus when Captain Bowen took an East Indiaman, he told the captain bluntly that he and his men were resolved to go on spoiling the East India Company's trade until they should receive a free pardon for all the piracies and murders, misdemeanours and other offences of which they had been guilty in England or elsewhere, the last pardon of December 1698 having been " a sham to entrap honest pirates ".

Captain Bowen's righteous indignation may have been a bit misplaced, but it is doubtful if the example of this sort of official trickery helped to keep seamen honest. The cunning part of the 1698 Act was that it offered pardon for piratical offences committed within certain dates and geographical limits. When they surrendered, the pirates usually naïvely confessed all their previous piracies, and were hanged for those that were not covered by the Act. This did not encourage the others to surrender, and when Captain Bowen decided to retire he wisely went to Mauritius and bribed the Governor to let him settle down on the island.

Most of the other pirates left in the Eastern Seas settled down in Madagascar. Some had already decided to stay on the island, and were living in colonial luxury. Internecine strife among the natives made it easy for them to ally with one or other of the tribes, and several set themselves up as planters, traders, and even kings. Robert Drury, in his book *Madagascar* (1729), described a meeting with the pirate King of St. Mary's, John Pro. Other kings lived at Masselege, Maritain, St. Augustine's, and Port Dauphin. They lived comfortably, with many slaves to attend them, and traded with merchant ships that called. Most of these were slavers, and the kings supplied them with cargo and provisions. How seriously they took their regal status may be judged from the document signed by Abraham Samuel, a mulatto from Jamaica who became pirate King of Port Dauphin, which is reproduced opposite page 161.

Once things were quiet again, the men-of-war left the Eastern Seas, and in 1704 another pirate ship arrived from America. It was commanded by Captain John Halsey, of Boston, who had been given a commission from the Governor of Rhode Island to cruise off Newfoundland. He attacked the Mocha fleet and took prizes worth about £50,000, and then he and his company retired to Madagascar. This seems to have been an isolated incident.

In 1711 a privateer under Captain Woodes Rogers called at Cape Town. The captain met some pardoned pirates who had lived until recently on Madagascar, and they told him that numbers there had dwindled to between sixty and seventy. "They added that they had no embarkations but one ship and a sloop that lay sunk; so that those pirates are so inconsiderable that they scarce deserve to be mentioned; yet if care be not taken after a peace to clear that island of them, and hinder others from joining them, it may be a temptation for loose straggling fellows to resort thither, and make it once more a troublesome nest of freebooters."

For a man who had not been to Madagascar this was a remarkably accurate prophecy.

His Excellencie Richard Coote. Earle of Bellomont.
Lord Coote Colooney in the Kingdome of Ireland.
Gouernour of New England. New york. New Hampshe
and vice admirall of those Seas.

THE EARL OF BELLOMONT, GOVERNOR OF NEW ENGLAND

Surprised New York by refusing bribes and enforcing the law against piracy.

CAPTAIN WOODES ROGERS AND HIS FAMILY

Woodes Rogers, the first honest Governor of the Bahamas, used pirates to catch other pirates while the Royal Navy stayed neutral.

CHAPTER FIFTEEN

Pirate Republic

IN 1710 Francis Nicholson was succeeded as Governor of Virginia by Colonel Alexander Spotswood. In one of his first letters to the Council for Trade the new Governor asked for a fort to be built, saying that "it would afford a retreat for ships when pursued by privateers in the time of war, or by pirates which must be expected in time of peace."

The expectation of a rise in piracy when the war ended was general, and when the Treaty of Utrecht was signed in 1713 the Government stationed men-of-war in the Caribbean as guard-ships. Virginia was allotted one man-of-war. This did not seem enough to the Virginian exporters, who in December 1713 urged Governor Spotswood to ask for another. He replied: "I am of opinion that the ship already here is sufficient, and that there's no occasion to put her Majesty to a further expense until it appears that the pirates are more formidable than there's yet reason to apprehend they are."

Spotswood was not a short-sighted man, and he cannot be blamed for having failed to anticipate the extent piracy would reach in the next few years. It is easy for us to look back and say it was inevitable. It is easy to look back on any historical event and prove its inevitability. This thought behoves us to be cautious in seeking the causes of the greatest era of piracy in modern history.

The end of the war was the first cause. "War is no sooner ended but the West Indies always swarm with pirates," wrote John Graves, Collector of Customs in the Bahamas in 1706. By 1713 fighting had been going on for a long time, and privateering had become an established occupation. Since an Act on privateering passed in 1708 the whole of the plunder had been shared by the owner and crew. It had been encouraged especially in the West Indies. In 1713 it stopped abruptly, and thousands of seamen were thrown out of work.

They had no alternative employment, and knew no trade other than plundering merchant-ships. Poverty drove them to crime, and experience turned them to piracy.

The Caribbean had a number of peculiar natural advantages for pirates. It was dotted with islands of all shapes and sizes, many offering safe anchorages and refuges, and often wood, water, and even provisions for the taking. Maritime trade was considerable, settlement thin, and defence difficult. Long voyages were unnecessary, and innumerable creeks and inlets allowed small pirate sloops easy escape from pursuing men-of-war. The only real danger to the pirates was interception by a guard-ship on the high seas; and this danger proved to be very slight.

One of the reasons for the tremendous expansion of piracy was simply the inertia and incompetence of those who were sent to prevent it. Men-of-war were sent out, but the pirates were hardly ever caught. There can be no better advertisement for any crime than that.

Unemployment in the British West Indies was general, and the pirates had plenty of recruits from men who had never served on privateers. Ever since the Restoration convicts had been 'dumped' on the colonies, and the increase in the slave-traffic had caused the growth of a large class of 'poor whites.' The Home Government provided fresh man-power for the pirates by extending the system of transportation. The execution of the law in England was declining in severity, and many pirates convicted at home, instead of being hanged, were transported to the colonies. In 1718 the Governor of Jamaica complained about these unwanted immigrants: "Those people have been so far from altering their evil courses and way of living and becoming an advantage to us that the greatest part of them are gone and have induced others to go with them a-pirating."

In spite of all these favourable circumstances the pirates could hardly have flourished as they did without a good permanent base. They found one at New Providence, in the Bahamas.

The Bahamas had been colonized by the British in the middle of the seventeenth century, but they had never been properly settled. Their natural wealth was too small to make them a worth-while proprietary colony. They had no trade of their own—and therefore the few inhabitants always gave a friendly welcome to pirates. It was not by accident that Captain Every put in at New Providence when he came back from the Eastern Seas. Nor should Governor Trott be censured too harshly for accommodating the pirates. His official income worked out at about £30 a year, and he had to live.

Trott was succeeded by Colonel Webb, who, according to Edward Randolph, " was directed and proved an apt scholar under Trott's discipline and advice." Bellomont said of him: " If he were to give an account of how he made £8000 in two years in such a paltry island, I believe he would [say] he but stood in the steps of his predecessor, Trott, the greatest pirate-broker that ever was in America."

Governors of the Bahamas continued to make a livelihood out of pirate-broking until the War of the Spanish Succession broke out. In 1703 Nassau, the chief town of New Providence, was destroyed by the French and Spanish. They plundered the settlement, but did not bother to take possession of the islands. Many of the inhabitants fled, and in the following year the British Governor abdicated. The Lords Proprietors seem to have lost interest in their property, and in 1713 the Bahamas were still without any government. In 1714 the pirates moved in.

At this time the Governor of Bermuda said that the islands were inhabited by " about two hundred families scattered up and down amongst them, who live without any face or form of Government, every man doing only what's right in his own eyes." He told the Council for Trade, " Till the Bahamas are settled in some form they will still be a nest for pirates," and offered to annex them. For the sake of the trade of Bermuda, he said, he was quite ready to "scour them clear of that sink or nest of infamous rascals."

Henry Jennings of Jamaica is credited with having been the first pirate captain to settle at Nassau, and he was soon joined by others. The harbour was ideal. It could take five hundred little ships, and yet was too shallow for naval ships-of-the-line. An island divided it into two inlets, so that it would need two men-of-war to bottle it up. New Providence itself was well wooded and had plenty of fresh-water wells, besides fruits, fish and turtle, wild hogs and cattle. Situated near to important trade-routes, it was a pirates' paradise.

The pirates were followed by merchants and traders, who arranged for smugglers to take the pirates' plunder to the Carolinas for disposal. Stores, taverns, and brothels opened, and a shanty town sprang up, consisting mostly of shacks built of driftwood and thatched with palm fronds. There were no laws, but by common consent the defence of the settlement was vested in whatever pirate captains and quartermasters happened to be in port at the time. A battery was raised, and the harbour kept a guard of fifty men.

Most of the former inhabitants of the Bahamas either threw in their lot with the pirates or fled to the American mainland. The only man who tried to resist the invasion was Captain Thomas Walker. On the strength of an out-of-date commission as a Vice-Admiralty Judge he even arrested some pirates and sent them under guard to Jamaica. They escaped on the way.

The Governors of American as well as West Indian colonies complained about the Bahamas, for by 1715 pirates from New Providence had extended their range and were plying off the American coast from Maine to Florida. By 1716 the situation in the West Indies had become so bad that the Governor of the Leeward Islands wrote from Antigua to explain that he could not visit the Virgin Islands: "I do not think it advisable to go from hence except upon an extraordinary occasion, not knowing but that I may be intercepted by the pirates." A few months later Governor Spotswood of Virginia sent home a deposition made by John Vickers, a former inhabitant of New Providence, which stated that the ringleader at Nassau was a pirate captain named Thomas Barrow. " He is the ' Governor ' of Providence and will make it a second Madagascar, and expects five or six hundred men from Jamaican sloops to join in the settling of Providence."

In August 1716 Thomas Walker was forced to flee to South Carolina. He reported: "The pirates daily increase to Providence, having begun to mount the guns in the fort for their defence and seeking the opportunity to kill me because I was against their illegal and unwarrantable practices and by no means would consent to their mounting of guns in the fort upon such accounts." The ringleader of the pirates then was Benjamin Hornigold, who threatened to burn down Walker's house and " said that all the pirates were under his protection."

In July 1717 the Governor of Bermuda wrote: " North and South America are infested with these rogues, but the Bahama Islands are their rendezvous and by a modest computation it's concluded they are at least 1000 distributed in ships, brigantines, and sloops, and certainly will increase, for when they take a vessel some of the sailors generally turn to them."

By this time trade in the West Indies was almost paralysed. "Our coast is now infested with pirates," reported the Governor of Virginia. All ships leaving Jamaica had to sail in convoy with a naval escort. Shipping in the Leeward Islands was brought almost to a standstill.

The new pirates got no help from the colonial Governors. This was not surprising, for they were not bringing plunder from the Eastern Seas, but robbed mostly ships carrying exports from the colonies themselves. Their prizes were not nearly so valuable as the Moorish ships in the Red Sea, but they were more numerous, and when they were not sailing under escort they were easy to take. This was not the most profitable era of piracy, but it was probably the least hazardous. The reason for this, according to the Governor of Bermuda, was " the little apprehension they have of the King's ships that are sent into the Indies to suppress them." The men-of-war, he said, " are commonly so much disabled by sickness, death and desertion of their seamen that they are often constrained to lie near two-thirds of the year in harbour; it not being possible for the captains thereof to recruit the loss they thereby sustain while the merchants have any employ for the mariners (their service being so much more advantageous to the seamen than the King's)."

There was ample confirmation of this view, but it only partly explained the utter failure of the guard-ships to take effective action against the pirates. The Governor of Jamaica wrote more bluntly. " There is hardly one ship or vessel coming in or going out of this island that is not plundered," he told the Council for Trade. " And this in great measure I impute to the neglect of the Commanders of His Majesty's ships of war, who are said to be appointed for the suppressing of pirates and for a security to this island, but in reality by their conduct have not the least regard to the service they are designed for."

It was a standing grievance among the Governors that they had no jurisdiction over the naval Commanders, who were just as keen on using their official positions for private gain as the Governors were themselves. The seamen could see little profit in chasing pirates; nor could their commanders. The seamen turned to more lucrative forms of employment; so did the commanders.

To begin with, the men-of-war hired themselves out for convoy duty. This was both legal and profitable. Merchants paid as much as twelve and a half per cent. of the value of the merchandise for this service. The money was easily earned, for pirates rarely attacked an escorted convoy. At the same time it became in the commanders' interests not to disturb the pirates. If the pirates were suppressed there would be no need for convoys, and no twelve and a half per cent. A kind of unwritten non-aggression pact seems to have been observed by the pirates and the commanders.

The merchants were the sufferers, and they sought to find a way of reducing freight costs. Some of the commanders helped them by offering to carry the goods themselves. This was illegal, but the commanders were outside the reach of the law. As they could offer lower rates than merchant ships, and much better security, their services were greatly in demand. The result in Jamaica was a slump in shipping and fresh unemployment among merchant seamen. The Governor of Jamaica summed up the causes of the slump in a letter to the Council for Trade: " I can attribute that to nothing more than the man-of-war's transporting goods and merchandise which otherwise would be done by vessels belonging to the island, and consequently be a livelihood to numbers of seafaring men, who now have not bread for want of employment, which is the chief occasion of so many of them going a-pirating." This final consequence completed the vicious circle. More men were driven to piracy, and the demand for the men-of-war for both carrying and convoy work became greater than ever. The pirates and the men-of-war were nearly exchanging salutes.

That was the state of affairs according to the Governors, and I cannot find any reason to disbelieve it. The explanations given by the naval commanders are unconvincing. In one letter to the Admiralty the Commodore of the Jamaica Squadron complained that the Attorney-General at Port Royal was protecting the pirates. That is easy to believe, but it does not explain why the Jamaican Squadron never took any pirates. In another letter the same Commodore said the pirates were being sheltered by the Spanish at Trinidad. This was like saying that the mouse was sheltering the cat from the dog.

The only possible remedy, said the Governor, was to place the guard-ships under their command. The Government refused to do this, and sent out some more men-of-war, who joined in the game. Then the Governors repeated their demands for action against the pirate republic on the Bahamas. The Lords Proprietors of the colonies at last promised to appoint a new Governor. The Council for Trade, remembering Trott and others, urged that the Governor should be appointed by the Crown. Joseph Addison (of the *Spectator*), then Secretary of State, supported this proposal and recommended that the appointment should be given to Captain Woodes Rogers.

Woodes Rodgers is one of the forgotten men of British history. In 1708 he sailed round the world in command of a privateer, with Dampier as his pilot, and brought back Spanish treasure worth £800,000. He also brought back Alexander Selkirk (" Robinson Crusoe ") from Juan Fernandez. His book, *A Cruising Voyage round the World*, is one of the finest works of its kind ever written.

In the autumn of 1717 Woodes Rogers was appointed " Captain-General and Governor-in-Chief in and over our Bahama Islands in America," and was given a commission to suppress piracy by whatever means he thought fit. Unlike other colonial Governors, he was not empowered to convene Vice-Admiralty courts to try pirates. He said he would need some soldiers to command, so Addison wrote to the Secretary of

State for War asking for a " company of a hundred men at least," and suggested that they might be " draughted out of the Guards, or any other regiments now on foot, or out of His Majesty's Hospital at Chelsea." Rogers got mostly Pensioners.

The expedition took some time to prepare, and meanwhile the Government published a new Royal Proclamation offering pardons for all piratical offences committed before January 5, 1718, provided that the offenders surrendered before September 5 of the same year. Unlike previous pardons, this was a genuine offer, and pirates could surrender to any Governor or Deputy Governor.

The Proclamation reached the Governor of Bermuda in December 1717, and he sent a sloop with a copy of it to the pirates on New Providence. It was, he said, " accepted of with great joy." Before surrendering, however, the pirates demanded an assurance that they would be allowed to keep their plunder, and the Governor of Bermuda had no choice but to agree. Then the pirates began to surrender. A few of them, who had made quite a lot out of piracy, retired from the trade altogether. Captain Jennings was one, Benjamin Hornigold was another. A few others genuinely repented and looked for honest employment; finding none, they returned to piracy. The majority surrendered simply because it cost nothing and wiped out past offences.

In February 1718, at the request of the Governor of Bermuda, H.M.S. *Phenix*, Captain Pearse, sailed to New Providence to encourage the sluggards to surrender. Some more agreed, provided that they were allowed to keep their loot. " They are a parcel of unthinking people," complained Captain Pearse, " and I am forced to treat with them only by persuasion not having any force to suppress them." Soon afterwards he had a clash with a pirate called Charles Vane, and got the worst of it. Vane impudently mocked the captain of the warship, who wrote: " I several times summoned the inhabitants together in His Majesty's name and used all the arguments possible to prevail with them to assist me in suppressing the said pirates, but they always rejected all methods I proposed, and entertained and assisted them with provisions and necessaries and on all occasions showed no small hatred to government." In May some of the pirates threatened to seize the warship unless Captain Pearse left them alone, so he sailed to New York. In the same month the Governor of Bermuda reported that most of those who had surrendered had already gone out a-pirating again. The Act of Grace, he said, had failed.

Meanwhile a fresh influx of recruits had come as a result of Spanish attacks on the English logwood-cutters in the Bay of Campeche. At a trial of pirates in South Carolina nearly a year later the Attorney-General said that this had forced many into piracy, and estimated that nine out of ten of the men turned out of Campeche had become pirates. They nearly all went to New Providence.

By June matters were worse still. There were fewer seizures in the West Indies, simply because hardly any ships dared to sail unescorted. So the pirates cruised to the north, taking ships entering and leaving the American colonies. "The pirates continue to rove on these seas, and if a sufficient force is not sent to drive them off our trade must stop," wrote the Governor of New England. The Governor of New York told the Council for Trade that he "must wait for a ship of war before sailing on leave, pirates being busy on the coast." Hardly any of the pirates were caught, and there were now estimated to be about three thousand operating from New Providence. The floating pirate population of the island was about five or six hundred, and there were another two hundred permanent inhabitants, mostly hangers-on. This was the community that awaited the new Governor, who arrived early in July in the ship *Delicia*, escorted by H.M.S. *Rose* and H.M.S. *Milford*.

Captain Vane had just returned to New Providence, and when he saw the ships arrive he sent a man out in a boat with a letter to Woodes Rogers. In this Vane said he was willing to accept the Act of Grace provided he was given a guarantee that he and his company would be allowed to keep all the plunder they had just taken, and threatened to resist if the request was refused. Rogers ignored the letter and blockaded the harbour. Vane then sailed out in his sloop, engaged H.M.S. *Rose*, using a plundered prize as a fire-ship, and escaped to sea.

There was no further resistance from the pirates of New Providence, and when Rogers landed he found their much-vaunted fort in ruins. He read out his commission to the assembled population, and invited the pirates to surrender. They did so to a man, although apparently none were required to surrender their plunder too. Apart from the pirates and hangers-on, there were a few men of good will on the island. These included Thomas Walker, who had now returned, and John Graves, the Collector of Customs. Rogers made Walker Assistant Chief Justice and appointed a Council of six.

The two men-of-war had been told to stand by until Rogers was settled in, and then to relieve the guard-ships at the Leeward Islands. H.M.S. *Milford* left almost immediately. At Rogers's request H.M.S. *Rose*, Captain Whitney, agreed to stay for another three weeks, but left after a week. Captain Whitney refused to go after Vane, who was standing off the island and threatening to return and drive out the new Governor.

Rogers was in an extremely difficult position. He had only the *Delicia* to defend Nassau, and his expeditionary force was too small and inefficient to be able to resist a determined attack. Nor was the only danger from the pirates. There were strong rumours of an impending invasion by the Spanish regular forces. Rogers turned this additional threat into a blessing. He found that the pardoned pirates sympathized with Vane but were ready to help to defend the island against the Spanish. " I don't fear but they'll all stand by me in case of any attempt except pirates," he wrote, " but should their old friends have strength enough to design to attack me, I must doubt whether I should find one-half to join me." He formed them into a militia and set them to work building a new fort, repeatedly emphasizing that it was for defence against the Spanish. " The people did for fourteen days work vigorously, seldom less than two hundred men a day, but nothing but their innate thirst of revenge on the Spaniard could prompt them to such zeal, which was so strong that they forgot they were at the same time strengthening a curb for themselves."

In fact the danger from Vane was much greater than the Spanish threat at this time, but Rogers pretended that the reverse was the case. His authority was very slender. Later he told the Council for Trade: "Had I not took another method of eating, drinking, and working with them myself, officers and soldiers, sailors and passengers, and watch at the same time, whilst they were drunk and drowsy, I could never have got the fort in any posture of defence, neither would they [have] willingly kept themselves or me from the pirates if the expectation of a war with Spain had not been perpetually kept up. It was as bad as treason is in England to declare our design of fortifying was to keep out the pirates. . . ."

The 'reformed' pirates made poor soldiers. "These wretches can't be kept to watch at night, and when they do they come very seldom sober, and rarely awake all night." To encourage them to become useful citizens Rogers proclaimed a sort of homestead act, under which anyone could have full title to one hundred and twenty square feet of land anywhere in or round the town if he would build a permanent house on it within a specified period of time. The response was disappointing. "For work they mortally hate it, for when they have cleared a patch that will supply them with potatoes and yams and very little else, fish being so plentiful . . . they thus live, poorly and indolently, seeming content, and pray for wrecks or pirates."

It seemed that their prayers might be answered, for Vane renewed his threats, promising to burn the *Delicia* and visit Rogers, and it was said that another pirate, Stede Bonnet, had agreed to join him in an expedition against Nassau. Rogers then took a bold step. He commissioned a former pirate vessel, with a crew of pardoned pirates, to try to do what Captain Whitney had refused to attempt—to seek out Vane. The captain of this 'privateer' was Benjamin Hornigold, the man who had once threatened to burn Thomas Walker's house about his ears.

Nothing was heard of the sloop for a few weeks, and Rogers feared that they had gone back to their old ways. Then they returned. They had not been strong enough to catch Vane, but they had achieved their purpose. Vane did not carry out his threat.

Thus Woodes Rogers, with little more force than a handful

of Chelsea Pensioners, took and held the pirate republic of New Providence. This was the first serious blow struck at the pirates since their re-emergence after the Treaty of Utrecht. Piracy in the West Indies continued, and was bound to continue so long as it was condoned by the Royal Navy; but it was not so easy now that the pirates had been robbed of their best base.

New Providence was not their only base. There were many uninhabited islands where the pirates could careen and refit their vessels, and the Danish Governor of St. Thomas was usually hospitable to them. Moreover, while Woodes Rogers was literally holding the fort at Nassau, some of the pirates who had formerly operated from New Providence were using new bases on the American mainland. The most important of these was Blackbeard.

CHAPTER SIXTEEN

Blackbeard

THE highwayman Dick Turpin is described by the *Dictionary of National Biography* as " a very commonplace ruffian, who owed all his fame to the literary skill of Ainsworth." A similar relationship may be adduced to the pirate Blackbeard and his biographer, Captain Johnson. Although Blackbeard was by no means commonplace, his real importance in the story of piracy has been forgotten; and, thanks to Johnson and his embellishers, he is remembered for quite different and erroneous reasons.

Romantic history has been kinder to Turpin than to Blackbeard. The highwayman, who was a brutal ruffian, has come down as a legendary hero. The pirate, who was not guilty of a single atrocity, is generally portrayed as the archetype of seafaring villainy. The main reason seems to have been the beard.

" Captain Teach," says Johnson, " assumed the cognomen of Blackbeard from that large quantity of hair which, like a frightful meteor, covered his whole face, and frightened America more than any comet that has appeared there a long time."

The *Dictionary of National Biography*, with unusual charity, seems to accept Johnson's picture of Blackbeard as a sort of flying black saucer, and describes his biography as " thoroughly accurate as far as it can be tested by the official records, which are very full." But the accuracy of Johnson's vivid picture of the beard, which is the highlight of his biography, cannot be tested, for the records say nothing about it except that it was black. Johnson more than made up for this official reticence:

" This beard was black, which he suffered to grow of an extravagant length; as to breadth, it came up to his eyes. He was accustomed to twist it with ribbons, in small tails, after the manner of our Ramilie wigs, and turn them about his ears. In time of action he wore a sling over his shoulders, with three brace of pistols hanging in holsters like bandoliers, and stuck lighted matches under his hat, which, appearing on each side of his face, his eyes naturally looking fierce and wild, made him altogether such a figure that imagination cannot form an idea of a fury from hell to look more frightful."

Lieutenant Maynard, who killed Blackbeard in action, gives a less picturesque description, and says nothing about any lighted matches; and as this was the only recorded occasion on which Blackbeard was ever in action, it seems fair to conclude that Johnson was romancing.

Johnson called him Edward Teach, but his name was more probably Tache or Thatch. In official records he is sometimes named also Tach, Tatch, and Thach; other alternatives are Drummond and Drumond. It does not matter greatly, because he was always called Blackbeard.

Of his early life nothing is known, although much has been invented. Johnson says that he was a Bristol man who served on privateers during the War of the Spanish Succession, and " often distinguished himself for his uncommon boldness or personal courage." None of this can be confirmed. Alternatively he is described as a native of the Carolinas, while Charles Leslie states that he was born in Jamaica, " of very creditable parents," and that his brother was captain of the train of artillery. Mr. Clinton Black, the archivist at Spanish Town, has kindly explored the registers and other records in Jamaica without finding any confirmation for this.

If Blackbeard served on privateers he would have been thrown out of work when the war ended in 1713. Johnson says he did not start piracy until the end of 1716, and it was at this time that his name began to appear in Admiralty documents. What he was doing during the previous three years is unknown. It is certain that he went to New Providence, and probably went a-pirating with Captain Hornigold. They parted company early in 1717. By then Blackbeard was captain of a large French Guineaman, mounting forty guns, which he had patriotically renamed *Queen Ann's Revenge*.

Blackbeard took several prizes, and nearly always put the crews ashore and then burnt their ships. He never had to fight, and in the depositions of witnesses against him there is no suggestion that he maltreated or terrorized his prisoners. He was active off the Carolinas, and sometimes careened in lonely spots on the coast of Virginia. He does not seem to have had much trouble from British men-of-war. Johnson describes a three hours' engagement with H.M.S. *Scarborough*, but there is no mention of this in the Captain's letters or the ship's log.

About May 1717 Blackbeard sailed to the pirates' southern rendezvous in the Bay of Honduras. On the way he fell in with a pirate sloop of ten guns commanded by Major Stede Bonnet.

Stede Bonnet is one of the curiosities of pirate literature. He has been called the " gentleman pirate," and certainly he had been granted the King's commission. A man of good family and education, he had fought in the war and retired with the rank of major when already middle-aged. He owned property in Barbados, and settled down on his estate. Then, for some unexplained reason, he turned pirate. Johnson suggests that he was driven to it by a nagging wife. It is an entertaining theory.

Bonnet began by buying a sloop, which was an unheard-of thing for a pirate to do. He called the ship the *Revenge*—a favourite name among pirates—and collected a crew of eighty men. That virtually ended his ownership of the sloop.

Beginning early in 1717, Bonnet was at first fairly successful. He took several ships off Virginia, and then off New England, and in August he was reported off the bar of Charleston, where he took two more prizes. He careened in North Carolina, probably in the region of Cape Fear River, and then sailed for the Bay of Honduras. Then he met Blackbeard.

According to Johnson, Blackbeard, " finding that Bonnet knew nothing of maritime life, with the consent of his own men, put in another captain, one Richards, to command Bonnet's sloop, and took the Major on board his own sloop, telling him that as he had not been used to the fatigues and care of such a post, it would be better for him to decline it and live easy at his pleasure." This has probably been taken too literally. Johnson had his moments of irony, and I think this was one. Bonnet had been successful enough so far, and it seems most likely that Blackbeard and his crew simply took the sloop.

In December Blackbeard took the sloop *Margaret* off Crab

Island. Her master, Henry Bostock, later deposed: "He was ordered on board, and Captain Tach took his cargo of cattle and hogs, his arms, books and instruments. . . . They did not abuse him or his men, but forced two to stay and one Robert Bibby voluntarily took on with them. . . . They owned they had met the man of war on this station [St. Christopher], but said they had no business with her, but if she chased them they would have kept their way. Deponent told them an Act of Grace was expected out for them, but they seemed to slight it." (Calendar of State Papers.)

Soon after this Blackbeard took some trading sloops off St. Christopher, where Walter Hamilton, Governor of the Leeward Islands, had just arrived after a tour of the Virgin Islands. Hamilton wrote to the Council for Trade: "This gave the people of St. Christopher such just apprehensions of my safety in turning up from thence to Antigua that they moved it to me in Council to give them leave to impress and man a good sloop to attend the man of war to see me up, which was done accordingly. . . . The man of war is so small as I formerly wrote your lordships that in case he should meet by himself these pirates it would be exposing the Captain's character and perhaps be the loss of H.M. ship."

In the same month (January 1718) Blackbeard and his two ships went to North Carolina and surrendered to the Governor, Charles Eden, under the Act of Grace. The surrender was evidently prearranged, for in return for a share the Governor allowed the pirates to keep their loot and to prepare for a fresh piratical voyage. Members of the Council—including Tobias Knight, Secretary and Collector of Customs—connived at this arrangement, which gave pirates their first protected base on the American mainland since the beginning of the century.

It was not by accident that the pirates went to North Carolina, nor was their welcome due to the especial corruptness of the Governor and other officials. The reason was simply that North Carolina was one of the few remaining places on the American mainland where pirates were a blessing rather than a curse. The cause of this was the Acts of Trade and Navigation, which had been responsible for the welcome given to the pirates by most American colonies in the sixteen-nineties.

BLACKBEARD

Probably the most maligned pirate in history. He treated his prisoners humanely and never fought if he could avoid it. He rarely had to fight, as he was avoided by the Royal Navy and protected by the Governor of North Carolina.

LIEUTENANT MAYNARD VERSUS BLACKBEARD
Blackbeard's first—and last—conflict with a naval officer.

THE END OF BLACKBEARD

But times had changed since then. The New England colonies had lost interest in the pirates after the break-up of the Red Sea trade. South Carolina had developed her natural resources and, like Virginia, now had a flourishing export trade—and therefore, again like Virginia, was hostile to pirates, but cordial to smugglers. For reasons of trade Robert Johnson, Governor of South Carolina, was just as strongly opposed to pirates as Governor Eden of North Carolina was friendly towards them. There is no reason to think that one was morally better than the other. Both were recently appointed, and the change had occurred before they took office. It seems reasonable to think that if a cross-posting had been arranged the two Governors would have inherited each other's principles.

Eden had no excuse for issuing commissions to the pirates, and so they could not enjoy his protection on the high seas. But North Carolina was a good base. There were excellent places for careening in the Cape Fear and Pamlico Rivers, and a ready market for merchandise at Bath. It was this rather than fear of men-of-war that made the pirates prefer their new base to New Providence, although Woodes Rogers had not yet arrived in the Bahamas. On New Providence the pirates could sell only to the middlemen—traders who had to smuggle the merchandise into the American colonies. In North Carolina the sale was direct to consumers, and even after the Governor and other officials had taken a percentage the profit was still higher.

In April 1718 Blackbeard sailed again to the Bay of Honduras and took the *Adventure*, whose sailing master, David Herriot, and most of the crew voluntarily joined the pirates. Blackbeard's sailing master, Basilica or Israel Hands, was elected to command the new prize.

After taking two or three more prizes Blackbeard sailed north again and lay off the bar outside Charleston. This was a favourite hunting ground for the pirates, who, Governor Johnson complained, had " at some times blocked up our harbour for eight or ten days together, and taken all that have come in or gone out."

Blackbeard now commanded quite a little fleet. With the

Adventure he had his flagship, *Queen Ann's Revenge*, and Bonnet's old sloop, the *Revenge*, still under the command of Richards. There were also another sloop and two smaller tenders. Altogether the pirates numbered about four hundred men. Bonnet was still with them, although without any command.

Lying off the harbour, Blackbeard took eight or nine ships. The last one was bound for England and carried $6,000 in specie. One of the passengers was a prominent citizen of Charleston, a member of the Governor's Council, named Samuel Wragg. Blackbeard held him hostage while he sent Richards and another pirate ashore in a tender. They took a passenger named Marks with them, and a list of medical supplies needed, made out by the pirates' surgeon. Marks had to present this list to the Governor and tell him that unless the demands were met Blackbeard would kill all his prisoners, including Samuel Wragg, and send their heads to the Governor; they threatened also, in the words of the Governor's report, to come over the bar " for to burn the ships that lay before the town and beat it about our ears." The Governor was given two days to get the supplies, which were estimated to be worth about £300 to £400.

The Governor at once convened the Council and put the case before them, while Marks waited in an anteroom and Richards and the other pirate strutted about the town. The Council did not want to give in to Blackbeard's demands, but there was no man-of-war at hand and the harbour was unprotected. They decided to yield.

The medical supplies were put in the tender, and Marks and the two pirates set off for the ship. On their way a squall upset their boat, and they had to put back to shore. They did not get away again until the following day, by which time Blackbeard's ultimatum had expired. But he did not carry out his threat, and Marks found his fellow prisoners none the worse. The pirate fleet sailed away without having inflicted any casualties.

This incident, which is fully reported in the Calendar of State Papers, has some puzzling features. The pirates had not been in an engagement recently, and no reason is given for their urgent need for medical supplies. They could have got emergency supplies from the eight or nine ships they had plundered, and further needs could have been made up openly when they returned to Bath. There is no suggestion of an epidemic of infectious disease among them. Probably the answer is that they wanted mercurial preparations for the treatment of syphilis. Brothel casualties were usually higher than battle casualties among the pirates.

What is more puzzling is that when holding a town to ransom the pirates did not make a higher demand. There does not seem to be any reason why they could not have got a few thousand pounds as easily as goods worth a few hundred. There is no clue to this mystery in the letters sent by Governor Johnson to the Council for Trade. He wrote:

" The unspeakable calamity this poor province suffers from pirates obliges me to inform your Lordships of it in order that His Majesty may know it and be induced to afford us the assistance of a frigate or two to cruise hereabouts upon them, for we are continually alarmed and our ships taken to the utter ruin of our trade. . . . I don't perceive His Majesty's gracious proclamation of pardon works any good upon them, some few indeed surrender and take a certificate of their so doing and then several of them return to the sport again. . . . I am credibly informed there are above twenty sail now in these seas, so that unless ships be sent to cruise upon them, all the trade of these American ports will be stopped, for hardly a ship goes to sea but falls into their hands."

In another letter Governor Johnson wrote:

" Those people are so accustomed to this easy way of living that nothing can reclaim, and most of those that took up with the proclamation are now returned to the same employment, which has proved more an encouragement than anything else, there now being three for one there was before the Proclamation was put out. They are now come to such a head that there is no trading in these parts, it being almost impossible to avoid them, and nothing but a considerable force can reduce them, which at first might have been done at an easy charge, had the Government but rightly appraised what sort of people they generally are and how most of them that first turned pirates have formerly lived, being such as had always sailed in these parts in privateers . . . that being of so near akin to their present way of living."

Governor Johnson had more reason to be worried when Woodes Rogers landed at New Providence and broke up the pirate republic. The neighbouring colony of North Carolina became the most important pirate base in American waters.

After the Charleston episode Blackbeard sailed to North Carolina and went into Topsail Inlet, where the *Queen Ann's Revenge* and the *Adventure* ran aground. This may have been a deliberate manœuvre by Blackbeard, who is said to have used it to break up his company and cheat most of the men out of their share of the plunder. This is plausible, as the shares from a division among three or four hundred would not have been large. There was certainly a quarrel, and Blackbeard went off in one of the sloops with only about forty of his men, including Israel Hands. Bonnet regained command of his old sloop the *Revenge*, and sailed away with about fifty men, including David Herriot. He seems to have chased Blackbeard without success, and then put in at Bath, where the Governor obligingly gave him a new pardon and clearance for his sloop. Bonnet changed the sloop's name to *Royal James* and his own to Captain Thomas, and sailed back to Topsail Inlet, where he rescued seventeen men who had been marooned on a small island by Blackbeard. Then he went on a long cruise, taking prizes off Virginia, Bermuda, and Philadelphia. There were rumours that Bonnet had joined forces with Charles Vane, who was said to be preparing an expedition to drive Woodes Rogers out of New Providence, but these are unconfirmed. All that is known for certain is that Bonnet returned to Cape Fear in August 1718 with two prizes. His sloop was leaking badly, and he put in for repairs.

Meanwhile Blackbeard had gone to Bath, where the Governor convened a Vice-Admiralty Court which solemnly condemned the pirate's sloop as a lawfully taken Spanish prize, although Britain and Spain were not at war and the real owners of the ship were English merchants. One of the judges on the Court was Tobias Knight, who was then acting Chief Justice.

It is not surprising that in London the judge of the High Court of Admiralty wrote to the Secretary of the Admiralty suggesting that it would be better to order privateers to bring all prizes to London for adjudication, instead of taking them to Vice-Admiralty Courts abroad, " since it is much to be feared that they are not well versed in the Laws of Nations, and Treaties between us and other states, and it is well known that they do not proceed in that regular manner as it is practised in His Majesty's High Court of Admiralty."

This was the position when news was brought to Governor Johnson that a pirate sloop and two prizes were lying in Cape Fear River.

The Governor knew he could not expect any help from the Navy. He knew also that to tell the Governor of North Carolina would be simply warning the pirates. So he fitted out two sloops, and on his own authority commissioned them as privateers with orders to seek out pirates. One sloop, the *Henry*, was under the command of Captain Masters, and the other, the *Sea Nymph*, under Captain Ball. Each mounted eight guns and carried a crew of about thirty-five men. Johnson placed the expedition under the command of the Receiver-General, Colonel William Rhett.

Rhett was about to sail when news was received that Vane was off the bar at Charleston in a brigantine. Johnson sent Rhett after him, and reports from men who had been taken prisoner suggested that Vane was sailing southward to careen. Rhett went in pursuit; but the scent was false, for in fact Vane had sailed northward past Cape Fear and put in at Ocracoke Inlet, where he found Blackbeard at anchor. The pirates exchanged salutes with their guns.

Sailing north again, Rhett reached Cape Fear River late in the day, and sighted the topmasts of Bonnet's sloop and the two prizes. Then both his sloops ran aground. He could not refloat them until late at night, and decided to wait till dawn before attacking.

The pirates had seen the two sloops, and Bonnet sent three armed boats to investigate. When they reported back, Bonnet ordered his men to turn to and clear the decks for action. They worked all night preparing for the engagement. There was similar activity on Rhett's sloops.

At dawn the pirates made a bid to get out of the river.

There was a good breeze, and with all sail set they went down the river, intending to make a running fight for the open sea. Rhett's sloops weighed anchor and sailed towards the *Royal James*, forcing the pirates to steer close to the shore. Unfortunately Rhett did not know the river, and all three sloops went aground. They were stuck hard and fast on the sandy bottom, with no hope of getting off until the next tide.

The pirates had the better position. The *Royal James* and the *Henry* had careened in the same direction in such a way that the pirates' deck was protected while the whole deck of the other sloop was exposed to their fire at pistol-shot range. The *Sea Nymph* was too far ahead to be able to help the *Henry*.

Rhett opened fire on the pirates' hull, but his gunners were forced to seek shelter when their deck was raked by the enemy. It was clear that the pirates had the upper hand—for the time being. All Rhett could do was keep his men under cover and wait for the tide.

The wait lasted five hours, and the *Henry* suffered heavy casualties. Then, late in the day, the flood poured up the river, and everything depended on who should get off first.

It was the *Henry*, and Rhett at once called on the pirates to surrender. Some of the men wanted to, but Bonnet used his authority. He swore he would fire the magazine and sink the crew with the ship unless they fought, and drew his pistol and threatened to spatter the deck with the brains of anyone who disobeyed. But there were too many against him, and just as Rhett was about to board the *Royal James* she flew the white flag. The Colonel had no idea of the identity of the pirate captain until he arrested him.

The *Henry* lost eight killed and fourteen wounded, several of whom died later. The casualties on the *Sea Nymph* were two killed and six wounded, while the pirates lost seven killed and five wounded. Bonnet and over thirty surviving pirates were taken back to Charleston without reference to the authorities in North Carolina.

David Herriot and the pirate boatswain, Ignatius Pell, decided to turn King's evidence, and were put in the residence of the Provost Marshal. So was Bonnet, as it was considered that a gentleman could not be kept in the public watch-house. The result of this rather odd arrangement was that Bonnet bribed the guards and escaped with Herriot. Governor Johnson offered a reward of £700 for their re-arrest, and Colonel Rhett followed them by boat to an island off the coast, killed Herriot, and took Bonnet prisoner for the second time. Bonnet was tried at Charleston and executed. So were thirty of his men.

Very soon after this Governor Johnson heard that another pirate ship was lying off Charleston. He commissioned four ships, including the *Sea Nymph* under Captain Hall and Bonnet's old sloop, now under Captain Masters. This time Governor Johnson led the expedition personally. In the course of an exciting sea-fight twenty-six pirates were killed, including their captain, Worsley. Twenty-four others were taken prisoner, tried, and executed.

Meanwhile Blackbeard had been out again on quite a long voyage. His men had been seen in Philadelphia, and in August 1718 the Governor of Pennsylvania issued a warrant for his arrest. He returned to Bath with a cargo including eighty or ninety slaves stolen from the French, which he sold openly. Then he went out again, ostensibly on a trading voyage to St. Thomas, and took two more French ships near Bermuda. One was laden with sugar and cocoa, but the other was in ballast. Blackbeard then put the crew of the former on board the latter, and sailed back to Bath with his prize. Then he went to the Governor, and swore on oath that he had found the ship at sea with no crew and no papers. The Governor convened another Vice-Admiralty Court, again with Tobias Knight as one of the judges, and the ship was solemnly condemned as a wreck. As the French were likely to look for it, Blackbeard suggested destroying it. Knight agreed, and prepared a warrant saying that it was leaky and in danger of sinking and blocking the river. The Governor signed the warrant, and Blackbeard beached and burnt the ship in an inlet near Bath. For their shares in this enterprise the Governor took sixty hogsheads of sugar and Knight twenty.

Blackbeard stayed in Bath, where, Johnson says, Governor Eden married him to a girl of sixteen; " and this, I have been informed, made Teach's fourteenth wife, whereof about a dozen might be still living."

Although he enjoyed the Governor's protection and had brought some wealth to the colony, Blackbeard was not universally popular in North Carolina. He helped himself to any ship that came his way, and some of the merchants had suffered heavily. Moreover, he seems to have been a rowdy, drunken braggart. There is one story of Johnson's that has a ring of truth. One day at sea, " a little flushed with drink," Blackbeard suggested to his crew that they should " make a hell of our own, and try how long we can bear it." Then he and three others went down into the hold, closed up all the hatches, and set fire to several pots full of brimstone and other combustible matter. They remained below until they were almost suffocated and the other three men were crying out for air. Then Blackbeard opened the hatches, " a little pleased that he held out the longest."

Another of Johnson's stories is undoubtedly true. This tells that one night Blackbeard, Hands, and another man were drinking below, and Blackbeard quietly drew out a small pair of pistols and cocked them under the table. The third man wisely excused himself and went up on deck. Then Blackbeard blew out the candle, crossed his hands under the table, and fired. It was only a practical joke, of course, but Hands got a bullet through his knee and was lamed for life. Still, the bullet saved his life in the end.

This sort of behaviour was tolerated on a pirate ship, but in Bath many citizens who were not profiting directly began to complain about the Governor's new favourite. He and his men made themselves free of private property, and there were some scandalous tales about their dealings with the women. It was no use complaining to the Governor or the Secretary, so the respectable citizens reported the state of affairs to the more sympathetic Governor Spotswood of Virginia.

Virginia had better protection against pirates than South Carolina, for two men-of-war, the *Pearl* (Captain Gordon) and *Lyme* (Captain Brand), were stationed as guard-ships in the James River. They do not seem to have gone looking for pirates, but their presence seems to have been a comfort to the

Virginians and a deterrent to the pirates. In the colony itself, although the planters were strongly opposed to piracy, there were some in high places who were ready to make money when their official positions gave them the chance. Governor Spotswood found this out when he ordered the arrest of William Howard, former quartermaster to Blackbeard, who had entered Virginia with two negro slaves who he openly admitted were taken piratically. When arrested, Howard at once began a lawsuit against the man who had taken him, and was released. Then he was heard persuading seamen to join him and seize a ship and go on the account. On the Governor's instructions he was taken before two Justices of the Peace, who sent him aboard the *Pearl* as a vagrant seaman. He was not there for long; and the next thing Spotswood heard was that Captain Gordon, his lieutenant Robert Maynard, and the Justice of the Peace who had signed the warrant against Howard, were all arrested at the order of John Holloway, a judge of the Vice-Admiralty Court of Virginia, each in an action of £500 damages for false imprisonment.

Spotswood ordered an enquiry to be held, and from this it was learned that Howard had feed Holloway as his lawyer, and also that Howard had committed acts of piracy since he had been pardoned at Bath in January. Spotswood wanted to bring him to trial, and was surprised to find some opposition to this in his Council. However, he had his way, and Howard was brought before the Vice-Admiralty Court. Captains Gordon and Brand refused to sit on this in company with Holloway, so Spotswood tactfully told the lawyer to keep out of it. This so annoyed Holloway that he said he would never sit again—" which," Spotswood reported, " I confess, I was not much displeased at since it gave me an opportunity of putting an honester man in his place." The court found Howard guilty of assisting in the taking of twelve vessels after the date of his pardon, and sentenced him to death. On the day fixed for execution a new Royal Proclamation was received, extending the period of grace to August 18, and Spotswood had to release Howard.

Citizens of North Carolina continued to complain to Spotswood about Blackbeard's activities, but the Governor could not do anything so long as the pirate was enjoying the protection of Eden and Knight in Bath. Then, in November, came the news that Blackbeard was with a prize in Ocracoke Inlet. The report added that Blackbeard was preparing to fortify the shore and make the place into " another Madagascar."

Spotswood at once held a conference with Captains Brand and Gordon. There was no question of the two men-of-war being able to go into the shallow and difficult waters of Ocracoke Inlet, and sloops were needed. The captains refused to hire sloops out of their own pockets, but agreed to supply the men if the Governor would pay for the hire of the sloops and pilots. Spotswood agreed, although it meant raising the money privately. He could not ask for a vote out of public funds, for he wanted to keep the expedition secret. He did not even tell his Council what he was going to do—" for fear of his [Blackbeard's] having intelligence, there being in this country . . . an unaccountable inclination to favour pirates."

However, Spotswood expected the pirates to fight, and, like his predecessor Francis Nicholson, he knew that naval ratings were reluctant to risk their lives unless there was some prospect of gain. So before the expedition left, and still without revealing his plans, he persuaded the Assembly to pass an Act " to encourage the Apprehending and Destroying of Pirates." Under this Act he was able to issue a Proclamation promising rewards out of public funds for the taking of pirates, dead or alive, " within one hundred leagues of the continent of Virginia or within the provinces of Virginia or North Carolina." (This, of course, was illegal. The Governor of Virginia had no right to claim jurisdiction over another colony.) The Proclamation went on to name the rewards, which were on a sliding scale: " for Edward Thatch, commonly called Captain Thatch, or Blackbeard, one hundred pounds; for every other commander of a pirate ship, sloop, or vessel, forty pounds; for every lieutenant, master, or quartermaster, boatswain, or carpenter, twenty pounds; for every other inferior officer, fifteen pounds; and for every private man taken on board such ship, sloop, or vessel, ten pounds." The Proclamation promised that the rewards would be " punctually and justly paid "; and as they were in addition to prize money, they provided an adequate incentive to the Navy to do its duty.

The Governor hired two sloops, and they were manned by fifty-five ratings from the men-of-war. The larger sloop was commanded by Lieutenant Maynard, and the other by the first officer of the *Lyme*. Captain Brand went overland to Bath, where he met Edward Moseley, a prominent politician, and Colonel Moore, both of whom were strongly opposed to the Governor and the Secretary. Brand then went to see the Governor and told him why he was there.

Meanwhile the sloops had reached the inlet, where they found Blackbeard on a sloop of nine guns, well fitted, with about twenty men. It was found later that, despite Spotswood's precautions, the pirates had received warning, but they had taken no advantage of it. It was evening when the expedition sighted the enemy, and Maynard decided to anchor close to the shore for the night. Blackbeard does not seem to have followed Bonnet's example of using the night for preparation for action.

At dawn, with a little breeze, Maynard ordered the smaller sloop to try to board the pirate vessel. He followed in his own sloop, but ran aground and had to heave ballast overboard to get off. By then the smaller vessel was aground. The advantage was with the pirates, who cut their cable and got under sail, and fired a broadside at the smaller sloop while she was trying to get off, killing the commander and several others.

Maynard kept up a running fight until the pirate ship ran aground. Then, seeing that the enemy meant to board, Blackbeard took up a bowl of liquor, drank damnation to anyone that should give or ask quarter, and discharged his great guns loaded with partridge shot, causing further heavy casualties. The pirates managed to board Maynard's sloop, but in fierce hand-to-hand fighting they lost nine killed and all the others wounded. Maynard personally killed the pirate captain, and sailed back to Bath with his head, complete with beard, hung up at the bowsprit's end. Naval casualties were ten killed and twenty-four wounded, some of whom died later.

Blackbeard had ordered a negro to blow up his sloop rather than let the Navy take her, but the man preferred to keep his own life. Searching Blackbeard's clothes, Maynard found a letter of recent date from Tobias Knight containing a memorandum of goods deposited and guardedly warning the pirate of the expedition. It ran: " My friend, If this finds you yet in harbour I would have you make the best of your way up as soon as possible. . . . I have something more to say to you than at present I can write . . . I expect the Governor this night or to-morrow, who I believe would be likewise glad to see you before you go. . . . Your real friend and servant, T. Knight."

Maynard showed this letter to Captain Brand at Bath, and when Governor Eden saw it he gave authority for Brand to take the goods from Knight. With Moseley and Moore, Brand went to see Knight, who denied that he had ever received any goods from Blackbeard. The letter was produced, and eventually Knight confessed. Brand searched Knight's barn and took away one hundred and forty sacks of cocoa and a cask of sugar. To round off the job he took the Governor's share as well as Knight's, and also arrested six more pirates in Bath, including Israel Hands. Then the expedition returned to Virginia.

When Governor Eden found that his own goods had been taken he sent a sharp note to Spotswood demanding the return of both the goods and the pirates. He said the goods had been taken lawfully from a wreck condemned as such, and complained—with perfect reason—that Spotswood had no right to send an expedition to abduct persons from another colony. If they were charged with piracy, then they could appear before a court in North Carolina.

Spotswood reminded Eden that he had given Brand permission to take the goods from Knight's barn, and refused to return either the pirates or the merchandise. The pirates were tried by a Vice-Admiralty Court in Virginia, and fourteen were executed. Israel Hands had turned King's evidence, and was pardoned when he had proved that he had left Blackbeard's company after the under-table shooting incident. His testimony included serious charges against Knight, and Spotswood sent a copy of it, with a copy of the letter found on Blackbeard's body, to Eden. He suggested that Knight should be sent to England for trial.

As Spotswood also reported the whole affair to the Council for Trade in London, Eden could not ignore the charges against his Secretary. He had Knight brought before his Council, and the documents were read out. Knight admitted that he had written the letter to Blackbeard, but denied any knowledge of piracy. The Council decided that the evidence of Hands was "false and malicious" and that Knight "hath behaved himself in that and all other affairs wherein he hath been instructed as becomes a good and faithful officer, and thereupon it is the opinion of this Board that he is not guilty and ought to be acquitted of the said crimes, and every one of them laid to his charge as aforesaid."

Meanwhile Edward Moseley had been trying to find evidence against the Governor himself. He went to Knight's office in Bath to examine the records, which, under the instructions of the Lords Proprietors, were open to public inspection. But Eden had had the records removed to a private house, and Moseley was denied admittance. Thereupon Moseley with Colonel Moore broke into the house to seize the documents. Eden at once issued a warrant for his arrest, and sent an armed posse to carry it out.

Moseley complained bitterly at this high-handed treatment, saying that the Governor "could easily procure armed men to come and disturb quiet and honest men, but could not (though such a number could have done) raise them to destroy Thack." He said of his own arrest, "It is like the commands of a German prince." For these and similar "seditious words" Moseley was indicted under a colonial statute "for the more effectual observing of the King's Peace" which had been passed in 1715. Ironically, Moseley himself had been Speaker of the Assembly at that time, and the statute bore his own signature.

The case was sensational, and Moseley had a good deal of public support; but he was found guilty, fined £100, and disqualified from holding any office or place of trust in the colony for three years. By the end of this period Eden had died in his bed and the Blackbeard affair was forgotten.

In May 1719 Spotswood informed the Council for Trade that "the effects of Thach the pirate have been condemned by the Court of Vice-Admiralty and sold at public auction." He enclosed an account, showing that the ship and cargo had fetched £2,500, " as there is likely to be some controversy about the property of those goods, being taken in a French ship, east of Bermuda, and brought into North Carolina. If the owners make out their property, the produce must be paid to them. But there is an unexpected pretence set up by the Government of North Carolina to these goods, as being taken within the seas and off the soil of the Lords Proprietors. They suffered these goods to remain in the possession of that piratical crew for divers months, some in chief stations having had too much correspondence with them, particularly one who held the office of Secretary, Chief Justice, one of the Council and Collector of the Customs."

Governor Eden had now altered his claim. He no longer said the ship was a wreck, but he repeated that the cargo ought to have been tried and condemned in North Carolina, and threatened to prosecute Brand in England for trespass. Spotswood replied that the cargo would not have been condemned in North Carolina, as the ship had been declared a wreck. Further, he said, if the Government of North Carolina could prove its title to the cargo, it would lose nothing by the fact that it had been sold in Virginia, where public sales fetched higher prices. At the same time Spotswood took Eden's threat seriously, and sent the proceeds to England, so that if Brand was convicted the money would be available for payment.

The result of all this wrangling was that the share-out of the prize-money was protracted. At the same time the payment of the rewards was not so prompt as had been promised, for Lieutenant Maynard had a dispute over this with Captains Brand and Gordon. The two captains said the money ought to be divided among the crews of the two men-of-war, while Maynard claimed that it should go only to those who had actually taken part in the capture of the pirates. In the end the captains won their case, and four years after Blackbeard's death the money was shared out.

This version of the story of Blackbeard, which I have pieced together from official records, differs considerably from the account given by Johnson which earned the description of "thoroughly reliable" from the *Dictionary of National Biography*.

Johnson started the legend of Blackbeard's buried treasure: "The night before he was killed he sat up and drank till the morning with some of his own men and the master of a merchant-man; and having had intelligence of the two sloops coming to attack him, . . . one of his men asked him, in case anything should happen to him in the engagement with the sloops, whether his wife knew where he had buried his money. He answered, ' That nobody but himself and the devil knew where it was, and the longest liver should take all.' "

Further reference to Blackbeard's supposed treasure was made by Clement Downing, writing in India a few years later. He said that he had been told about it by a Portuguese named Anthony de Silvestro, who said that " he had been amongst the pirates, and that he belonged to one of the sloops in Virginia when Blackbeard was taken. He informed me that if it should be my lot ever to go to York River on Maryland, near an island called Mulberry Island, provided we went on shore at the watering-place where the shipping used most commonly to ride, that there the pirates had buried considerable sums of money in great chests well clamped down with iron plates." Downing added: " If any person who uses those parts should think it worth while to dig a little way at the upper end of a small sandy cove, where it is convenient to land, he would soon find out whether the information I had was well grounded. Fronting the landing place are five trees, amongst which he said the money was hid. I cannot warrant the truth of this account; but if I was ever to go there I would by some means or other satisfy myself, as it could not be a great deal out of my way. If anybody should obtain any benefit by this account, if it please God that they ever come to England, 'tis hoped they will remember the author for his information."

I echo Downing's hope, but without any expectations. The treasure has been sought and not found. This is hardly sur-prising. If this mysterious de Silvestro had really known where it was, he would not have given the information to Downing for nothing. Besides, pirates did not bury their treasure together, and Blackbeard never took enough loot to make his share worth burying.

Johnson says that among the documents taken was Blackbeard's journal, and he quotes two typical extracts from it: " Such a day rum all out; our company somewhat sober; a damned confusion amongst us; rogues a-plotting; great talk of separation; so I looked sharp for a prize "—and: " Such a day took one with a great deal of liquor on board, so kept the company hot, damned hot, then all things went well again." I cannot find any reference to this journal in the official records, but the extracts ring true. So does Johnson's picture of Blackbeard as a drunken braggart. But otherwise his character seems far removed from the popular conception.

Blackbeard fought bravely at the end, but this was the only occasion on which he ever had to fight. He did not terrorize his prisoners, and there is not a shred of evidence to show that he ever ill-treated one of them. He threatened murder at Charleston, but did not keep his word when the time-limit expired. When he took prizes he usually put the crews ashore and burnt their vessels. If this was not possible he merely took the cargoes and let the men keep their ship, although it would have been safer to sink her with all hands. His conduct when he took the two French ships off Bermuda was typical.

It would be unfair to blame Johnson entirely for the Blackbeard legend as it is usually told to-day. It has been greatly coloured by later writers.

Although Blackbeard was more important, Stede Bonnet was the more interesting character. It is still a mystery why a middle-aged gentleman of means should have taken up piracy in this way. The suggestions that Bonnet was an incompetent captain are entirely unfounded, and in his last engagement he showed courage and a good deal more sense than Blackbeard.

According to some pirate historians, Bonnet was the only pirate captain who made his prisoners walk the plank. I have been unable to find a scrap of evidence to support this. Bonnet's career is even more fully documented than Blackbeard's, for a full report of his trial has been preserved. The

ALEXANDER SPOTSWOOD, GOVERNOR OF VIRGINIA (1710–22)

Exceeded his duties by sending an expedition to North Carolina to catch Blackbeard.

MAJOR STEDE BONNET ON THE GALLOWS
Bonnet is said to have been driven to piracy by a nagging wife.

evidence against him was considerable, yet not one of the witnesses accused him of ill-treatment of prisoners. It seems as if this is another myth.

The end of Blackbeard was virtually the end of American piracy. No other pirates tried to establish North Carolina as a base. Thanks to the energy of Governors Johnson and Spotswood, well over a hundred pirates had been killed in action or executed in a few months. This death-rate was unprecedented in the history of piracy. Like most criminals, pirates do not seem to have been greatly influenced by the severity of punishment awaiting them if caught; but, again like most criminals, they were easily deterred by the probability of being caught. An efficient, if irregular, police drove them away from North Carolina.

In 1719, after the struggle was over, the Home Government belatedly answered Governor Johnson's appeals and sent two additional men-of-war as guard-ships. One was stationed off Charleston, and another cruised off the coast of the Carolinas. Neither had much work to do.

With the death of George I in 1727 the colonial Governors' commissions to try pirates expired. Neither in Virginia nor South Carolina was it thought necessary to apply for their renewal.

CHAPTER SEVENTEEN

Woodes Rogers of Nassau

SHORTLY before the death of Blackbeard, Thomas Gale wrote from North Carolina: " The pirates yet accounted to be out are near two thousand men, and of these Vane, Thatch and others promise themselves to be repossessed of Providence in a short time; how the loss of that place may affect the Ministry I cannot tell, but the consequence of it seems not only to be a general destruction of the trade to the West Indies and the main of America but the settling and establishing of a nest of pirates."

Vane was still out, and the pirates at sea had been joined by about a hundred who had left New Providence after accepting the Act of Grace from Woodes Rogers. At the same time the Spanish threat to the island increased. It was learnt at Nassau that the King of Spain had already appointed a Spanish Governor for New Providence, and that he was at Havana with an expeditionary force of sixteen hundred men and two men-of-war and three galleys. To defend the island Woodes Rogers still had only the *Delicia*, his unreliable militia, and the privateer under Captain Hornigold. He commissioned two more ex-pirate vessels, also officered and manned by pardoned pirates, to assist in the defence, and in November he caught three pirates. He sent them to Bermuda for trial, for he feared an insurrection if he brought them before a court at Nassau. " I was at that time too weak to bring them to a trial, most of the people here having led the same course of life."

In December an attempt was made to kill Woodes Rogers and restore pirate rule to New Providence. Some of the soldiers whom Rogers had brought from England were in the plot. Rogers was forewarned, and he had three of the ringleaders flogged—" but having no power to hold a Court Martial and cannot spare the men to send them hence I shall release them and be more on my guard." He added feelingly: " I would not undergo the like fatigue and risk as I have done ever since I have been here for the profits of any employ upon earth."

Meanwhile stocks of food were running out, and Rogers sent three ships with trade goods to exchange for fresh supplies. The little fleet was commanded by Captain Henry White, the other two captains being William Greenway and John Augur. The pilot was Richard Turnley. All were pardoned pirates. To watch over them Rogers sent James Ker, who had come with him from England, as supercargo.

Two days out of New Providence, the ships anchored off a little island called Green Key, where the crews mutinied under the leadership of a man called Phineas Bunce. They had decided to return to piracy. Captain Augur joined them voluntarily, and they kept Captain White as a forced man, needing him to sail his ship. Ker, Turnley, and five others were put ashore. Greenway was to have been forced, but he joined the men who were marooned. After many hardships they got back to Nassau.

When Woodes Rogers heard the news he sent Hornigold out in his sloop to try to catch the pirates. However, they had already fallen foul of three Spanish coastguard vessels, and many had been killed, including Bunce. Hornigold caught thirteen, including Captain Augur, and took them back to Nassau. " I am glad of this new proof Captain Hornigold has given the world to wipe off the infamous name he has hitherto been known by, though in the very acts of piracy he committed most people spoke well of his generosity," wrote Rogers.

Not having a gaol at Nassau, and fearing that the pirates would be rescued if they were confined in the guardroom of the fort, Rogers kept them aboard the *Delicia* while he convened a special meeting of the Council to discuss their disposal.

Having no authority to set up a Vice-Admiralty Court himself, Rogers ought to have sent the pirates to Jamaica for trial. But their capture occurred just when the news was received that the long-expected war with Spain was about to break out. Rogers could not possibly spare the *Delicia* or Hornigold's sloop, and there was no other means of transport. He proposed to stretch the law and try them himself.

The Council agreed, and passed a resolution that a Vice-Admiralty Court should be set up by the Governor, "notwithstanding he has made known to us all that he has no direct commission for trial of pirates."

The court sat in the guardroom at Nassau on December 9 and 10, 1718. Three of the pirates had died of wounds; of the other ten, nine were found guilty and sentenced to death. Sentence was ordered to be carried out on December 12. The condemned men asked for more time to prepare themselves for death, but Rogers regretted that as he had no guards and no gaol, and needed every able-bodied man " because of the expected war with Spain, and there being many more pirates amongst these islands," he found himself " indispensably obliged for the welfare of the settlement to give them no longer time."

Rogers sent the proceedings of the court back to England, together with an account of the execution of the condemned men. Guarded by one hundred carefully chosen men, the nine pirates were taken to the top of the ramparts facing the sea, where the gallows had been erected. At the last moment Rogers reprieved one of the nine. The others spent three-quarters of an hour under the gallows in prayers and speeches.

Augur was hanged first. His last request was for a glass of wine, and he " drank it with wishes for the good success of the Bahama Islands and the Governor." The next man, Will Cunningham, who had been Blackbeard's gunner, expressed himself penitent. The third was Dennis McKarthy, whom Rogers had made an ensign of his militia. He appeared in a new suit of clothes, " adorned at neck, wrists, knees and cap with long blue ribbons ", and on the rampart " he looked cheerfully around him, and saying he knew the time when there was many a brave fellow on the island that would not suffer him to die like a thief, at the same time pulled off his shoes, kicking them over the parapet of the wall, saying he had promised not to die with his shoes on." One other man besides Cunningham was penitent, and when offered wine said that " water was more suitable to them at that time." Another said he had always wished to die drunk, and achieved his ambition.

A few weeks later the gallows were used again, after Rogers had been " forced to condemn and hang a fellow for robbing and burning a house." In reporting this he told the Council for Trade: " If for want of lawyers our forms are something deficient, I am fully satisfied we have not erred in justice."

Meanwhile the long-expected war with Spain had broken out, and the threat of invasion increased. Rogers pleaded again for a man-of-war, reporting that Captain Chamberlain, Commodore of the Jamaica Squadron, " was but twenty leagues hence, but thought fit to pass me with a compliment of being glad to hear I was well and wished me a merry Christmas, without giving me hope of seeing him or any of the other two that came with us here." To Sir Richard Steele he wrote more bluntly: " Every capture made by the pirates aggravates the inclinations of the commanders of our men-of-war, who having [i.e. have] openly avowed that the greater number of pirates makes their suitable advantage in trade, for the merchants of necessity are forced to send their effects in the King's bottoms, when they from every part hear of the ravages committed by the pirates."

In January 1719 Rogers wrote: " I have now an account of one Captain Congon [i.e. Condent] that commands two pirates of thirty-six guns each, who designs to come hither, to offer to surrender themselves and embrace His Majesty's gracious pardon, and the time being so far elapsed, I would if I could resist them, but the inhabitants here are so much their friends that I fear I shall be forced to receive them at all hazards." But Condent sailed instead to the Eastern Seas, where he made a highly successful cruise that will be reported in a later chapter.

The threat of invasion by the Spanish was now worrying Rogers more than the pirates. Before the war it had been useful as a means of persuading the inhabitants of New Providence to look to their defences; now it had become an immediate danger. " Should the pirates come first," Rogers told the Council for Trade, " it may be best to receive them to defend myself against the Spaniards, for if I refuse to receive them most of those I have now with me will either join them or quit me, and then they'll possess the place maugré all I can prepare to do against them." Fortunately Captain Hornigold remained loyal, and Rogers strengthened his defences by commissioning two more ex-pirate ships as privateers, choosing the captains and men with great care. He kept them as guard-ships; to clear the seas of pirates was beyond his power.

Meanwhile the British Government issued a new Royal Proclamation, extending the time limit of the Act of Grace. On receiving this the Governor of Jamaica wrote (March 1719): " I am of opinion the pirates will now come in, war with Spain being declared, which they have long wished for." Some did go in, but mostly surrendered on their own terms. In June the Governor of Bermuda reported: "Another sloop brought to just without our bar, the commander whereof sent his boat ashore with written proposals to me wherein they owned themselves pirates and inserted that if I would allow all they had on board to be their own they would come in and surrender, or otherwise be gone by such an hour; and I thought proper for the service to agree to their demands, and hope I was right."

Many pirates accepted the transition to lawful plundering offered by the war, and their threat to New Providence decreased. The Spanish danger remained throughout the year; and at last, in February 1720, the long-awaited invasion came.

The Spanish attacked with five men-of-war, three brigantines, and three sloops. Their expeditionary force of two thousand included fourteen hundred regular soldiers. A man-of-war had arrived to assist Rogers, but was unable to prevent the Spanish from landing. The militia of ex-pirates drove them off, Rogers's combined naval forces forcing the enemy fleet to withdraw. Thus, with hardly any resources Rogers had succeeded in holding New Providence against both the pirates and the Spanish.

The war ended soon afterwards, and with the withdrawal of commissions from the privateers piracy increased again. The old threat returned, and the Home Government took no measures to deal with it. "We may expect as it's peace there will be more than ever the vast detriment if not destruction of the American trade," warned Rogers. What disturbed him most was that New Providence was still virtually unsettled as well as unprotected, and he had received no indication of the Government's plans for the Bahamas. In April 1720 he wrote: " It's about twenty-one months since my arrival here, and I have yet no account from home what is or will be done for the preservation of this settlement." Three months later he remarked that he had received " none of your Lordship's commands nor no news from home for above this twelve months past." At last, in November 1720, his Council wrote this remarkable letter to the Secretary of State: " Governor Rogers having received no letter from you dated since July 1719, and none from the Board of Trade since his arrival, given him and us great uneasiness lest this poor colony should be no more accounted as part of His Britannic Majesty's dominions."

Since his arrival at Nassau Rogers had been forced to subsidize the settlement mainly out of his own pocket. He had borne most of the cost of defence and had paid for food imports. He had given accounts of his expenses to the Council for Trade, expressing the hope that he would be reimbursed. In January 1720 he had reported that " the credit of the King's garrison is quite extinct." Now, over two years after his arrival, he was still waiting for a reply to his first letter, and was already heavily in debt.

At this point Rogers seems to have lost his patience. In February 1721 he wrote bluntly: " It is impossible that I can submit here any longer on the foot I have been left ever since my arrival." He sailed to Carolina, where he ordered provisions for New Providence to last until the following Christmas, and then returned to London. His financial dealings with the Government are outside the scope of this history, but it may be said that Rogers did not get all his money back. He refused to return to Nassau, so a new Governor, George Phenney, was appointed, and Rogers was retired on half-pay as captain of the foot.

In 1728 Woodes Rogers was reappointed Governor of the Bahamas, with a salary of £400 a year and the power to convene an Assembly. By the time he returned the Age of Piracy was over, and he devoted his energies to encouraging cotton and sugar industries. He died in office in 1732. It is doubtful if any empire-builder has been so shabbily treated both by his contemporaries and by posterity. Without any force worth the name he won and held the Bahamas against two much stronger enemies, and in the final reckoning he probably did more than any other man to bring the Age of Piracy to an end.

CHAPTER EIGHTEEN

" *My Lord, We Plead Our Bellies* "

AMONG the pirates who sailed out from New Providence when Woodes Rogers first sailed in was a bold young fellow named John Rackham. At that time he was quartermaster on Vane's ship. Some months later he disputed Vane's decision not to pursue a French man-of-war. Vane, says Johnson, " made use of his power to determine this dispute, which in these cases is absolute and uncontrollable, by their own laws, viz. the captain's absolute right of determining in all questions concerning fighting, chasing, or being chased. . . . But the next day the captain's conduct was obliged to stand the test of a vote, and a resolution passed against his honour and dignity, which branded him with the name of coward, deposed him from the command, and turned him out of the company with infamy; and with him went all those who did not vote for boarding the French man-of-war." Rackham was elected captain in Vane's stead.

Not much can be found out about Rackham outside the pages of Johnson, but he seems to have commanded an un-usually daring company, and later they got the best of a Spanish man-of-war. They were still at sea in October 1720, when the Governor of Jamaica, weary of the unco-operative attitude of the British guard-ships, commissioned a merchant sloop, under Captain Barnet, to try to catch these elusive pirates. Barnet caught them at anchor, apparently the worse for drink, and succeeded in capturing the whole company. He took them to San Jago de la Vega, Jamaica, where they were tried by a Vice-Admiralty Court.

The story runs that when the pirates had all been sentenced to death, and were asked the conventional question whether there was any reason why sentence should not be carried out, two of them said :

" My lord, we plead our bellies."

This was not an unusual plea at that time, nor was the wording original. Even in the eighteenth century a court was not allowed to order the killing of an unborn child, and a condemned woman escaped the gallows if she could prove that she was pregnant. But it was not the sort of plea that one expected to hear from a couple of pirates.

The story goes that the plea was greeted with ribald laughter. Bravado was always appreciated in such circumstances, and there was a nice touch of bawdiness about this. But the two pirates were not joking, and insisted on being examined by the surgeon. Sure enough, they were pregnant women.

So much for the popular tale, for which Johnson cannot be blamed. The laughter in court was not heard until the nineteenth century. But the rest of the story was written up by Johnson only four years after the trial, and it is as strange a blend of fact and fiction as that indefatigable historian ever concocted.

One of the women pirates was named Anne Bonny, or Bonney, and Johnson gives a pornographically circumstantial account of her conception in County Cork. It is too blatantly invented to merit repetition and examination here. It is enough to say that according to Johnson, Anne's father, a lawyer, had to abandon his practice and emigrated to Carolina, taking Anne and her mother with him. The mother died, but the father built up a good practice and bought some plantations. Anne was heiress to a large fortune when she eloped with a pirate named James Bonny. He took her to New Providence, and they were still there when Woodes Rogers arrived. Then Bonny not only took the pardon but turned informer. This upset Anne, who liked the pirates so much that she started to stray into their hammocks. After some promiscuity she reserved her favours for one Calico Jack, so called from the striped seaman's trousers he always wore. This was Jack Rackham.

The story is confused by some inconsistencies here, but it seems that eventually Anne put on seaman's clothes and went off a-pirating with her lover. So far as the rest of the crew were concerned she was just another seaman, and she wielded a cutlass with the best of them until she had to take shore leave in

Cuba to have a baby. Apparently abandoning the child, she rejoined the ship, and all went well until her fancy was taken by a new member of the crew. She took him aside one day and revealed her sex. The revelation does not appear to have been entirely verbal, for when Rackham saw them together he drew his cutlass and threatened to kill them both. But fortunately for Anne her lover turned out to be a woman too.

Her name was Mary Read, and Johnson has another racy story to tell about the circumstances leading to her birth. He also says that she was fighting in Flanders until the Treaty of Ryswick, which would make her at least middle-aged in 1720. After a fine military career Mary married a fellow trooper, and when he died she took to the sea and sailed to the West Indies. After various adventures she became one of Rackham's crew.

Mary's virtue was not so easy as Anne's, but before long she fell in love with a forced man and gave him an opportunity " by carelessly showing her breasts, which were very white." (Johnson does not state the source of this intimate piece of information.) The forced man, being " made of flesh and blood," took this for an invitation, but Mary refused to allow him any liberties until " they plighted their troth to each other, which Mary Read said she looked up to be as good a marriage in conscience as if it had been done by a minister in church."

A little later Mary's " husband " quarrelled with one of the pirates and was challenged to a duel. Mary thereupon deliberately picked a quarrel with the same man, and arranged a duel with him first. After a long and bloody fight she ran him through with her cutlass.

When Barnet and his men ultimately boarded the pirate ship, only Anne and Mary put up any sort of fight, and they vigorously upbraided the others for their cowardice. But they were taken at last, and, says Johnson—correctly—when their sex was discovered by the authorities they were given a separate trial. Johnson says that Anne was acquitted but Mary was convicted because of a statement she was supposed to have made on the pirate ship. It was almost certainly ' ghosted ' by Johnson, but it is worth quoting, if only to hearten those who believe in the deterrent effect of capital punishment:

" As to hanging, she thought it no great hardship, for, were it not for that, every cowardly fellow would turn pirate, and so infest the seas that men of courage must starve: that if it was put to the choice of the pirates, they would not have the punishment less than death, the fear of which kept some dastardly rogues honest: and that . . . the ocean would be crowded with rogues, like the land, and no merchant would venture out: so that the trade, in a little time, would not be worth following."

Mary, says Johnson, was saved from the gallows because she was pregnant, but died in childbirth. Anne survived, and her release was obtained by some influential friends of her father. Seeing Rackham on the way to the gallows, she said " she was sorry to see him there, but if he had fought like a man he need not have been hanged like a dog."

That is Johnson's story, and to make sure it was believed he wrote a little preface:

" As to the lives of our two female pirates, we must confess they appear a little extravagant. Yet they are never the less true for seeming so, but as they were publicly tried for their piracies, there are living witnesses to justify what we have laid down concerning them." Johnson admitted that he had included " some particulars which were not so publicly known," but this was because " we were more inquisitive into the circumstances of their past lives than other people." He ended his note, " If there are some incidents and turns in their stories which may give them a little the air of a novel, they are not invented or contrived for that purpose."

Johnson's story has been repeated credulously for over two hundred years, usually without any such apology, although some writers have drawn attention to similar male impersonations in the eighteenth century. The ones generally mentioned are those of Mrs. Christian Davies (" Mother Ross ") and Hannah Snell.

A biography of Mother Ross was published in the year after her death (1739). It has been attributed to Daniel Defoe, although he died in 1731. This book gives a long account of Mother Ross's service under the Duke of Marlborough in the Low Countries. It is almost certainly fictitious; but Mother Ross existed and, according to the *Gentleman's Magazine* (July 1739), served as a dragoon—but in Ireland, not Flanders. The story of Hannah Snell, who is said to have served in both the Army and the Navy, lacks confirmation.

Male impersonation in the Forces would have been easier then than now, in that medical examinations could be avoided more easily; on the other hand, there was a good deal less privacy in sanitary arrangements. This matter caused some scepticism at the time when the stories were published. The second edition (1740) of the biography of Mother Ross contains a " Bookseller's Note " designed to satisfy the curiosity of the many readers who had written to say that they were " greatly puzzled to conceive how a woman could so long perform a certain natural operation without being discovered; since soldiers are obliged to perform it, not only standing but often publicly, and even at the head of the regiment." The bookseller's answer was ingenious. " This indeed seems to have been a difficult task; and yet it was very easy to her by means of a silver tube painted over, and fastened about her with leather straps." Without this " urinary instrument," continued the bookseller, " she could never have hoped to pass long concealed." The bookseller excused himself from giving a specification of " this notable engine " as he did not want to " offend nice ears "; but he added that Mother Ross " sold the toy in Flanders for seven pistoles, which she much repented ever after; for on her return to England she soon became sensible, by the great resort of persons who had heard of this circumstance, among others relating to her history, that she might have gotten a handsome subsistence by showing it as a curiosity."

I do not want to offend nice ears either, but it is impossible to discover the truth about these unique women pirates without some consideration of the usual sanitary arrangements on a sloop. Anne Bonny and Mary Read would have been faced with much more difficult problems of concealment than Hannah Snell, for on a man-of-war special wooden seats were rigged in a secluded part of the deck. On a small vessel like a sloop there were no such refinements. In those days ' the head ', which survives only in name, meant what it said. The men had to make do perched on the forechains of the bow.

There is another puzzle here. While Hannah Snell is said to have kept her secret to herself, both Anne and Mary had lovers. We know that not even the captain of a pirate ship had private quarters, and there is plenty of evidence that any collusive secrecy aroused the suspicions of the rest of the crew and was often expressly forbidden by the articles. In these circumstances it is difficult to visualize how Anne and Mary could have carried on their respective amours on an over-crowded sloop without anyone else finding out.

The only explanation I can think of is that they may have passed off their affairs as homosexual. It is extremely difficult to discover how much homosexuality there was among pirates, for in their age, even more than now, there was a strong taboo on the mention of the subject in print. That it existed to some extent seems certain from the specific ban on catamites in the articles of Bartholomew Roberts. Provided that homo-sexuality was practised or even tolerated on Rackham's ship, it was perhaps possible, with reasonable restraint, to disguise heterosexual activity in this way. If this is not physically plausible, I cannot think what could have gone on.

Fortunately much of Johnson's story can be verified without speculation. The records of the Vice-Admiralty Court are lost, but a report of the trial was published in Jamaica at the time by a printer named Robert Baldwin. Its claim to authenticity is strong, for it was sent to the Council for Trade in lieu of an official report by the Governor of Jamaica, who presided over the court. It is fortunate that it was sent, for this copy, now in the Public Record Office, seems to be the only one extant. I understand that a photostat was made recently for the Colonial Archives at Spanish Town.

Anne Bonny and Mary Read were tried at San Jago de la Vega on November 28, 1720, over a week after Rackham and the others were hanged.

The first witness against them was a woman named Dorothy Thomas, who had been in a canoe when the pirates attacked her and stole her store of provisions. She testified that the accused were among them—" dressed in men's jackets, and long trousers, and handkerchief tied about their heads." She added that she knew their sex " by the largeness of their breasts." She seems to have been rash enough to mention the fact at the time, for she said that they "cursed and swore at the men to murder me, to prevent me from coming [i.e. bearing witness] against them."

Thomas Dillon, the master of a sloop taken by the pirates, confirmed this evidence. When he was attacked, he said, "Anne Bonny had a gun in her hand." He added that "they were both very profligate, cursing and swearing much, and very ready and willing to do anything."

Then came the evidence of two Frenchmen, whose names were given as John Besneck and Peter Cornelian. They had been taken prisoners by the pirates and claimed to be forced men. A single sentence in their evidence destroys most of Johnson's impersonation story:

"When we saw any vessel, gave chase, or attacked, they wore men's clothes; at all other times they wore women's clothes."

I think this may almost be taken as a complete explanation of the impersonation story. Women's fashions in those days were unsuitable for piracy. Anne and Mary wore trousers for the same reason that women often wear slacks to-day. It was a matter not of disguise, but of physical convenience.

The evidence of the Frenchmen makes it clear that the sex of the women was no secret from the crew. The witnesses added that Anne and Mary "did not seem to be kept or detained by force," but served "of their own free-will and consent." Both were "very active on board, and willing to do anything."

None of the evidence for the prosecution was disputed or contradicted. Both the accused were found guilty and sentenced to death. When they were asked if there was any reason why sentence should not be carried out, both pleaded their bellies and were reprieved.

There is just one possible explanation that might make the impersonation story valid. The Frenchmen were recent captives, and it may be that the sex of the two women had only recently been discovered by the rest of the crew. In that case previous events could have occurred as Johnson reported them. But I think this is an unjustifiably charitable theory. It would still not explain how physical privacy was maintained; and if Johnson had known the full facts as well as he professed, he would surely have mentioned the discovery. Besides, there are too many other discrepancies between the report of the trial and Johnson's version.

Johnson says that Mary Read was the more valiant of the two, but the court record suggests the reverse. The speech attributed to Mary on the virtue of capital punishment does not appear in the report of the proceedings; and while Johnson says that only Mary was sentenced to death, the report shows that Anne received the same sentence.

The printed account of the trial contains no information about their previous history, beyond the description of them both as " spinsters of New Providence." However, Johnson's story of Anne's marriage to James Bonny may well be correct, for a pirate of this name did surrender to Woodes Rogers and was employed by him. The account of Anne's early life in Carolina rests on no better authority than the story of her conception, and her father's name is still unknown.

The story of Mary Read's duel to save her lover is unconfirmed, as is Johnson's account of her military adventures in Flanders. I am struck by the close resemblance between this and the story of Mother Ross, and there may be some significance in the fact that both tales have been independently attributed to Daniel Defoe. Mother Ross certainly fought in the dragoons, although not in Flanders, and received a life pension of a shilling a day after being wounded at Aughrim in 1691. The story was probably famous for many years, and may well have been fathered—or mothered—on to Mary Read.

Why the two women were allowed on board Rackham's ship is a mystery, for as a rule pirates were extraordinarily strict on this matter. Possibly they joined the crew disguised as men and their sex was not discovered until they were at sea; if so, it is unlikely that they hit on the same idea independently. Another possibility is that the crew voted to waive their articles for once, perhaps partly because the two women were lusty fighters and partly because they were lustful women. They would have had ample opportunities to show both propensities at New Providence. But as the case is exceptional in

ANNE BONNY AND MARY READ

An illustration from Captain Johnson's *History of the Pirates* (1726). The picture suggests that these female pirates wore men's clothes for physical convenience rather than sexual disguise. The artist thus missed the point of the story, but thereby probably got nearer the truth than the author.

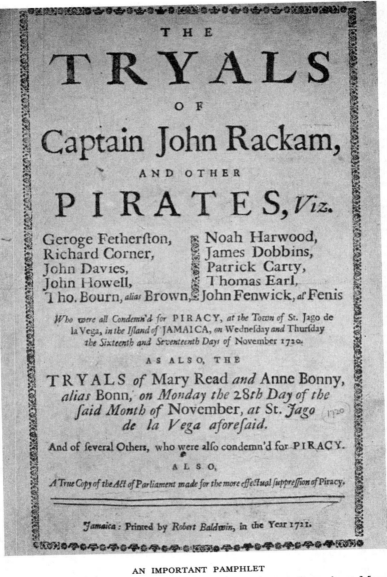

THE
TRYALS
OF
Captain John Rackam,
AND OTHER
PIRATES, *Viz.*

Geroge Fetherston,	Noah Harwood,
Richard Corner,	James Dobbins,
John Davies,	Patrick Carty,
John Howell,	Thomas Earl,
Tho. Bourn, *alias* Brown,	John Fenwick, *al'* Fenis

Who were all Condemn'd for PIRACY, *at the Town of* St. Jago de la Vega, *in the Island of* JAMAICA, *on* Wednesday *and* Thursday *the Sixteenth and Seventeenth Days of* November 1720.

AS ALSO, THE
TRYALS *of* Mary Read *and* Anne Bonny, *alias* Bonn, *on Monday the* 28th *Day of the said Month of* November, *at* St. *Jago de la Vega aforesaid.*

And of several Others, who were also condemn'd for PIRACY.

ALSO,

A True Copy of the Act of Parliament made for the more effectual suppression of Piracy.

Jamaica : Printed by *Robert Baldwin,* in the Year 1721.

AN IMPORTANT PAMPHLET

Title-page of a pamphlet containing the only known facts about Mary Read and Anne Bonny. The pamphlet is important because it disproves most of the popular story about these two female pirates.

pirate history I am more inclined to think it was probably unpremeditated.

The articles of Captain Bartholomew Roberts, which were drawn up in the West Indies about this time, contained this extension of the normal ban on women: " If any man were found seducing any of the latter sex, and carried her to sea disguised, he was to suffer death." Pirates did not legislate against hypothetical contingencies, and the mere existence of this article strongly suggests that the subterfuge had at least been attempted. The fact that no other cases came to light is further evidence of the difficulty of maintaining the deception. With Anne and Mary it was not maintained, and they could only have remained on board with the general consent of the company.

However they became pirates, it is most unlikely that either would have been allowed to remain monandrous. The captain was perhaps the last person who would have been allowed a private concubine. The crew—which in this case was relatively small—would certainly have invoked the traditional pirate principle of fair shares for all; and as the women " did not seem to be kept or detained by force " it may be assumed that they agreed to forming a common pool. They must have been, in the words of the Frenchmen at their trial, " very active on board and willing to do anything."

The characters of Mary Read and Anne Bonny are without parallel in pirate history, and it is a pity that their story is incomplete. Unless new evidence is discovered their full story will never be known. The evidence that exists may serve at least to show the danger of over-reliance on Captain Johnson.

CHAPTER NINETEEN

Another Madagascar

SO long as the pirates held New Providence they were mainly content to cruise in the West Indies and, when plunder was scarce, off the Atlantic seaboard of America. The loss of their island base, and of careening and market facilities in North Carolina, made them go farther afield. The West Indies were not so attractive after Woodes Rogers had blocked up their best bolt-hole, and there was no suitable alternative to New Providence. The Governor of Bermuda received threats that his island would be seized and turned into " another Madagascar," as the pirates put it, but no attempt was made to carry out these threats. Some of the more adventurous pirates had a better idea. They decided to make " another Madagascar " of Madagascar itself.

In an earlier chapter I reported a prophecy made by Woodes Rogers when he met some pirates from Madagascar in 1711. Shortly after the signing of the Treaty of Utrecht this far-seeing man had repeated his warning to the British Government, and had proposed that he should lead an expedition to take possession of Madagascar and turn it into a British colony. He suggested that this would be the easiest way of preventing another threat by the pirates against British trade with the East. His proposal was ignored; and it is a little ironical that by driving the pirates out of New Providence, Woodes Rogers himself turned the thoughts of the pirates back to Madagascar.

The return to the Eastern Seas was led by a pirate named Christopher Condent, who left New Providence shortly before Woodes Rogers arrived. He sailed to the Cape Verde Islands, took some prizes, and then shaped his course for Madagascar, where he arrived about June 1719. He was joined here by some of Captain Halsey's old company and a few other stragglers, and then followed the traditional route to the Red

Sea. But he missed the Mocha fleet, and sailed to the west coast of India. He took a few small prizes, but nothing of any real value. However, his presence was regarded as sufficiently dangerous for the East India Company to ask the Government to send a squadron of men-of-war. The request was ignored, and in October 1720 Condent's persistence was rewarded with the capture of a very valuable Moorish ship near Bombay. No resistance was offered, although the ship was taken close to the shore and, indeed, her passengers and crew were put on the mainland. Condent then took his prize to St. Mary's.

The value of the ship and cargo was estimated at thirteen lakhs of rupees, or about £150,000. It was easily the richest prize taken since the old days of the "pirate round," and each pirate had a share of about £1500 to £2000. Valuable merchandise, including drugs, spices, and silks, were left strewn on the beach at St. Mary's, where the company broke up. Most of the pirates now decided to retire from the trade, and they started to negotiate with the Governor of Réunion for a French pardon. The negotiations were successful, and Condent and about forty others sailed to the island.

Meanwhile other pirates had come into the Eastern Seas. Among these were a Frenchman named Oliver La Bouche and an Irishman named Edward England. England had better luck than Condent in the Red Sea, and took several Indian ships. The plunder was rich, and as the women passengers were coloured, they were abused in the usual way. England took his prizes to St. Mary's, which he found deserted except by natives, who gave the pirates an agreeable welcome. They secured their base and promised to return after another cruise; but when they sailed they took their plunder with them.

England's ship was the *Fancy*, a former Dutchman; her consort, the *Victory*, was commanded by a pirate named John Taylor. They sailed to Johanna, and found two East Indiamen and an Ostender in the bay. The East Indiamen were the *Cassandra*, Captain Macrae, and the *Greenwich*, Captain Kirby, and both carried commissions to take pirates. At the time of their arrival Macrae and Kirby were about to seek out La Bouche, who was reported to have lost his ship and to be building another. When Macrae saw the *Fancy* and *Victory* he changed his plans and prepared for an engagement. Kirby agreed to take part, but the Ostender sheered off.

The *Fancy* came in, flying the black flag at the maintopmast, the red flag at the foretopmast, and the cross of St. George at the ensign staff. The *Cassandra* engaged her, and when the *Victory* came in too Macrae called to Kirby for help. But Kirby followed the Ostender out of the battle. Outgunned and outnumbered, Macrae fought bravely for several hours, but after he had lost thirteen men killed and twenty-four wounded he was forced to yield. Knowing that he could not expect quarter now, Macrae, who was himself wounded in the head, fled to the shore with the other survivors. Here he was granted asylum by the native Prince.

The pirates had suffered much heavier casualties, and they were in a murderous mood. When they boarded the *Cassandra* they found three wounded men whom Macrae had been forced to leave behind, and slashed them to pieces. Then they went ashore to look for Macrae. But a report was spread that he had died of his wounds, and he was able to lie low for ten days. He and his men were now in wretched circumstances, and without any prospect of getting a ship; so, hoping that the pirates had got over their wrath, he let them know he was alive and asked if he could go aboard for a parley. He was promised safe-conduct, but it was only the fact that he knew some of the pirates, including England, that saved him from being murdered.

The pirates were now refitting the *Cassandra* and intended to burn the *Fancy*, which had been badly disabled in the battle. Macrae pleaded for the ship, and in the end they let him have it and also gave him back some of the cargo from the *Cassandra* which they did not want. Macrae managed to return to India, and as a reward for his valour he gained rapid promotion in the Company's service, eventually becoming Governor of Madras. The salary for this appointment was only £500 a year, but when Macrae retired after eight years he had amassed a fortune of £800,000.

The loot from the *Cassandra* was estimated as worth about £75,000, but according to one contemporary account " no part of the cargo was so much valued by the robbers as the doctor's chest, for they were all poxed to a great degree." It seems that Macrae owed his life mainly to England, who had managed to persuade a bare majority of the pirates to agree to let him go. A strong minority, led by Captain Taylor, protested against the decision and finally turned the general feeling against England, who was deposed and turned out of the company. With a few others who suffered the same fate he managed to reach Madagascar, and for a time they lived at St. Augustine's Bay on the charity of other pirates. Taylor was elected captain in England's place.

The second mate of the *Cassandra*, Richard Lazenby, was not so lucky as Captain Macrae, for he was taken as a forced man and had to remain with the pirates as pilot. When he was finally released he wrote an account of his experiences, which has fortunately been preserved.

After leaving Johanna with the *Cassandra* and *Victory* the pirates took two Moors, and tortured the captains and merchants until they revealed where their money was hidden. They attacked and scattered a fleet of ships of the East India Company, although the odds were against them, and after taking more prizes they put in at the port of Cochin, where the Dutch Governor accepted their bribes. They spent Christmas (1720) at sea, and feasted so riotously that they used up nearly all their fresh provisions. Lazenby says that quite two-thirds of the food was wasted. The *Victory* was now leaking badly, and they decided to sail to Mauritius. Their remaining provisions had to be strictly rationed, and when they reached Mauritius they were half-starved. After resting, they re-sheathed the *Victory* and sailed to Réunion, where they found a large Portuguese ship lying at anchor, with the Viceroy of Goa aboard. They took her easily, and found themselves in possession of a prize with three or four million dollars' worth of diamonds and about half a million crowns in cash. They accepted a ransom for the Viceroy, released Lazenby, and sailed away.

Lazenby understandably says nothing about his own share of the plunder. He reports that he spent a few months at Réunion, where he met Condent and his men. Fifteen of them eventually sailed with Lazenby when a French ship took him to Europe. Condent stayed at Réunion, and Johnson says that he married the Governor's sister-in-law and later went to St. Malo and set up in business as an " honest merchant." Some of Condent's crew spent the rest of their lives at Réunion. One of them, named Adam, was still living there in 1770, aged one hundred and four.

The pirates had abandoned their old *Victory* at Réunion, and the *Cassandra*, with the Portuguese prize—renamed the *Victory*—sailed to St. Mary's. After the final share-out each man had £4000 in cash and about forty diamonds. This was probably the most successful cruise in the history of piracy.

Meanwhile the British Government had at last heeded the requests of the East India Company, and a squadron of four men-of-war, under Commodore Thomas Mathews, was sent east. Mathews in his flagship reached St. Augustine's Bay ahead of the rest of his fleet, and, finding the bay deserted, wrote a letter to his other captains explaining his plans and ordering them to join him at Bombay. He left this letter with the natives, who handed it over to the first captains who came into the harbour. They happened to be Taylor and La Bouche.

Mathews reached Bombay just when the Governor was planning a joint attack with the Portuguese against the native Angrian pirates. The arrival of the naval squadron seemed to make success certain, but Mathews quarrelled with the Governor about the question of who should fire the first salute, and then he quarrelled with the Portuguese. After the attack had failed he returned to Madagascar. He anchored at Charnock Point, about three leagues from St. Mary's, and sent a boat up to the island, which was found deserted. The beach was strewn with drugs, spices, and chinaware, and the entrance to the harbour was blocked by sunken wrecks. One of them was the *Victory*.

Mathews had among his crew a seaman named Clement Downing, who wrote an account of the expedition and included it in his *History of the Indian Wars* (1737). It is not entirely reliable, for it contains a good deal of hearsay information; but Downing's account of what he saw himself is confirmed in many particulars by the stories of other members of the expedition, including one of Mathews's captains. According to Downing, the first person to greet them at Charnock Point was an Englishman who appeared wearing two pistols in his sash and introduced himself as John Plantain. He said that he had helped to take the *Cassandra*, but had now left off pirating and lived at Ranter (Antogil) Bay. Captain Cockburn, of Mathews's expedition, tried to arrest the man, but found that he was protected by an armed guard of about twenty natives. Then Plantain explained that he was not just a resident of Ranter Bay. He was the King.

Plantain went on to say that he was born of English parents at Chocolate Hole, Jamaica. He had become a pirate with the fixed intention of making enough to give him a start in life and then accepting the King's pardon and settling down in honest business. He had sailed on a pirate ship off the Guinea coast, where he had joined Captain England. He had remained with Captain Taylor on the *Cassandra*, and after the share-out he had decided to stay for a while at Madagascar. He said that the others had already sailed back to the West Indies with the intention of seeking a pardon under the Spanish Act of Grace.

Plantain had two other retired pirates with him, and they invited Mathews's officers to visit them at Ranter Bay. They had built a fort there, and their rule had been accepted by the natives, whom they provided with arms for their wars against other tribes. When Mathews visited the fort, Plantain ran up the flag of St. George and provided a lavish feast. He offered to supply Mathews with cattle, and the Commodore did some private trading as well. Finally, without having made any attempt to look for active pirates, the men-of-war returned to England.

Downing gives a long account of Plantain's life on Madagascar after the departure of the naval squadron. I shall not draw on this material, for it is irrelevant to this history and not wholly reliable. It is, however, a fascinating story, and Downing's book deserves to be read.

When Mathews got back to England he was charged with neglect of duty and trading with pirates and was relieved of his

command. Most historians have described his expedition as a
complete failure. It seems to have been a complete success.
Mathews had been sent to suppress piracy in the Eastern seas,
and after his appearance there piracy ceased. Surprisingly it
looks as if this was a case of cause and effect.

It was simply the appearance of the naval squadron that
drove the pirates away. After Taylor and La Bouche had read
Mathews's letter to his captains they left Madagascar for good.
Shortly before this two English merchant captains had reported
that there were at least fourteen well-armed pirate ships in
those seas. By the time Mathews returned to Madagascar
they had all vanished. The only pirates that remained were
those who, like Plantain, settled down in Madagascar in retirement.

Considering the value to pirates of a secure base, and the
trouble they took to fortify their bases, it is strange that they
never tried to defend them. The small force under Woodes
Rogers that landed at Nassau was unopposed, and the pirates'
fort there seems to have been deliberately destroyed beforehand. St. Mary's, described as easily defensible and also
fortified, was never defended either. When Commodore
Warren appeared off the harbour in 1699 the pirates dis-
mantled their guns, sank their ships, and fled to the mainland.
When another generation of pirates heard of the arrival of
Mathews's squadron they sailed away without waiting to see
what it was like.

I find this conduct difficult to understand. It can hardly
be explained by saying that pirates were seamen, not soldiers,
and therefore unwilling to fight on land. A more likely reason,
perhaps, is that they did not fight at all when there was a
chance of escape, and the history of their sea-engagements with
men-of-war goes some way to bearing this out. Moreover,
while at sea they were bound by a single set of articles and led
by a single captain, on land they had no common bond or
leader. Yet the explanation is still not entirely satisfactory.
If they did not mean to defend their bases, why did they
fortify them?

It is easier to find explanations for the fact that after each
abandonment of St. Mary's the pirates left the Eastern Seas

HISTORIE DER ZEE-ROOVERS.

JOHNSON IN HOLLAND

Frontispiece of the first Dutch edition of Captain Charles
Johnson's *History of the Pirates* (1725). In Holland, Johnson
seems to have been regarded as a second Exquemelin; with good
reason.

ATROCITY PICTURE FROM JOHNSON

The picture illustrates an apocryphal story of the murder of a wounded Spaniard.

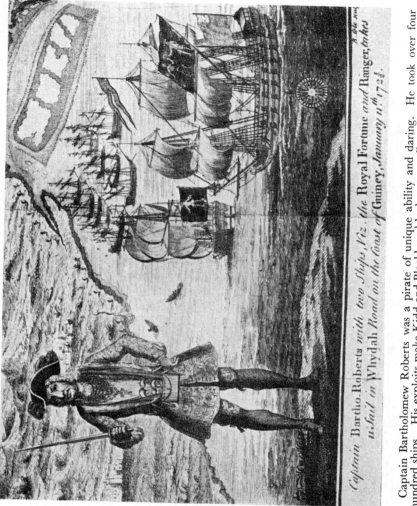

Captain Bartho. Roberts with two Ships, Viz. the Royal Fortune and Ranger, takes usail in Whydah Road on the Coast of Guiney, January 11th 1722.

Captain Bartholomew Roberts was a pirate of unique ability and daring. He took over four hundred ships. His exploits make Kidd and Blackbeard look very small.

A THREATENING LETTER

This threatening letter from Captain Bartholomew Roberts was addressed to Lieutenant-General Mathew of the Leeward Islands. (The text is printed on page 241.)

PIRATES DRINKING

Some of Captain Roberts's crew on the Guinea coast.

altogether, although in the West piracy continued after the loss of New Providence. In the West Indies there were innumerable small creeks and inlets where pirate sloops could hide and careen, and even when they had no base they could still ply their trade in comparative safety so long as the men-of-war remained benevolently neutral. In the Eastern Seas, where larger ships had to be used, conditions were less favourable for hit-and-run piracy, and a good base was necessary for the thorough careening and refitting required before the return voyage across the Atlantic. Moreover, the East India Company, which had to pay compensation and suffer reprisals, was becoming increasingly active against the pirates. Lazenby estimated that in the engagement with the *Cassandra* the pirates lost between ninety and a hundred killed. With the strengthening of the anti-piratical forces by a naval squadron the pirates may have considered that they had lost the freedom of the sea as well as their base. They knew that they could not rely on the neutrality of the Navy, which had not the same opportunity for easy pickings as in the West Indies.

It all seems plausible enough, once you admit that the pirates had to give up St. Mary's for good, but that is what I find so difficult to understand. The squadron commanded by Warren that arrived in 1699 had cruised off the island for nearly a year, and then had been replaced by two other men-of-war; moreover, the outbreak of war brought a revival of privateering soon afterwards. Even so, Captain Halsey ran the gauntlet to make a further successful piratical cruise in the Red Sea, and retired to Madagascar. But after Mathews's brief and rather wretched intervention piracy in the Eastern Seas came to a full stop.

I can understand also why Taylor and his company sailed away at the first sign of danger. They had already made enough to retire on. But I have been unable to discover what happened to the other dozen-odd pirate ships in the Eastern Seas at the time. They seem to have fled also, without even attempting to take one of the rich Moors; and no more pirates came after Mathews had gone again.

What worries me most is the fact that if the pirates had not left the Eastern Seas when they did, I should have found it very easy to explain why they were bound to stay until someone better than Mathews was sent out to stop them. This seems to bring out the danger of drawing inferences from historical facts. Even if you steel yourself against the temptation to select the facts that please you most, you are still liable to err because no records are complete and so you never get more than a selection of the facts.

CHAPTER TWENTY

The Great Pirate Roberts

ABOUT the same time that Condent sailed to Madagascar, other pirates from New Providence went to the Guinea Coast. It was less hospitable, for the Royal African Company had established some forts there, and the negroes, used to the ways of slavers, could be very unfriendly to strangers with white skins. But there were valuable prizes, and for men of daring the reward was worth the risk.

Most of the Guinea pirates were exceptionally daring, and one of them was possibly the most daring pirate who ever lived. His name was Bartholomew Roberts, and he bestraddles the Age of Piracy like a colossus. A Welsh poet has honoured " Black Barty," but he has never become a household name like Kidd and Blackbeard. I cannot imagine why. Not only was he immeasurably bolder, braver, and more successful—not only is his story far more exciting and dramatic—but in his lifetime he achieved a far greater fame. For nearly three years he was feared more than any other man at sea. Moreover, Johnson, on whose history most popular pirate books are based, did Roberts full justice, giving him five times as much space as Blackbeard or any other pirate.

Johnson's biography of Roberts is unusually reliable. The chronology is sometimes confused, and there are errors of detail, but generally the story agrees with the facts. Johnson got some of his information from Surgeon Atkins, who was in at the death, and also had access to the proceedings of the trial of Roberts's crew. These proceedings have been preserved in the Public Record Office; and with captains' letters and logs and Colonial Office papers, they make the story of Roberts one of the best documented in pirate history. This is very fortunate, for Roberts was of considerable historical as well as personal importance. He was not only the greatest of the pirates, but he was virtually the last.

He was tall, dark, and handsome, according to Johnson, and he went to sea as a boy. If that is true, he must have been at sea throughout the War of the Spanish Succession, for he was about thirty-seven years old when he entered pirate history at the beginning of 1719. He was then third mate of the *Princess*, a galley commanded by Captain Abraham Plumb of Stepney, which was taken within sight of a Royal African Company fort on the Gold Coast. The *Princess* did not resist, for the pirates had two well-armed ships, the *King James* and the *Royal Rover*, and they came in with their decks crowded with fierce-looking men.

The captain of the pirates was another Welshman, Howell Davis—a man of daring and character, renowned for his generosity and humanity. Davis boasted that he never forced a man to become a pirate, but he took Roberts aboard to give him some time to make a decision. At first reluctant, Roberts came over in the end, and at once proved himself a man of exceptional courage and ability. A few weeks later Davis was killed in action, and this new recruit was elected captain in his place.

The *King James* had sprung a leak and been abandoned, so it was the *Royal Rover*, mounted with thirty-two cannon and twenty-seven swivel guns, that Roberts commanded. He quickly took two prizes, and then resumed the cruise off the Guinea coast. Having no further success, the company voted to try their luck off Brazil. They found nothing there, and were about to sail to the West Indies when they fell in unexpectedly with a fleet of forty-two Portuguese ships preparing to sail for Lisbon.

Several of the ships were well armed, and an escort of two men-of-war was anchored near by; but Roberts, sending most of his crew below, sailed into the fleet. Coming alongside one of the ships, he ordered the captain aboard, introduced himself, and told the man he had nothing to fear if he would only indicate which was the richest ship in the fleet. The Portuguese pointed to the *Sagrada Familia*, a ship of forty guns and a hundred and fifty men, obviously stronger than the *Royal Rover*. Roberts sailed towards this ship and tried to take her by a ruse; but his purpose was discovered, and when he saw that the crew of the *Sagrada Familia* were preparing to defend her he poured in a broadside and followed it quickly with a boarding party. The other Portuguese ships fired their guns to summon the men-of-war; but by the time these sailed in Roberts had already sailed his prize out of the fleet, covering her with the *Royal Rover*.

It was said afterwards that the men-of-war were slow to answer, and the armed merchantmen cowardly. The fact remains that for sheer daring this seizure has no parallel in the history of piracy. Outgunned and outnumbered by over forty to one, Roberts had won a rich prize for the loss of only two men. The *Sagrada Familia* was laden with sugar, skins, and tobacco, and contained the large sum of forty thousand moidores of gold (about £50,000 sterling).

The pirates took their prize to Devil's Island (then a Spanish possession), where the Governor and inhabitants gave them a friendly welcome and helped the pirates to dispose of their booty. As usual, hard liquor and soft women were the favourite commodities, and the pirates lived merrily for a few weeks. Then a sloop came in from Rhode Island, and was seized. The facts about the sequel to this are confused, although Johnson's version is circumstantial. According to this, the captain of the sloop revealed that he had sailed in company with a brigantine laden with provisions; and Roberts and forty of his crew then boarded the sloop and went to take the consort. Bad winds and tides drove them off their course, and they not only missed the brigantine, but were stranded far from their base without adequate food or water. After having lived in luxury for weeks, the pirates were suddenly reduced to paddling a home-made raft ashore to get enough water to keep themselves alive.

Johnson says that when the rest of the company learnt what had happened they deliberately deserted Roberts and his party, and after giving their Portuguese prize to the captain of the Rhode Island sloop, made off in the *Royal Rover*. This is unconfirmed, and Roberts may still have been in command of the *Royal Rover* when she put in at the Danish island of St. Thomas, which the Governor of St. Christopher described as a place that "harbours all villains and vagabonds." But Walter

Hamilton, the Governor of the Leeward Islands, decided to
take a firm attitude towards the Danes, and he persuaded the
captain of a man-of-war to bring the pirate sloop in. The
pirates fled before the man-of-war arrived, although some were
caught later at Nevis and six were hanged. This Palmer-
stonian action by Hamilton seems to have forced the Governor
of St. Thomas to close the island to pirates.

Shortly afterwards Roberts appeared off Barbados in the
Rhode Island sloop, which he had renamed *Good Fortune,*
together with the brigantine that Johnson says he failed to take.
Governor Lowther of Barbados thereupon commissioned two
merchantmen, a galley and a sloop, to try to take the pirates.
The galley, commanded by Captain Rogers of Bristol, boldly
engaged the *Good Fortune* and, according to the Boston *News
Letter,* killed several of the pirates and made a hole in the sloop.
Roberts had to abandon his brigantine to get away, and retired
to Granada for repairs and careening.

Meanwhile, according to Johnson, Roberts had drawn up
a fresh set of articles. Roberts's articles were never found,
although their existence was freely admitted by the men who
had signed them, when they were eventually brought to trial.
Johnson gives what he calls "the substance of articles as taken
from the pirates' own information." This substance is unconfirmed and must be treated with reserve, but there is no reason
to assume it was an invention. It conforms mainly with other
pirate articles, and therefore does not need to be reprinted in
full. It had a few less conventional features, and these need
comment because most of Johnson's successors have probably
read too much between the lines.

The articles were stricter than usual, and it has been suggested that Roberts was a stern disciplinarian. But the
events of his career show that he had no more authority over
his crew than any other pirate captain, and the suggestion that
he was able to enforce the articles against the popular will
does not agree with the evidence. Nor does the other common
suggestion that Roberts was puritanical and insisted on a high
standard of moral behaviour on " his " ship. It was not his
ship; and the articles that are usually quoted in support of this
view can be more easily explained.

There was the usual ban on women on board, for the usual reason.

" No person to game at cards or dice for money." The reason was the same: gambling was a common cause of quarrels.

" The lights and candles to be put out at eight o'clock at night. If any of the crew after that hour still remained inclined for drinking, they were to do it on the open deck." This was a logical extension of the usual fire precaution. There was no worse fire hazard than heavy drinking below by candlelight.

" The musicians to have rest on the Sabbath day, but the other six days and nights none without special favour." The Sabbath was made for man, not man for the Sabbath. The original purpose of the Jewish Sabbath was to give people a weekly rest from work. In the eighteenth century, as now, Sunday was the usual day off from work. There is no reason to believe that Roberts was a sabbatarian. Nor was he a puritan or an ascetic. Johnson says he was a teetotaller, but adds that he dressed gaily, loved costly jewels, and enjoyed music and mirth. Where Roberts differed from most pirate captains was that he was exceptionally intelligent and commanded an unusual measure of respect. This accounts for his ability to persuade his fellows to impose extra restrictions on themselves for the sake of common security.

Roberts is heard of next a few months later (June 1720) in another daring exploit. According to Governor Spotswood of Virginia, Roberts, " with no more than a sloop of ten guns and sixty men, ventured into Trepanny in Newfoundland, where there were a great number of merchant ships, upwards of 1200 men and forty pieces of cannon, and yet, for want of courage in this heedless multitude, plundered and burnt divers ships there and made such as he pleased prisoners." Two other versions give the number of ships in the harbour as twenty-two, and all agree that Roberts took them without a fight. He went further. With his sixty men he took the whole harbour and plundered the port. " One cannot withhold admiration for his bravery and daring," wrote the Lieutenant-Governor of New England in reporting the invasion. It was not made by stealth. According to another account

(Boston *News Letter*) Roberts went in with " drums beating, trumpets sounding, and other instruments of music, English colours flying, the pirate flag at the topmast head with death's head and cutlass." Johnson gives a similar account.

Roberts stayed in the harbour for ten days, during which he mounted sixteen guns on a Bristol galley that he had taken, and signed on more hands. Then, cruising upon the banks, he met nine or ten French sail, plundered them all, and kept the best, a ship of twenty-six guns. He gave the French captain the British galley in exchange, and christened his new ship *Royal Fortune.*

Roberts quickly took several more prizes, including the *Samuel,* Captain Curry, of London. She was a rich prize, and had several passengers on board, who, according to the report in the Boston *News Letter* (August 22, 1720), were robbed of all their money and clothes. The reporter describes the pirates as " a parcel of furies "; but no one was hurt. " They often ridiculed and made a mock of King George's Acts of Grace with an oath, that they had not got money enough, but when they had, if he then did grant them one, after they sent him word, they would thank him for it." The *Samuel*'s cargo was estimated to be worth £10,000, but the pirates already numbered well over a hundred, and according to one of them " seven or eight hundred pounds each " was their ambition. It seems that several of the more thrifty ones achieved it and retired, but Roberts never had trouble in making up his crew. He was becoming a legend.

Roberts forced four men out of the *Samuel,* including Harry Glasby, the sailing master. Like Howell Davis, he did not force men if he could avoid it, although he always obliged recruits who wanted an insurance policy. " I must oblige these fellows with a show of force," he said once. In common with all other pirate captains, he had to rely on conscription for specialists, and these included musicians. This was not due merely to his love of music, but because he regarded trumpets and drums as useful aids in frightening victims into asking for quarter. Another peculiarity about Roberts was that he insisted that only experienced seamen should be allowed to join.

SIR CHALONER OGLE

The only naval captain ever knighted for action against pirates. One of the very few naval captains who ever took any action.

SENTENCE OF DEATH

Extract from the proceedings of the Vice-Admiralty Court held at Cape Corso in 1722. This was probably the biggest trial of pirates ever held. Fifty-two were hanged outside the castle gates.

A month after taking the *Samuel,* Roberts was back in the West Indies, plundering freely and putting in to shore even in fortified harbours. Once he sailed boldly into Basseterre road (St. Christopher) and looted and burnt shipping while under the fire of the shore batteries. Just afterwards he sent this impudent letter to the Lieutenant-Governor of the Leeward Islands:

Royal Fortune, September the 27th, 1720

Gentlemen,

This comes axpressly from me to lett you know that had you come off as you ought to a done and drank a Glass of wine with me and my Company I should not harmed the least vessell in your harbour. Farther it is not your Gunns you fired that affrighted me or hindred our coming onshore, but the wind not proving to our expectation that hindred it. The Royall Rover you have already burnt and barbarously used some of our men but we have now a ship as good as her and for revenge you may assure yourselves here and hereafter not to expect anything from our hands but what belongs to a pirate as farther Gentlemen that poor fellow you now have in prison at Sandy point is entirely ignorant and what he hath was gave him and so pray make conscience for once let me begg you and use that man as an honest man and not as a C if we hear any otherwise you may expect not to have quarters to any of your Island.

Yours (signed) Bathll. Roberts.

To Lieutenant General Mathew.

This letter shows an unusually paternal consideration for an unlucky pirate, and it also throws some doubt on Johnson's story that some of Roberts's crew absconded with the *Royal Rover.*

Roberts now plundered shipping off Dominica. According to the Governor of the French Leeward Islands, " between 28th and 31st of October [1720] these pirates seized, burned or sunk fifteen French and English vessels and one Dutch interloper of forty-two guns at Dominica." A newspaper report said that " the men they took they barbarously abused, some they almost whipped to death, others had their ears cut off, others they fixed to the yard arms and fired at them as a mark and all their actions look like practising of cruelty." There is no confirmation for this. Roberts and his company seem to have observed the pirate code when quarter was asked for, and there is no reliable evidence of their having committed atrocities even when they met with resistance—which was not very often. The Dutch interloper, a ship of ninety men and thirty guns, was one of the few prizes they had to fight for, the engagement lasting four hours.

When Roberts stood off Santa Lucia, French shipping suffered so seriously that the Governor of Martinique appealed to the Governor of Barbados for help. Unfortunately the British guard-ship had gone to New England for the winter, and the Governor of Barbados had no help to send. However, the two Governors agreed on joint action against Roberts, and at Barbados a merchantman was fitted out as a privateer and sent to a rendezvous with a French frigate at Fort Royal. Nothing more is heard of this expedition. A few months later, when the guard-ship H.M.S. *Rose*, Captain Whitney, came south again, the Governor of Martinique sent another appeal for help, with two barrels of red wine, to Governor Hamilton of the Leeward Islands, who ordered Whitney to go and catch Roberts. Whitney replied that he took his orders only from the Admiralty, and a sharp exchange of letters followed. Hamilton told Whitney that it was his duty to try to catch pirates; Whitney answered, " You know, sir, you have no power to give me orders, but I will concert any affairs that shall be for my King's service, and am sorry I am forced to say I wish you'd do the same." Hamilton replied by telling Whitney where Roberts was, and Whitney then sailed in the opposite direction.

Roberts replied to the efforts of the Governors of Martinique and Barbados by having a special jack-flag made showing himself standing with each foot on a skull, one of which was subscribed ABH (A Barbadian's Head) and the other AMH (A Martinician's Head). He even had his cabin plate stamped with the same device.

Unopposed by the Navy, Roberts ranged freely in the West Indies, and in May 1721 Governor Spotswood of Virginia told the Council for Trade that he was putting up batteries with fifty-four pieces of cannon at strategic places along the coast in case this pirate should attack the American mainland.

The Governor of the Leeward Islands insisted that only resolute action by men-of-war could stop the depredations of " the great pirate Roberts," who took ships as he willed without having any permanent base.

Then Roberts suddenly sailed away from the West Indies. He was not driven away; he had nearly driven merchant shipping off the sea, and found it harder to take prizes. So about the middle of 1721 he went back to the Guinea coast. Here he ravaged the shipping of the Royal African Company, and by the end of the year his total number of prizes was over four hundred. In August he took the Royal African Company frigate *Onslow*, which he refitted and renamed *Royal Fortune*, giving the previous ship of that name to the captain of the *Onslow*. He sailed with two consorts, *Great Ranger* and *Little Ranger*, and continued to cruise off the Guinea coast.

Some months before Roberts's return to these waters two men-of-war had been sent to protect African shipping. Both were hampered by sickness among the crew, but in January 1722 H.M.S. *Swallow*, Captain Chaloner Ogle, sighted Roberts at anchor off Cape Lopez. The pirates thought the *Swallow* was a Portuguese merchantman, and the *Great Ranger* went out after her. Ogle lured the pirates out to sea, and took her after a fierce fight. The pirates lost ten men killed and twenty wounded.

Meanwhile Roberts had taken another prize, and as she had plenty of liquor aboard the pirates were mostly drunk when H.M.S. *Swallow* returned to Cape Lopez. However, Roberts prepared for battle, and the *Royal Fortune* bore down on the man-of-war. The *Swallow* fired a broadside—and in that first burst Bartholomew Roberts was killed.

The pirates continued the fight, but they had relied on their leader for so long that they were lost without him. After only two more had been killed they asked for quarter.

Captain Ogle took his prisoners to Cape Corso Castle, where they were tried by a Vice-Admiralty Court. The proceedings of this court are full of interesting information about Roberts in particular and pirates in general. One hundred and sixty-nine men were charged, of whom four died before the trial. All the rest pleaded not guilty, their defence in every case being that they were forced. Eighteen were Frenchmen who had been taken after the defeat of the *Great Ranger*, and they were acquitted at once. Fifty-six others were acquitted, including the sailing master, Harry Glasby, who was the chief witness for the prosecution of the remainder. Ninety-one were found guilty, and fifty-two of them were hanged before a large crowd of sailors and negroes. Their bodies were taken down and hung in chains from gibbets, as a warning to would-be pirates. The others were given long prison sentences.

Cape Corso was, as Johnson said, " among other happinesses, exempted from lawyers and law-books; . . . but perhaps if there was less law there might be more justice than in some other courts." Certainly the court seems to have been fair and even generous, and some of the men who were acquitted had been with Roberts for quite a long time. But most of these were specialists, like Glasby, for all the evidence showed that Roberts did not force men if he could avoid it. One man, Stephen Thomas, was acquitted because the court considered that " it was unlikely a master of a vessel at six pounds a month should be a volunteer among such villains." All but one of the surgeons were similarly acquitted, as were the musicians.

Only about half a dozen of the pirates had served with Howell Davis. There were a few other veterans, including two who had been with Stede Bonnet in 1718; but the majority had been recruited from various prizes taken by Roberts in 1720 and 1721. They admitted that once they signed the articles they had equal voting rights with the others, and when the court asked why, if they were unwilling to serve, they had not deposed Roberts, they had no reply.

Johnson gives an account of the execution of some of the pirates. One of them was David Symson, who had been quartermaster for a time but was deposed. When the *Onslow* was taken she was carrying a woman passenger, Elizabeth Trengove, and Johnson says that Symson was appointed her " sentinel." He says also that Symson saw her when he was walking to the gallows and remarked that " he had lain with that bitch three times, and now she was come to see him hanged." However, Symson was not charged with rape and

Elizabeth Trengove was not called as a witness against him, although she appeared in court to give evidence in defence of Harry Glasby.

Glasby was one of the few forced men who tried to escape. For this he was sentenced to be shot, but sentence was remitted after the intervention of one of the pirates who, Glasby said, was friendly to him and " bullied the others " into reversing their judgment. This was not Roberts, but a man named Valentine Ashplant, and indeed it seems that Roberts had no power to veto a sentence of death on his most valuable technician.

In general Roberts's powers seem to have been limited just as much as those of any other pirate captain. The difference was that he was respected and valued more highly for his personal ability. On one occasion, according to Johnson, in a fit of temper Roberts killed a drunken man who insulted him. The dead man's messmate, a fellow called Jones, protested, and Roberts went for him with his sword; but Jones, although wounded, threw his captain over a gun and gave him a thrashing. The quartermaster restored order, and suggested that the captain's dignity ought to be upheld, and the company thereupon voted that Jones should get two lashes from each of them.

Roberts and his company do not appear to have been particularly brutal. Contemporary newspapers printed some atrocity stories about them, but depositions of witnesses against them and all the evidence at their trial refute these. Roberts terrorized merchantmen with a show of force, in the Blackbeard tradition; usually he went in with the black flag flying and his musicians blowing and banging as hard as they could, while on deck his men waved their cutlasses ferociously. This nearly always discouraged resistance, and when quarter was asked for Roberts gave it readily. It was reported that he captured the Governor of Martinique and hanged him at the yard-arm. I cannot find confirmation for this, but the act would have been in character. Johnson says that on one occasion eighty negroes in a slaver were killed because the pirates were too lazy to remove their shackles before firing the ship. This also is unconfirmed, but there is no reason to suppose that the pirates regarded human cargo any more humanely than the captain of the *Zong* sixty years later.

Captain Ogle was knighted for destroying Roberts. I think this is the only case of such an honour being granted for taking pirates, and it is a measure of the importance that was attached to the event. Bartholomew Roberts was indeed the terror of the seas, and the news of his death was acclaimed by Governors in places as far apart as New York, Port Royal, and even Bombay. Clement Downing says that when John Plantain heard the news on Madagascar he took it very badly, saying that he had always hoped to return to Chocolate Hole, but that after this it would be unsafe for any pirate to try to cross the Atlantic.

It would be false to suggest that Sir Chaloner Ogle brought the Age of Piracy to an end single-handed. Woodes Rogers, who died in the Bahamas a few years later, deserved more than a knighthood for his part. Yet Ogle had done more than rid the seas of the most dangerous pirate captain and company since the Treaty of Utrecht. His action was important because it was the Navy's first really effective blow against the pirates, and only the Navy could clear the seas.

It was said that the end of " the great pirate " would be the end of the great days of piracy. It was, too.

CHAPTER TWENTY-ONE

Captain Snelgrave's Story

I HAVE already quoted some passages from an author named Captain William Snelgrave. They were all taken from his book *A New Account of Some Parts of Guinea and the Slave-Trade*. Although not published until 1734, most of this was written several years earlier, apparently without thought of publication. The author dedicated it to " the merchants of London trading to the coast of Guinea," and does not seem to have aimed at a wider public. The book had a small circulation, and it has been out of print for two centuries.

The book is in three parts. The first deals with the Guinea coast in general and the conquest of the Kingdom of Whidaw by the King of Dahomey in particular. The second part is a quiet, well-reasoned defence of the slave-trade (" designed at first only for a friend's satisfaction, who had objected against the lawfulness of that trade "). The third part, which seems to have been included as a makeweight, is an account of the author's experiences in the hands of pirates. This part is exciting and informative and, in my opinion, one of the most valuable single works in the whole vast pirate bibliography.

Both by precept and example Snelgrave was an unusually humane sea-captain for his age. He believed in treating human cargo as human beings, and he thought that seamen could be persuaded to work without being flogged. In character he seems to have been honest, intelligent, and modest. As a writer he observed well and reported accurately. Much of the third part of his book can be verified from other sources, and it does not contain a single palpable error. I cannot think of any reason for doubting the author's integrity or reliability.

Sailing in the *Bird Galley*, with a cargo from Holland, Snelgrave arrived at the River Gambia on April 1, 1719. He anchored at about seven in the evening in the mouth of the river. An hour later, when he was at supper, the officer of the watch on deck sent down word that " he heard the rowing of a boat." Snelgrave knew there might be pirates in the neighbourhood, so he went on deck and ordered Simon Jones, the first mate, " to go into the steerage, to put all things in order, and to send me forthwith twenty men on the quarter deck with firearms and cutlasses." It was too dark to see the boat, but the sound of the oars was getting louder, and she was hailed. An evasive answer was received, followed by " a volley of small shot at the ship, though they were then above pistol shot from us."

Snelgrave " called aloud to the first mate to fire at the boat out of the steerage port-holes; which not being done, and the people I had ordered upon deck not appearing, I was extremely surprised; and the more when an officer came and told me the people would not take arms. I went thereupon down into the steerage, where I saw a great many of them looking at one another. . . . I asked them with some roughness why they had not obeyed my orders, calling upon some brisk fellows by name, that had gone on a former voyage with me, to defend the ship, saying it would be the greatest reproach in the world to us all if we should be taken by a boat. Some of them replied they would have taken arms, but the chest they were kept in could not be found.

" By this time the boat was along the ship's side, and there being nobody to oppose them, the pirates immediately boarded us; and coming on the quarter-deck, fired their pieces several times down into the steerage, and shot a sailor in the reins, of which wound he died afterwards. They likewise threw several granado-shells, which burst amongst us, so that it's a great wonder several of us were not killed by them or by their shot.

" At last some of our people bethought themselves to call out for quarter; which the pirates granting, the quartermaster came down into the steerage, enquiring where the captain was. I told him I had been so till now. Upon that he asked me how I durst order my people to fire at their boat out of the steerage, saying that they had heard me repeat it several times. I answered I thought it my duty to defend the ship, if my people would have fought. Upon that he presented a pistol to my breast, which I had but just time to parry before it went off; so that the bullet passed between my side and arm. The rogue finding he had not shot me, he turned the butt-end of the pistol and gave me such a blow on the head as stunned me, so that I fell upon my knees; but immediately recovering myself, I forthwith jumped out of the steerage upon the quarter-deck, where the pirate boatswain was. He was a bloody villain, having a few days before killed a poor sailor because he did not do something so soon as he had ordered him. This cruel monster was asking some of my people where their captain was. So at my coming upon deck one of them, pointing to me, said, ' There he is.' "

Lifting up his broadsword, the boatswain swore that " no quarter should be given to any captain that offered to defend his ship," and aimed " a full stroke at my head." To avoid it Snelgrave " stooped so low that the quarter-deck rail received the blow, and was cut in at least an inch deep, which happily saved my head from being cleft asunder; and the sword breaking at the same time, with the force of the blow on the rail, it prevented his cutting me to pieces."

The boatswain was trying to hit Snelgrave with the butt-end of a pistol when some of his crew pleaded, " For God's sake don't kill our captain, for we were never with a better man." This " turned the rage of him and two other pirates to my people and saved my life; but they cruelly used my poor men, cutting and beating them unmercifully." However, none of them was killed or suffered any permanent injury.

" All this happened in a few minutes, and the quartermaster, then coming up, ordered the pirates to tie our people's hands." The quartermaster did not attempt any further violence against Snelgrave, but " took me by the hand and told me my life was safe provided none of my people complained against me. I replied I was sure none of them could." Snelgrave had his wound dressed, and was robbed of his watch. Then he was put in the boat and rowed to the pirate ship, the *Rising Sun*. " When we arrived along the side of the pirate vessel I told them I was disabled in the arm, and so desired their help to get me into their ship, which was readily done."

Snelgrave was frankly ashamed of the way his ship had been

taken. " There was in the boat only twelve of them, as I understood afterwards, who knew nothing of the strength of our ship, which was indeed considerable, we having sixteen guns and forty-five men on board." He attributed his failure mainly to the treachery of Simon Jones, who had been hoping to be taken by pirates and had hidden the chest of arms and denied the others access to it. But this was not the only reason. As the pirates told him, " they depended on the same good fortune as in the other ships they had taken, having met with no resistance; for the people were generally glad of an opportunity of entering with them: which last was but too true."

Snelgrave admitted further that he was bound to be taken by pirates the moment he anchored in the mouth of the Gambia. By bad luck he had arrived just when three pirate ships were keeping a rendezvous there. One was the *Rising Sun*, commanded by Captain Cocklyn. The other two were commanded respectively by Howell Davis and the Frenchman La Bouche. Snelgrave considered himself especially unlucky in being taken by the worst of the three. Davis, he said, was " a generous man, and kept his crew, which consisted of near one hundred and fifty men, in good order "; but " I found Cocklyn and his crew to be a set of the basest and most cruel villains that ever were." Cocklyn himself was the worst of them, and his crew told Snelgrave frankly that " they chose him for their commander on account of his brutality and ignorance, having resolved never to have again a gentleman-like commander as, they said, Moody was." Moody, the former captain of the company, had apparently cheated them over the plunder.

Boarding the *Rising Sun*, Snelgrave "was ordered to go on the quarter-deck to their commander, who saluted me in this manner: 'I am sorry you have met with bad usage after quarter given, but 'tis the fortune of war sometimes. I expect you will answer truly to all such questions as I shall ask you, otherwise you shall be cut to pieces; but if you tell the truth, and your men make no complaints against you, you shall be kindly used, and this shall be the best voyage you ever made in your life, as you shall find by what shall be given you.' "

The questions were confined to the sailing performance of

the *Bird Galley*, and Cocklyn was satisfied with Snelgrave's answers. Next " a tall man, with four pistols in his girdle, and a broadsword in his hand, came to me on the quarter-deck, telling me his name was James Griffin, and that we had been schoolfellows." Snelgrave remembered the man, but pretended not to, " having formerly heard it had proved fatal to some who had been taken by pirates to own any knowledge of them." Then Griffin said " he supposed I took him to be one of the pirate's crew, because I saw him armed in that manner, but that he was a forced man." Griffin went on to explain that " since his being forced they had obliged him to act as master of the pirate ship, and the reason of his being so armed was to prevent their imposing on him ; for there was hardly any amongst the crew of pirates belonging to Captain Cocklyn but what were cruel villains." Finally Griffin promised that " he would himself take care of me that night, in which would be my greatest danger, because many of their people would soon get drunk with the good liquors found in my ship."

Having said all this to Snelgrave privately, Griffin " turned to Captain Cocklyn and desired a bowl of punch might be made ; which being done, the captain desired Mr. Griffin my schoolfellow to show me the way to the great cabin, and he followed himself. There was not in the cabin either chair or anything else to sit upon, for they always kept a clear ship ready for an engagement : so a carpet was spread on the deck, upon which we sat down cross-legged. Captain Cocklyn drank my health, desiring I would not be cast down at my misfortune, for one of the boat's crew who had taken us had told him my ship's company in general spoke well of me, and they had goods enough left in the ships they had taken to make a man of me."

More healths were drunk, and the captain continued to entertain Griffin and Snelgrave until midnight, when " my schoolfellow desired the captain to have a hammock hung up for me to sleep in, for it seems every one lay rough, as they called it, that is, on the deck ; the captain himself not being allowed a bed." The hammock was provided, but Snelgrave was too dejected to sleep, and he was kept awake by " the execrable oaths and blasphemies I heard among the ship's company."

Griffin kept his promise and " walked by me, with his broad sword in his hand, to protect me from insults." At about 2 a.m. the boatswain appeared, " very drunk," and threatened Snelgrave with his cutlass. " Griffin bid the boatswain keep his distance, or else he would cleave his head asunder with his broad sword. Nevertheless that bloody-minded villain came on to kill me; but Mr. Griffin struck at him with his sword, from which he had a narrow escape, and then ran away; so I lay unmolested till daylight." Then Griffin " complained to the quartermaster and company of the cruel intentions of the boatswain towards me, representing they ought to observe strictly that maxim established amongst themselves not to permit any ill usage to the prisoners after quarter given. At the hearing of this many voted for his being whipped, though he was a great favourite of several others. But though I wished him hanged in my mind yet I thought it prudent to plead for him, saying I believed it was his being in liquor that was the cause of his using me in that manner. So he received a general order not to give me the least offence afterwards."

Next Simon Jones saw Snelgrave and told him that " his circumstances were bad at home, moreover he had a wife whom he could not love, and for these reasons he had entered with the pirates and signed their articles." Snelgrave gave his former mate a little lecture, but he wrote in his book: " I must do him the justice to own he never showed any disrespect to me; and the ten people he persuaded to enter with him remained very civil to me, and of their own accord always manned the side for me whenever I went on board the ship they belonged to." Some of these men later regretted their decision, and " desired me to intercede for them, that they might be cleared again; for they durst not themselves mention it to the quartermaster, it being death by their articles; but it was too nice a matter for me to deal in, and therefore I refused them."

Meanwhile the quartermaster had found two official documents among Snelgrave's papers, and, " not being able to read, he brought them to me and bid me read them aloud to all then present." One of the documents was a Royal Proclamation for a pardon to pirates; and when Snelgrave began to read the rewards offered for taking or destroying pirates there was a roar of anger, and they tore the document to pieces. At Cocklyn's command Snelgrave read the other paper, which was a report of the declaration of war against Spain. This was received not angrily but rather wistfully. " When I had read it some of them said they wished they had known it before they left the West Indies." Snelgrave advised them to take the pardon and use this " opportunity of enriching themselves in a legal way, by going a-privateering, which many of them had previously done."

The pirates had decided to abandon the *Rising Sun* and convert the *Bird Galley* for their future use, and they began to jettison bales of goods. " Before night they had destroyed between three and four thousand pounds' worth of cargo." Snelgrave did not protest, " for my schoolfellow told me I was still under displeasure of many of them on account of my ordering my people to fire on their boat when they took me."

Meanwhile the news of the capture had reached some private traders who lived ashore. Among these was an old friend of Snelgrave's, Captain Henry Glynn, who later became Governor for the Royal African Company at Gambia : " an honest generous person, and of so much integrity that though he had suffered by the pirates when he first landed, yet he would never accept of any goods from them, which they often pressed him to receive for his own use. This conduct, with an engaging deportment, so gained him the goodwill of the pirates that they were ready to oblige him in whatever he requested."

When Glynn heard that Snelgrave was taken he went aboard the *Rising Sun* accompanied by Captains Howell Davis and La Bouche, both of whom greeted the prisoner civilly. Davis went further, making a speech to the whole company. He said that " he was ashamed to hear how I had been used by them; that they should remember their reasons for going a-pirating were to revenge themselves on base merchants and cruel commanders of ships; that as for the owner of the prize, he had not his fellow in London for generosity and goodness to poor sailors; . . . that as for my part, no one of my people, even those that had entered with them, gave me the least ill character, but by their respect since shown me it was plain they loved me; that he indeed had heard the occasion of my ill-usage and of the ill-will some still bore me was because I had ordered my people to defend the ship: which he blamed them exceedingly for, saying if he had had the good fortune to have taken me, and I had defended my ship against him, he would have doubly valued me for it; that as he was not in partnership with them he would say no more at present, but he hoped they would now use me kindly, and give me some necessities, with what remained undamaged of my private adventure."

This frank speech was " by no means relished by this pack of miscreants," but Cocklyn took it with as good grace as he could manage and invited Glynn, Snelgrave, Davis, and La Bouche to go on board the *Bird Galley*, where he entertained them with Snelgrave's liquor in Snelgrave's old cabin. Cocklyn's quartermaster was there too, and Glynn asked him to put aside "several necessaries" for Snelgrave; "which being readily granted, they were tied up in bundles, and Captain Glynn designed to take them on shore with him to his home. But an unlucky accident happened which made me lose them all again."

The accident was caused by one of Davis's crew, " a pert young fellow of eighteen," who went aboard the prize and " broke open a chest to plunder it." The quartermaster went out and asked him what he was doing, and got the reply that " as they were all pirates he thought he did what was right." The quartermaster aimed a blow with his broadsword, which missed, and the youngster " fled for protection into the great cabin to his master Captain Davis. The quartermaster pursued him in a great passion; and there not being room amongst so many of us to make a stroke at him, he made a thrust with his sword and slit the ball of one of the young man's thumbs, and slightly wounded at the same time Captain Davis on the back of one of his hands. Davis upon that was all on fire, and vowed revenge, saying that though his man had offended, he ought to have been first acquainted with it, for no other person had a right to punish him in his presence."

Davis then returned to his ship and prepared for action. Cocklyn returned to the *Rising Sun* and did the same, but then thought better of it and went back to the *Bird Galley* and " desired Captain Glynn to go on board Davis with him in order to make up matters." Reluctantly Glynn agreed, and persuaded Davis to keep the peace in exchange for a share of the " liquors and necessaries " on the prize and a public apology by Cocklyn's quartermaster.

Snelgrave was now left alone on his old ship with only three or four members of Cocklyn's crew. " There being no boat along the side at that time, I resolved to stay where I was all night, and not hail their pirate ship to send their boat for me. The pirate carpenter was then lying on my bed in the state room, so I sat some time by myself in the cabin, having a candle by me on a table. When he awoke he civilly desired me to go and take some rest, saying he feared I had not had any since I was taken. I returned him thanks saying I would sit up till eight o'clock, whereupon he came and sat down by me on the lockers abaft in the cabin.

" The boatswain came down soon after, and being a little in liquor, began to abuse me. On that the carpenter told him he was a base villain and turned him out of the cabin."

The boatswain returned later, " presented a pistol and drew the trigger, swearing at that instant he would blow my brains out. By good fortune the pistol did not go off, but only flashed in the pan. By the light of which the carpenter, observing that he should have been shot instead of me, it so provoked him that he run in the dark to the boatswain, and having wrested the pistol out of his hand, he beat him with that and his fist to such a degree that he almost killed him.

" The noise that was made in this fray being heard on board the pirate ship that lay close to us, a boat was sent from her; and they being informed of the truth of the matter, the officer that was in her thought fit to carry away the wicked villain who had three times attempted to murder me." This was the last Snelgrave saw of the boatswain.

More of the pirates came over to the *Bird Galley* and spent the day drinking and looting, causing much wanton destruction. Entering Snelgrave's cabin, they tripped over the bundles of " necessaries " that had been made up for Glynn to take ashore. Complaining that " they had like to have broken their necks by those things lying in their way," they threw all but one bundle overboard, and that was taken forcibly from Snelgrave soon afterwards. However, " I must own that whenever they plundered me, no affront was ever offered to my person; but several brought me liquor, and slices of ham broiled, a biscuit being my plate, saying they pitied my condition."

A drunken pirate stole Snelgrave's hat and wig; but when he left the cabin he ran into Cocklyn's quartermaster, who asked him " how he came to be by the things he had on. To which the fellow not returning a direct answer, the quartermaster beat him very severely for taking things he had no right to; then, coming to me, he asked in a kind manner how I had fared in the hurly-burly of that day. When I told him I had lost all the necessaries he had given me the day before, he expressed much concern and said he would take care the next day to recover what he could for me. But he did not prove so good as his word."

On the following day La Bouche's men boarded the *Bird Galley* to take their share of the " necessaries " and liquor. " Being quite weary of such company, and understanding the three pirate captains were on shore at my friend Captain Glynn's home, I asked leave of their quartermaster to go to them, which he readily granted. When I came to Captain Glynn's, he and the pirate captains received me in a very civil manner; and upon my telling them how I had lost all my necessaries that had been given me the captains promised that the next day they would do what they could to recover some of them again for me. Then I begged a shirt of my friend Captain Glynn, for I had been three days without shifting, which is very uneasy in so hot a country, where people sweat so much."

Snelgrave stayed the night with Captain Glynn, and the next day returned to the *Rising Sun* with the three pirate captains. Howell Davis made another speech in his favour,

A CAPTAIN WITHOUT A SHIP

Edward England was captain of the *Cassandra* until he was deposed by popular vote. The peculiarly democratic constitution of the pirates made despotism impossible.

VICE-ADMIRAL THOMAS MATHEWS

Sent to Madagascar in 1722 to destroy the pirates, Commodore Mathews traded with one and successfully avoided all the others. Promoted Vice-Admiral in 1742; court-martialled and dismissed the service in 1747.

" which they relishing better than that he had formerly made, it was resolved to give me the ship they designed to leave, in order to go into the prize, with the remains of my cargo that was undestroyed. And there being a large quantity of goods likewise remaining in several prizes, they concluded to give me them also: which, with my own, were worth several thousand pounds. One of the leading pirates proposed to the rest that they should take me along with them down the coast of Guinea, where I might exchange the goods for gold, and if in order to make a quick sale I sold them at price cost, I should get money enough by them; that no doubt as they went down the coast they should take some French and Portuguese vessels, and then they might give me as many of their best slaves as would fill the ship; that then he would advise me to go for the island of St. Thomas in the West Indies, a free port belonging to the Danes, and sell them there with the vessel, and after rewarding my people in a handsome manner I might return with a large sum of money to London, and bid the merchants defiance."

This proposal was approved by everyone except Snelgrave, who said " it would not be proper for me to accept of such a quantity of other people's goods as they had so generously voted for me." This offended them, " for many of them were so ignorant as to think their gift would have been legal." But Howell Davis explained that Snelgrave had peculiar views on the ownership of property, and the suggestion was dropped. The pirates then gave Snelgrave the use of a brigantine for taking his cargo off the *Bird Galley.* He was also given permission to move on to their store-ship, a prize called *Two Friends.* Captain Elliott, the commander of this ship, had been taken as a forced man. Snelgrave was also allowed " to go on shore when I pleased to my friend Captain Glynn's home. . . . And now, the tide being turned, they were as kind to me as they had been at first severe."

It took Snelgrave four days to get the cargo off the *Bird Galley* and take it ashore. Cocklyn's pirates as well as his own men helped him in this work. Meanwhile a French ship had come in, and Snelgrave saw her taken by the pirates. Her captain did not ask for quarter at once, and when he was captured Cocklyn's men " put a rope about his neck and hoisted him up and down several times to the main yardarm till he was almost dead." But La Bouche, " highly resenting this their cruel usage to his countryman," had him set free, and " protested he could remain in partnership no longer with such barbarous villains; so to pacify him they left the Frenchman with the ship in his care."

Captain Elliott of the *Two Friends* " had a great ascendant over the leading pirates, so that he had seldom had the company of the common sort, having orders to drive them away whenever they came on board. And I have often been amazed at to hear and see what he has done to some of them when they were impudent, beating them and saying he was sure he should see them hanged in due time at Execution Dock."

Then Cocklyn's quartermaster fell sick and begged for Snelgrave to see him. He said "that at the time I was taken he designed to have killed me, when he presented the pistol to my breast, begging I would forgive him for his cruel intention." The quartermaster also claimed to repent for his wicked life, and sent a boy to the chest to give Snelgrave all the " necessaries " he needed. But he died " cursing his maker in a shocking manner."

Snelgrave still had three embroidered coats of his own, and one day the pirate captains asked for them as they were "going on shore amongst the negro ladies." This caused some trouble among the other pirates. " The pirate captains having taken these clothes without leave from the quartermaster, it gave great offence to all the crew, who alleged if they suffered such things the captains would for the future assume a power to take whatever they liked for themselves. So upon their returning on board next morning, the coats were taken from them and put into the common chest, to be sold at the mast. And it having been reported that I had a hand in advising the captains to put on these coats, it gained me the ill-will in particular of one Williams, who was quartermaster of La Bouche's ship." This man threatened to kill Snelgrave " for the advice I had given the captains "; but Captain Elliott said that Williams always talked like that, and advised

Snelgrave to call him " captain." This had a wonderful effect, and Williams " gave me a keg of wine and was my friend ever after."

By April 20 " the ship they had taken from me was completely fitted, and the next day was appointed to name her, to which ceremony I was invited. When I came on board the pirate captains told me it was not out of disrespect they had sent for me, but to partake of the good cheer provided on this occasion. So they desired I would be cheerful, and go with them into the great cabin. When I came there bumpers of punch were put into our hands, and on Captain Cocklyn's suggestion saying aloud ' God bless the *Windham Galley* ', we drank our liquor, broke the glasses, and the guns fired."

The pirates now decided to burn the *Rising Sun* and three prizes, but Snelgrave persuaded Howell Davis to ask for one prize to be left so that he and his crew could return to England. The pirates agreed, and in the end they burnt only the *Rising Sun*, leaving the other three ships.

" Now obtaining, through Captain Davis's means, my entire liberty, I went on shore to my friend Captain Glynn's home again." Before he left, however, Snelgrave was asked by Captain Elliott for a certificate that he had been forced, which he gave readily. Then he was invited to a farewell party on Howell Davis's ship. " Supper was brought up about eight o'clock in the evening, and the music was ordered to play, amongst which was a trumpeter that had been forced to enter out of one of the prizes." In the middle of supper a fire broke out, and there was considerable alarm, as " there was on board at least thirty thousand pounds of gunpowder, which had been taken out of several prizes, it being a commodity much in request amongst the negroes." Snelgrave was almost the only sober man on board, and he took charge of the fire-fighting. The only other officer who was of any use was Davis's master, Taylor, later captain of the *Cassandra*, of whom Snelgrave spoke very highly. The way Snelgrave got the fire under control impressed the men on Davis's ship so much that they did not want to lose such an able officer. One man said, " I propose in behalf of the ship's company that this man shall be obliged to go down the coast of Guinea with us, for I am told we cannot have a better pilot." But Howell Davis told the man they did not need a pilot, and "caned him off the quarter-deck." Snelgrave returned to Captain Glynn's house.

"The 29th of April such of the pirates as were my friends sent me word on shore that the sale of necessaries was to begin that day in the afternoon in the *Windham Galley*, Captain Cocklyn." He went to the sale, and "several of the pirates bought many of the necessaries that had been mine and gave them to me. Likewise Mr. James Griffin, my schoolfellow, was so civil as to beg from those that were not so kind to me as he hoped they would have been."

Snelgrave took his goods ashore, and saw the pirates sail away. On May 10 he and his crew embarked in one of the ships left for them, and returned safely to England.

Such is the story of Captain William Snelgrave, and after testing it as far as I could, I am unable to cast doubt on any part of it. It was written as an indictment of the pirates: against the popular conception of pirates as abominable brutes it is an impressive defence. Considering that by offering resistance Snelgrave forfeited his life under the pirate code, the treatment he received was humane and sometimes generous. The status of the two forced men, James Griffin and Captain Elliott, was equally in contradiction with conventional pirate histories.

Snelgrave's book has every mark of honest writing. He considered that he had been hardly done by, and included every detail to support his case; but there is no reason to think that he invented or exaggerated anything, and he put down also many facts that told in the pirates' favour. He made it clear from the beginning of his story that in his eyes all pirates were bad, but some were worse than others. His chief complaint was against his bad luck in falling into the wrong hands. He continually bemoaned the fact that instead of being taken by Howell Davis—"a most generous humane person"—he became a prisoner of "a set of the basest and most cruel villains that ever were." I think this was an exaggeration; more probably Cocklyn and his company were about average in villainy.

Anyone brought up on the traditional pirate atrocity stories may wonder if Snelgrave was not writing with his tongue in his cheek. I hope I have quoted enough from his book to show that it was utterly innocent of irony. There was no guile in the man. Not being a professional writer, he told the truth. In consequence he failed to give the public what it wanted, and that is why his book has not enjoyed a fraction of the popularity of the more imaginative histories of Exquemelin and Johnson.

It would be unreasonable to generalize from Snelgrave alone, but fortunately he was not the only man who wrote an account of his experiences in the hands of the pirates. There is a considerable amount of other first-hand testimony by men who suffered personally in much the same way. Most of this was given on oath, either as depositions against the pirates or as evidence in court. A smaller amount was published in books. One of the most interesting of these is *The Four Years' Voyages of Captain George Roberts, written by Himself* (1726). There is no need to quote from this, for, although captured by a different company of pirates, Roberts received much the same treatment as Snelgrave. The special importance of Roberts's book is that he was taken by the notorious Edward Low, captain of the *Good Fortune*. Johnson singled out Low as the most brutal of all pirate captains: Roberts found him civil and courteous; and although Roberts, like Snelgrave, complained bitterly about the way he was treated, his account makes nonsense of Johnson's assertion that " of all the piratical crews belonging to the English nation, none ever equalled Low in barbarity." It may be noted that Johnson could write about Low without fear of contradiction, as this pirate was never brought to trial. It may also be noted that some of the barbaric actions attributed to Low strongly resemble the atrocities of the buccaneers as described by Exquemelin.

I have devoted this chapter to Snelgrave because he was the best observer of all who left accounts of their experiences in the hands of pirates. It is clear from the other first-hand evidence that has been preserved that the treatment Snelgrave received was fairly typical. The atrocity stories do not date farther back

R 2

than the second-hand versions of Johnson and other popular writers. The number of men that were killed by pirates must have been very small; for at their trials they were hardly ever accused of murder, or even of brutality, although the evidence against them was nearly always provided by forced men and other members of their company who turned informers.

CHAPTER TWENTY-TWO

The Decline of Piracy

THE Caribbean was the grave as well as the cradle of British piracy.

It has sometimes been suggested that the decline of piracy dates from 1721, when the British Government passed an Act that was designed to encourage merchant seamen to resist pirates. Under this Act seamen who were wounded in the defence of their ship were to be rewarded and admitted to Greenwich Hospital, while seamen who failed to defend their ship were to forfeit their wages and be liable to a sentence of six months' imprisonment. This Act seems to have been ineffective, as it was not strictly enforced; if it had been, I imagine it would have driven more men to piracy.

The decline of piracy in the West dates from 1718, when the pirates were deprived of their bases. After this only the peculiar topography of the West Indies and the peculiar laxity of the men-of-war allowed the pirates to continue as long as they did.

In 1721–22 many of the guard-ships against which the Governors had complained were replaced. It seems that the new commanders were chosen more carefully, for they began to take pirates. In May 1722 the Governor of Jamaica reported, with evident surprise, that a new guard-ship had captured fifty-eight pirates. He put it down to " a very fortunate accident." Forty-two of the pirates were hanged.

In April 1723 the *Cassandra* turned up off Portobello, and Taylor sent a message to the Governor of Jamaica asking for a pardon. The Governor disregarded the request and asked the captain of H.M.S. *Mermaid* to bring in the pirates. The latter reported that he had " sent his lieutenant to persuade William Taylor and the other pirates on board the *Cassandra* to surrender, and thinks they will not do so without force or promise of pardon. He cannot attack these pirates, but is waiting off the lagoon where they lie. The Governors of Panama and Portobello have sent a sloop with an offer of pardon to the pirates, if they will come in to their port. There is not one Spaniard among them."

Two weeks later the captain of the *Mermaid* reported: " The Spaniards are all mad to get the pirates into their port, and the Governor of Panama is coming down to that occasion." A week later: " The pirates having been told they would get no pardon from Jamaica, and that men-of-war were coming there to attack them, have accepted a pardon from the Spaniards, upon condition that they should retain their liberty."

It seems that the pirates were also allowed to retain their plunder, the Spanish Governor asking for only twenty per cent. of it in the name of his King. There is an unconfirmed report that Taylor accepted a commission in the Spanish service and commanded a man-of-war that attacked English logwood-cutters in the Bay of Honduras.

The Governor of Jamaica did not think the *Mermaid* had done very well. In reporting the affair he remarked: " It is surprising that when the *Cassandra* came out of the place where she had lain, the man-of-war who had been in the very way all the time should just then have altered her station." He alleged also that when the *Mermaid* was in port the captain kept some of his petty officers in irons to stop them from going ashore and revealing what had really happened.

Colonial Governors had been making complaints of this kind for several years, and the Governor of Jamaica continued to complain. Soon after the *Cassandra* incident he wrote: " The trade of the island is become the property of the men-of-war, and none partake with them in it but those they favour. The merchants in general are most of them discouraged if not undone ; the captains of men-of-war, now they can't trade with their ships, hire sloops or buy them, then load them with things of their own, put but few hands on board, without being at the charge of victualling them, because they send men and victuals on board when required out of the man-of-war as soon as they are out of sight of land; and then, instead of clearing away the pirates, go from place to place with the sloops that are their own a-trading. This is their constant practice."

But Governors of other colonies had changed their tune. The Leeward Islands had received two new guard-ships, one of them H.M.S. *Hector* under Captain Ellis Brand; and in June 1723 the Governor wrote: "I do not hear of any more pirates in these seas except the brigantine *Good Fortune*. It is to the indefatigable care of Captain Brand and Captain Orme in pursuing these pirates wherever they hear of them that the trade is so well secured from that press, for which they can't be too much commended."

In the same month two pirate ships, each with a crew of about seventy, were pursued by Captain Solgard, commander of the guard-ship stationed off New York. Solgard captured one ship and crippled the other, and the Governor of New York, after praising Solgard, wrote: "This blow, with what they received from Captain Ogle, will, I hope, clear the seas of these accomplished villains."

Merchantmen commissioned as privateers continued to play their part, and in October 1723 the notorious Captain Lowther was caught careening in the Leeward Islands by the sloop *Eagle*. Twenty-four of the pirates were caught, and Lowther committed suicide. Reporting the incident in March 1724, the Governor of the Leeward Islands wrote: "I do not hear that there are any more pirates, except a ship commanded by one Lowe with about fifty pirates in his crew." Two months earlier Governor Phenney of the Bahamas had written of the inhabitants of New Providence: "They call those their good days when fine silks, lace, and other rich commodities were so plentifully brought in here by the pirate crews."

The Calendar of State Papers includes an anonymous paper on the sugar trade dated July 1724 that says the guard-ships, "although a very great expense to the nation, yet have done little or no service for many years past in the West Indies . . . pirates, becoming masters of those seas, have risen up like mushrooms under the very noses of the said men-of-war for near nine years, and we never heard they took more than two in America." This seems to be generally true, but it was already out of date; so was the petition of the Council for

Trade, also dated July 1724, complaining about the negligence of the men-of-war and asking for them to be put under the colonial Governors. By 1724 the Age of Piracy was over; and it was the men-of-war, after all, that finally brought it to an end.

Occasional acts of piracy continued to occur during the eighteenth, nineteenth, and twentieth centuries. I have placed these outside the scope of this history because they were isolated crimes without any general significance.

The last white man to be executed for piracy was Captain Nathaniel Gordon, who was hanged in New York in 1862. His crime was trading in slaves. This was one of the few offences for which a man could be executed at that time. A hundred years earlier Captain Gordon could have been hanged for most other crimes, but not for trading in slaves.

Among the reasons that have been given for the decline of piracy are the resumption of war, the rebuilding of the Navy, the abolition of privateering, better pay and conditions in the Navy and on merchant ships, better social conditions, the rise of Methodism, and the tax on gin. The Age of Piracy came to a rather abrupt end before any of these events, so their effect need not be considered.

I have tried to resist the temptation to give simple answers to difficult historical questions, and I think it would be misleading to try to show exactly why piracy declined when it did. It may serve a better purpose to consider the matter in more general terms.

Human beings usually only do anything when the incentives outweigh the deterrents. Piracy flourished most when the incentives were highest and the deterrents lowest. It declined when the balance changed.

I do not think it is an over-simplification to say that the only real incentive to any form of robbery is material gain, and that the only real deterrent is fear of being caught. This may seem too obvious to need to be stated, but it has often been suggested that pirates were inspired by love of adventure and deterred by severity of punishment. In spite of a careful search I have found no evidence of any pirate having been influenced by either consideration. Nor, I am afraid, could I discover any results of moral or religious influence. It was consistently simply a matter of gain versus risk.

Gain is a relative term. A loaf of bread is a big prize to a hungry man. Poverty and unemployment increase the incentive to rob. So do penalties for honesty, such as tax on the rewards of lawful work. But these are only aggravations. Robbery is older than taxation, and it survives under full employment. It is an irremovable corollary of the institution of private property. It is as much a consequence of the division of the world's wealth among individuals as international conflict is a consequence of the division of the world itself into nations. It is equally idle to talk about removing the causes of crime against property and the causes of conflicts between nations. Private property, like national sovereignty, is an expensive luxury. All that a property-owning society can do against crime is to try to suppress it. This is possible because fortunately there is no truth in the saying that crime does not pay. Crime only exists when it pays. Piracy ceased to exist when it ceased to be a paying proposition.

The most attractive way of fighting crime is to reduce the incentive by reducing poverty and unemployment and tax on lawful gain. Regrettably this seems to be less effective than increasing the deterrent, for the strongest incentive remains untouched. The final decline of piracy owed nothing to social or fiscal reform. It did not even occur in time of war, when there was alternative employment for seamen. It happened at a time when every incentive remained as strong as ever. But the incentives were overtaken by the deterrents, and then the game was no longer worth the candle.

The only thing that effectively deters professional criminals is an efficient police; and, in a rather haphazard way, it was a police that destroyed piracy.

Superficially sea-robbers may seem to have run less risk of capture than land-robbers like highwaymen. It was impossible to police the high seas, or even the main trade routes, in the same way as the roads. But a highwayman's horse was less conspicuous than a pirate ship, and it did not have to have its bottom scraped. A highwayman could lose himself and his horse in any large town.   Pirates had to have a base.   Therein lay their vulnerability.

The first step in the suppression of piracy was the removal of pirate bases.   Sending an incorruptible Governor to New England was one step forward.   Restoring government to New Providence was another.   Making Madagascar untenable was a third.   But the process could not be completed, owing to the peculiar topography of the West Indies, the existence of uninhabited coastland in other parts of the world, and the survival of gubernatorial corruption, as in North Carolina.

The second step was police action at sea.   This was delayed by the failure of the Royal Navy against pirates in the West Indies, where it was more profitable to fail than to succeed. Eventually irregular police action by Governors Nicholson, Johnson, and Spotswood was followed by regular naval action by Captains Ogle and Solgard, and piracy was destroyed.

I think that four lessons may be learnt from the history of piracy.

The first is that legislation alone cannot reduce crime, but it can increase it.   The Age of Piracy is remarkable for a series of Acts made up of threats and bribes.   No means were provided to enforce these Acts.   Some of them stimulated the crime they were designed to prevent; none of them had any other effect.

The Acts of Trade and Navigation, which were designed for the financial benefit of the British at the expense of the American colonists, gave a tremendous stimulus to piracy.   Not only did they provide a good market for the pirates' plunder, but they caused widespread bribery and corruption in the colonies and thus gave the pirates official protection and valuable bases.   I have quoted the statement of the Editor of the Calendar of State Papers that at one period British pirates practically swept British trade with the East Indies off the seas.   This was a direct cause of the Acts that were designed for the exclusive benefit of British trade.   Every law contains the seeds of crime, but none more than laws that confer privilege.

The second lesson to be learnt from the pirates is that public servants serve the public according to the way the public pays them.   A colonial Governor could hardly be expected to remain honest on a salary of £30 a year.   Ill-paid naval seamen could not be expected to risk their lives to defend the property of wealthy merchants. Public officials and policemen need financial incentives as much as anyone else.

The third lesson is that the incidence of crime varies indirectly with the strength and efficiency of the police. As crime costs more than its prevention, it would be sound economy to maintain a police strong enough to be almost continually idle. The Age of Piracy lasted as long as it did only because successive Governments held the erroneous belief that a country could afford crime better than a police. This belief seems to have survived.

The last lesson that may be learnt from the history of piracy is so well known to penologists that I apologize for restating it.

There is a theory that the threat of punishment causing physical pain or death has a special deterrent effect on criminals. This theory has persisted through the ages, and every reduction of the physical severity of the law has been opposed on the grounds that it would lead to an increase in crime. The opposition seems to have been based on assumptions rather than facts, and it has clung to these assumptions even after they have been disproved. Thus as recently as June 1952 Earl Howe asked in the House of Lords for consideration of the restoration of corporal punishment. He was told that since the abolition of this form of punishment the incidence of robbery with violence had gone down, not up (from 842 cases in 1947, the last year in which corporal punishment was in force, to 633 cases in 1951). Yet only three weeks after the announcement of these figures Lord Goddard, the Lord Chief Justice, in a speech to judges at the Mansion House, also asked for the restoration of flogging and whipping. He was reported to have said: " You can seldom hope to open your newspaper without seeing a report of some great robbery " (*News Chronicle*, 3rd July, 1952). The Press report did not state which newspaper Lord Goddard reads. At the same time Mr. Justice Streatfeild was reported to have said: " I do not know, nor am I particularly concerned, whether, statistically, crimes of violence have decreased or not since the abolition of corporal punishment. But I do know that the degree of violence is much more brutal and cruel than it ever was " (*Daily Express*, 8th

July, 1952). The report did not divulge the source of this knowledge, which apparently extends back to the beginning of the world.

Judges have always led the opposition to reductions in the severity of punishment. Every reform has been carried out in the face of hostility from the judiciary. This has been especially strong in the matter of capital punishment.

Piracy flourished when the penalty was execution. It declined at a time when the death sentence was beginning to be commonly commuted to transportation. The decline of highway robbery, smuggling, forgery, and other felonies coincided with a similar substitution of non-lethal for lethal penalties. This is no proof that capital punishment is an incentive to crime, but it does not support the theory that it is a deterrent. It is worth noting also that crime was most brutal when the law was most brutal.

It seems ironical that capital punishment continues to be applied in Britain—ostensibly as a deterrent—for the one crime that it is least likely to affect. In a recent murder case counsel for the prosecution reminded the jury that most murders are unpremeditated and unintentional. It is difficult to see how the threat of any form of punishment can be expected to deter people from crimes they do not intend to commit. The only logical reason for the retention of capital punishment would seem to be that it makes it impossible for a convicted murderer to murder again. The weakness in this argument is that most chronic murderers are insane and therefore—in theory, at least—immune from the death penalty.

The deterrent value of capital punishment is an attractive theory. Unless we are a nation of criminologists, or unless the newspapers do not know what the public wants, the publicity given to murders and executions can only be explained by our lust for revenge and our taste for vicarious sadism. The deterrent theory provides a handy moral justification for the satisfaction of these base instincts. It enables us to break the Sixth Commandment by proxy and feel self-righteous about it.

The deterrent theory appeals also to our parsimony. It is cheaper to kill a criminal than to keep him in prison for life, just as it is much cheaper to threaten severe punishment than to maintain an adequate police. The flaw in these economics is that criminals are deterred less by the probable consequences of arrest than by the probability of being arrested. And as we no longer kill all felons, it is probably costing us more to build and maintain new prisons than it would to pay enough policemen to make them unnecessary.

CHAPTER TWENTY-THREE

The Character of the Pirate

THERE is no such thing as group character, but there are group characteristics—national, vocational, social, and so on. Pirates were individuals, like artists, cooks, and bottle-washers. The average or typical pirate did not exist. But most pirates had some common characteristics, and I hope that the more important of these will have emerged in my book, and I only want to add a few reflections based also on the material that I have not been able to include.

In my first chapter I mentioned the romantic and ' realistic ' conceptions of the pirate character. I suggested that both were false—that pirates have been credited with exceptional virtues and vices that few of them possessed. Usually they have been admired or condemned, according to the inclinations of the beholder, as bold, bad men. Generally speaking, I think, they were not very bold, and not very bad.

Among the pirates there were a few men of exceptional courage and daring, like Bartholomew Roberts; but Roberts, as much as any other captain, avoided fighting whenever possible. Pirates did not like fighting, although when they were attacked they defended themselves valiantly.

In the conduct of their profession the pirates were conservative and imitative. They copied their articles from the privateers, and made few innovations. The most striking of these was the division of command between the captain and the quartermaster. Honest service in the Navy or on merchant ships had made them loathe and dread authority, and if they gloried in anything it was their freedom from the fear of being flogged. They had no discipline, and therefore much self-discipline.

In private life most pirates were sensual and profligate, but probably no more than their contemporaries. They spent more on drinking, whoring, and gambling because they had more to spend. They sometimes cheated one another, but there was no less honour among them than in other communities.

Pirates had no sentimental feeling for their ship and no love of piracy. Their motive was gain, and those who saved their share of the plunder retired as soon as they could.

Pirates were not abominable brutes. Although the legal penalty for murder was no greater than that for piracy, very few of them killed wantonly. Mostly they treated their captives humanely, and advertised their clemency in order to deter others from making them fight for their loot. For the same reason they showed little mercy when they did have to fight. Their cruelties were not exceptional in the age in which they lived.

BIBLIOGRAPHY

MY main source has been the Calendar of State Papers, especially the Colonial Series, America and the West Indies. I have drawn also on the Journal of the Commissioners for Trade and Plantations, and on various unpublished documents in the Public Record Office, London, mostly under the headings Colonial Office, Admiralty (especially Captains' Letters and Logs), and High Court of Admiralty. As this is not a scholarly book I have not included annotations, but the more important references to unpublished documents are given below.

I am indebted also to two published collections of documents: *Privateering and Piracy in the Colonial Period : Illustrative Documents*, edited by J. F. Jameson (The Macmillan Company, New York, 1923); and *Notes on Piracy in Eastern Waters*, compiled by S. C. Hill (Bombay, 1923).

Pirate literature is enormous. It began with *A General History of the Robberies and Murders of the Most Notorious Pyrates*, by Captain Charles Johnson (London, first edition, 1724; fourth edition, enlarged, 1726), to which I have already made many references. Most other pirate histories follow Johnson so closely that they do not need to be mentioned. The outstanding exceptions are *The Pirates' Who's Who* (London, 1924) and *The History of Piracy* (London, 1930), both by Philip Gosse, based on a very wide range of printed works. These two books have rightly joined Johnson as classics of pirate literature. Another entertaining history, more limited in scope, is *The Pirates of the New England Coast*, 1630–1730, by G. F. Dow and J. H. Edmonds (Marine Research Society, Salem, Massachusetts, 1923).

General books that I have consulted include the following:

Bartlett, H.: *A History of the Merchant Navy* (London, 1937).
Beer, C. L.: *The Old Colonial System* (New York, 1912).

Butler, N.: *Boteler's Dialogues* (Navy Records Society, 1929).

Hannay, D.: *Short History of the Navy* (London, 1909).

Hargraves, F.: *A Complete Collection of State Trials* (London, 1776–81).

Oppenheim, M.: *A History of the Administration of the Royal Navy and of Merchant Shipping in Relation to the Navy* (London, 1896).

Osgood, H. L.: *The American Colonies in the Eighteenth Century* (New York, 1930).

Richardson, W.: *A Mariner of England* (edited by Colonel Spencer Childers: London, 1908).

Specific references follow.

CHAPTER ONE

The quotation from Raymond Postgate is taken from his book *Murder, Piracy and Treason* (London, 1925). As I have quoted only to dispute, I think I should add that my criticism of these three sentences does not extend to the rest of this entertaining book.

The facts about the slave trade were taken mainly from the following books:

Donnan, E.: *Documents Illustrative of the History of the Slave Trade to America* (Carnegie Institution of Washington, 1930).

Dow, G. F.: *Slave Ships and Slaving* (Marine Research Society, Salem, Massachusetts, 1927).

Falconbridge, Alexander: *An Account of the Slave Trade on the Coast of Africa* (London, 1788).

Snelgrave, Captain William: *A New Account of Some Parts of Guinea and the Slave-Trade* (London, 1734).

Some of the information about the punishment of criminals in England was drawn from *The Old Bailey and Newgate*, by Charles Gordon (London, 1903), and *History of Newgate and the Old Bailey*, by W. Eden Hooper.

CHAPTER TWO

Much information was drawn from an article by David Matthew entitled " Cornish and Welsh Pirates in the Reign of Queen Elizabeth " published in the *English Historical Review*, Volume XXXIX (1924). My other main source was the Calendar of State Papers (Domestic).

CHAPTER THREE

I have drawn some facts from *Drake and the Tudor Navy*, by J. S. Corbett (London, 1898) and *The Age of Drake*, by J. A. Williamson (London, 1946), but neither author is responsible for my inferences.

CHAPTER FOUR

The quotation from Captain John Smith is taken from his book *The True Travels, Adventures and Observations of Capitaine J. Smith* (London, 1630). Other sources include the following:

Corbett, J. S.: *England in the Mediterranean* (London, 1904).
Ewen, Cecil H. L'E.: *Captain John Ward, " Arch-Pirate "* (London, 1939).
Forster, John: *Sir John Eliot* (London, 1836).
Mainwaring, Sir H.: *Life and Works* (edited by G. E. Manwaring: Navy Records Society, 1920).
Monson, Sir William: *Naval Tracts* (London, 1703).
Prowse, D. W.: *A History of Newfoundland* (London, 1896).
Ward, John: *Newes from the Sea* (London, 1609).
Whitbourne, Sir Richard: *Discourse and Discovery of Newfoundland* (London, 1622).

CHAPTERS FIVE TO SEVEN

The " Johnson " of the buccaneers is *Bucaniers of America*, by A. O. Exquemelin (Amsterdam, 1679; first English translation, London, 1684), and the material for Chapter Five has been based mainly on this work, read in conjunction with the Calendar of State Papers (Colonial, America and West Indies).

For Chapter Six, I have drawn also on *The Life of Sir Henry Morgan*, by E. A. Cruikshank (Toronto, 1935). This seems to be the only biography of Morgan based on the mass of material in the Calendar of State Papers. The others mostly repeat Exquemelin and therefore need not be mentioned.

The story of the later buccaneers (Chapter Seven) is drawn

partly from *History of the Buccaneers of America*, by James Burney (London, 1816). The story of the Sawkins–Sharp expedition is based mainly on *The Voyages and Adventures of Captain Bartholomew Sharp*, by Basil Ringrose (London, 1684); Sharp's own narrative (Sloane MSS); *A New Voyage Round the World*, by William Dampier (London, sixth edition, 1717); and *A New Voyage and Description of the Isthmus of America*, by Lionel Wafer (London, 1699).

Many books have been written on the buccaneers, but only a few add to or subtract from the history of Exquemelin. I think the best is still *The Buccaneers in the West Indies in the Eighteenth Century*, by C. H. Haring (London, 1910). Other books on the subject are *On the Spanish Main*, by John Masefield (London, 1906) and *The Spanish Main*, by P. A. Mean (New York, 1935). A shorter but more valuable study is " Privateers and Pirates in the West Indies," by Violet Barbour, published in the *American Historical Review*, Vol. XVI (April 1911).

Other books consulted for these three chapters include *The History of Jamaica*, by Edward Long (London, 1774); *The Memoirs of Père Labat*, 1693–1705 (first English edition, London, 1931); and *The Inquisition in the Spanish Dependencies*, by H. C. Lea (London, 1908).

CHAPTER EIGHT

Good books on the history of privateers are *Private Men-of-War*, by C. W. Kendall (London, 1931); *Privateer Ships and Sailors*, by H. M. Chapin (Toulon, 1926); and *Bristol Privateers and Ships of War*, by J. W. D. Powell (Bristol, 1930).

CHAPTER ELEVEN

The pamphlet *Piracy Destroy'd* was published in London in 1701. Nearly all the other material for this chapter, including the extracts from Adam Baldridge's journal, came from the Calendar of State Papers.

CHAPTER TWELVE

The story of Every is based mainly on the Calendar of State Papers and S. C. Hill's *Notes on Piracy in Eastern Waters*.

CHAPTER THIRTEEN

The story of Kidd is based partly on the same sources as
Chapter Twelve, and also on Jameson's *Privateering and Piracy*
and many unpublished documents in the Public Record
Office. Kidd has quite a literature of his own, but most of the
books about him are too prejudiced, one way or the other, to be
of much value. I think the best is *Captain Kidd and his Skeleton
Island*, by H. T. Wilkins (London, 1935), although the author
was more concerned with the treasure than with Kidd. The
discovery of the French passes was reported by Ralph D. Paine
in his *Book of Buried Treasure* (New York, 1911). The *Trial
of Captain Kidd* was published in William Hodge's " Notable
British Trials " series (Edinburgh, 1930) with an Introduction
by Graham Brooks, on which I have already commented.
Lord Birkenhead's essay appeared in *Famous Trials of History*
(London, 1926). Sir Cornelius Neale Dalton's book, *The Real
Captain Kidd* (London, 1911), is interesting because it was the
first defence of Kidd.

CHAPTER FOURTEEN

This chapter is based almost entirely on the Calendar of
State Papers and unpublished documents in the Public Record
Office.

CHAPTER FIFTEEN

The main source is the same as for Chapter Twelve. P.R.O.
documents under C.O. 23/1, 23/2, and 23/13 were especially
useful. Almost incredibly, Woodes Rogers has never had a
biographer. There is, however, an excellent biographical
sketch by G. E. Manwaring in the 1928 edition of Rogers's
Cruising Voyage round the World (first published 1712). The only
other book I know of that does Rogers justice is *The Great
Days of Piracy in the West Indies*, by George Woodbury (Norton,
New York, 1952).

CHAPTER SIXTEEN

The material for this chapter came from many sources. The
first was the Calendar of State Papers. Another was *The*

Official Letters of A. Spotswood, published by the Virginia Historical and Philosophical Society (1882–5), supplemented by *Alexander Spotswood*, by Leonidas Dobson (London, 1932). Other printed sources include *The Tryals of Major Bonnet and Other Pirates* (London, 1719); *History of North Carolina*, by R. D. W. Connor (London, 1919); and especially *The Carolina Pirates and Colonial Commerce*, 1670–1740, by Shirley Carter Hughson (Johns Hopkins University Studies in Historical and Political Science, Series 12, Nos. 5, 6, 7: 1894).

Unpublished sources (in the Public Records Office) include Board of Trade, Bahamas 1 (C.O. 23/1); Captains' Letters (Brand, Gordon, Hume and Pease); and Order in Council, 24th August, 1721 (with memorial from Robert Maynard).

CHAPTER SEVENTEEN

References are as for Chapter Fifteen. The proceedings of the trial of the pirates at Nassau may be found in the Public Record Office under C.O. 23/1, No. 18.

CHAPTER EIGHTEEN

The trial of Mary Read and Anne Bonny is calendared in the P.R.O. under C.O. 137/14, No. 9.

CHAPTER NINETEEN

The main references are as for Chapter Twelve.

CHAPTER TWENTY

The proceedings of the trial of the pirates at Cape Corso are calendared in the P.R.O. under HCA 49, Bundle 104. Additional information was drawn from the Calendar of State Papers and Captains' Letters (Ogle).

CHAPTER TWENTY-ONE

The main source is Snelgrave, *op. cit. The Four Years' Voyages of Captain George Roberts, written by Himself*, was published in London in 1726 and reprinted in the Travellers' Library in 1930.

INDEX

All ships are indexed under the heading Ships

A CATALOG OF SELECTED
DOVER BOOKS
IN ALL FIELDS OF INTEREST

A CATALOG OF SELECTED DOVER
BOOKS IN ALL FIELDS OF INTEREST

CONCERNING THE SPIRITUAL IN ART, Wassily Kandinsky. Pioneering work by father of abstract art. Thoughts on color theory, nature of art. Analysis of earlier masters. 12 illustrations. 80pp. of text. 5⅜ x 8½. 23411-8 Pa. $4.95

ANIMALS: 1,419 Copyright-Free Illustrations of Mammals, Birds, Fish, Insects, etc., Jim Harter (ed.). Clear wood engravings present, in extremely lifelike poses, over 1,000 species of animals. One of the most extensive pictorial sourcebooks of its kind. Captions. Index. 284pp. 9 x 12. 23766-4 Pa. $14.95

CELTIC ART: The Methods of Construction, George Bain. Simple geometric techniques for making Celtic interlacements, spirals, Kells-type initials, animals, humans, etc. Over 500 illustrations. 160pp. 9 x 12. (Available in U.S. only.) 22923-8 Pa. $9.95

AN ATLAS OF ANATOMY FOR ARTISTS, Fritz Schider. Most thorough reference work on art anatomy in the world. Hundreds of illustrations, including selections from works by Vesalius, Leonardo, Goya, Ingres, Michelangelo, others. 593 illustrations. 192pp. 7⅛ x 10¼. 20241-0 Pa. $9.95

CELTIC HAND STROKE-BY-STROKE (Irish Half-Uncial from "The Book of Kells"): An Arthur Baker Calligraphy Manual, Arthur Baker. Complete guide to creating each letter of the alphabet in distinctive Celtic manner. Covers hand position, strokes, pens, inks, paper, more. Illustrated. 48pp. 8¼ x 11. 24336-2 Pa. $3.95

EASY ORIGAMI, John Montroll. Charming collection of 32 projects (hat, cup, pelican, piano, swan, many more) specially designed for the novice origami hobbyist. Clearly illustrated easy-to-follow instructions insure that even beginning papercrafters will achieve successful results. 48pp. 8¼ x 11. 27298-2 Pa. $3.50

THE COMPLETE BOOK OF BIRDHOUSE CONSTRUCTION FOR WOOD-WORKERS, Scott D. Campbell. Detailed instructions, illustrations, tables. Also data on bird habitat and instinct patterns. Bibliography. 3 tables. 63 illustrations in 15 figures. 48pp. 5¼ x 8½. 24407-5 Pa. $2.50

BLOOMINGDALE'S ILLUSTRATED 1886 CATALOG: Fashions, Dry Goods and Housewares, Bloomingdale Brothers. Famed merchants' extremely rare catalog depicting about 1,700 products: clothing, housewares, firearms, dry goods, jewelry, more. Invaluable for dating, identifying vintage items. Also, copyright-free graphics for artists, designers. Co-published with Henry Ford Museum & Greenfield Village. 160pp. 8¼ x 11. 25780-0 Pa. $10.95

HISTORIC COSTUME IN PICTURES, Braun & Schneider. Over 1,450 costumed figures in clearly detailed engravings–from dawn of civilization to end of 19th century. Captions. Many folk costumes. 256pp. 8⅜ x 11¾. 23150-X Pa. $12.95

THE BEST TALES OF HOFFMANN, E. T. A. Hoffmann. 10 of Hoffmann's most important stories: "Nutcracker and the King of Mice," "The Golden Flowerpot," etc. 458pp. 5⅜ x 8½.
21793-0 Pa. $9.95

FROM FETISH TO GOD IN ANCIENT EGYPT, E. A. Wallis Budge. Rich detailed survey of Egyptian conception of "God" and gods, magic, cult of animals, Osiris, more. Also, superb English translations of hymns and legends. 240 illustrations. 545pp. 5⅜ x 8½.
25803-3 Pa. $13.95

FRENCH STORIES/CONTES FRANÇAIS: A Dual-Language Book, Wallace Fowlie. Ten stories by French masters, Voltaire to Camus: "Micromegas" by Voltaire; "The Atheist's Mass" by Balzac; "Minuet" by de Maupassant; "The Guest" by Camus, six more. Excellent English translations on facing pages. Also French-English vocabulary list, exercises, more. 352pp. 5⅜ x 8½. 26443-2 Pa. $9.95

CHICAGO AT THE TURN OF THE CENTURY IN PHOTOGRAPHS: 122 Historic Views from the Collections of the Chicago Historical Society, Larry A. Viskochil. Rare large-format prints offer detailed views of City Hall, State Street, the Loop, Hull House, Union Station, many other landmarks, circa 1904-1913. Introduction. Captions. Maps. 144pp. 9⅜ x 12¼. 24656-6 Pa. $12.95

OLD BROOKLYN IN EARLY PHOTOGRAPHS, 1865-1929, William Lee Younger. Luna Park, Gravesend race track, construction of Grand Army Plaza, moving of Hotel Brighton, etc. 157 previously unpublished photographs. 165pp. 8⅞ x 11¾.
23587-4 Pa. $13.95

THE MYTHS OF THE NORTH AMERICAN INDIANS, Lewis Spence. Rich anthology of the myths and legends of the Algonquins, Iroquois, Pawnees and Sioux, prefaced by an extensive historical and ethnological commentary. 36 illustrations. 480pp. 5⅜ x 8½.
25967-6 Pa. $10.95

AN ENCYCLOPEDIA OF BATTLES: Accounts of Over 1,560 Battles from 1479 B.C. to the Present, David Eggenberger. Essential details of every major battle in recorded history from the first battle of Megiddo in 1479 B.C. to Grenada in 1984. List of Battle Maps. New Appendix covering the years 1967-1984. Index. 99 illustrations. 544pp. 6½ x 9¼.
24913-1 Pa. $16.95

SAILING ALONE AROUND THE WORLD, Captain Joshua Slocum. First man to sail around the world, alone, in small boat. One of great feats of seamanship told in delightful manner. 67 illustrations. 294pp. 5⅜ x 8½. 20326-3 Pa. $6.95

ANARCHISM AND OTHER ESSAYS, Emma Goldman. Powerful, penetrating, prophetic essays on direct action, role of minorities, prison reform, puritan hypocrisy, violence, etc. 271pp. 5⅜ x 8½. 22484-8 Pa. $7.95

MYTHS OF THE HINDUS AND BUDDHISTS, Ananda K. Coomaraswamy and Sister Nivedita. Great stories of the epics; deeds of Krishna, Shiva, taken from puranas, Vedas, folk tales; etc. 32 illustrations. 400pp. 5⅜ x 8½. 21759-0 Pa. $12.95

THE TRAUMA OF BIRTH, Otto Rank. Rank's controversial thesis that anxiety neurosis is caused by profound psychological trauma which occurs at birth. 256pp. 5⅜ x 8½.
27974-X Pa. $7.95

A THEOLOGICO-POLITICAL TREATISE, Benedict Spinoza. Also contains unfinished Political Treatise. Great classic on religious liberty, theory of government on common consent. R. Elwes translation. Total of 421pp. 5⅜ x 8½. 20249-6 Pa. $10.95

CATALOG OF DOVER BOOKS

PERSPECTIVE FOR ARTISTS, Rex Vicat Cole. Depth, perspective of sky and sea, shadows, much more, not usually covered. 391 diagrams, 81 reproductions of drawings and paintings. 279pp. 5⅜ x 8½. 22487-2 Pa. $9.95

DRAWING THE LIVING FIGURE, Joseph Sheppard. Innovative approach to artistic anatomy focuses on specifics of surface anatomy, rather than muscles and bones. Over 170 drawings of live models in front, back and side views, and in widely varying poses. Accompanying diagrams. 177 illustrations. Introduction. Index. 144pp. 8⅜ x11¼. 26723-7 Pa. $9.95

GOTHIC AND OLD ENGLISH ALPHABETS: 100 Complete Fonts, Dan X. Solo. Add power, elegance to posters, signs, other graphics with 100 stunning copyright-free alphabets: Blackstone, Dolbey, Germania, 97 more–including many lower-case, numerals, punctuation marks. 104pp. 8⅛ x 11. 24695-7 Pa. $8.95

HOW TO DO BEADWORK, Mary White. Fundamental book on craft from simple projects to five-bead chains and woven works. 106 illustrations. 142pp. 5⅜ x 8. 20697-1 Pa. $5.95

THE BOOK OF WOOD CARVING, Charles Marshall Sayers. Finest book for beginners discusses fundamentals and offers 34 designs. "Absolutely first rate . . . well thought out and well executed."–E. J. Tangerman. 118pp. 7¾ x 10⅝. 23654-4 Pa. $7.95

ILLUSTRATED CATALOG OF CIVIL WAR MILITARY GOODS: Union Army Weapons, Insignia, Uniform Accessories, and Other Equipment, Schuyler, Hartley, and Graham. Rare, profusely illustrated 1846 catalog includes Union Army uniform and dress regulations, arms and ammunition, coats, insignia, flags, swords, rifles, etc. 226 illustrations. 160pp. 9 x 12. 24939-5 Pa. $10.95

WOMEN'S FASHIONS OF THE EARLY 1900s: An Unabridged Republication of "New York Fashions, 1909," National Cloak & Suit Co. Rare catalog of mail-order fashions documents women's and children's clothing styles shortly after the turn of the century. Captions offer full descriptions, prices. Invaluable resource for fashion, costume historians. Approximately 725 illustrations. 128pp. 8⅜ x 11¼. 27276-1 Pa. $11.95

THE 1912 AND 1915 GUSTAV STICKLEY FURNITURE CATALOGS, Gustav Stickley. With over 200 detailed illustrations and descriptions, these two catalogs are essential reading and reference materials and identification guides for Stickley furniture. Captions cite materials, dimensions and prices. 112pp. 6½ x 9¼. 26676-1 Pa. $9.95

EARLY AMERICAN LOCOMOTIVES, John H. White, Jr. Finest locomotive engravings from early 19th century: historical (1804–74), main-line (after 1870), special, foreign, etc. 147 plates. 142pp. 11⅜ x 8¼. 22772-3 Pa. $12.95

THE TALL SHIPS OF TODAY IN PHOTOGRAPHS, Frank O. Braynard. Lavishly illustrated tribute to nearly 100 majestic contemporary sailing vessels: Amerigo Vespucci, Clearwater, Constitution, Eagle, Mayflower, Sea Cloud, Victory, many more. Authoritative captions provide statistics, background on each ship. 190 black-and-white photographs and illustrations. Introduction. 128pp. 8⅞ x 11¾. 27163-3 Pa. $14.95

CATALOG OF DOVER BOOKS

PIANO TUNING, J. Cree Fischer. Clearest, best book for beginner, amateur. Simple repairs, raising dropped notes, tuning by easy method of flattened fifths. No previous skills needed. 4 illustrations. 201pp. 5⅜ x 8½. 23267-0 Pa. $6.95

HINTS TO SINGERS, Lillian Nordica. Selecting the right teacher, developing confidence, overcoming stage fright, and many other important skills receive thoughtful discussion in this indispensible guide, written by a world-famous diva of four decades' experience. 96pp. 5³/₈ x 8¹/₂. 40094-8 Pa. $4.95

THE COMPLETE NONSENSE OF EDWARD LEAR, Edward Lear. All nonsense limericks, zany alphabets, Owl and Pussycat, songs, nonsense botany, etc., illustrated by Lear. Total of 320pp. 5⅜ x 8½. (AVAILABLE IN U.S. ONLY.) 20167-8 Pa. $7.95

VICTORIAN PARLOUR POETRY: An Annotated Anthology, Michael R. Turner. 117 gems by Longfellow, Tennyson, Browning, many lesser-known poets. "The Village Blacksmith," "Curfew Must Not Ring Tonight," "Only a Baby Small," dozens more, often difficult to find elsewhere. Index of poets, titles, first lines. xxiii + 325pp. 5⅜ x 8¼. 27044-0 Pa. $8.95

DUBLINERS, James Joyce. Fifteen stories offer vivid, tightly focused observations of the lives of Dublin's poorer classes. At least one, "The Dead," is considered a masterpiece. Reprinted complete and unabridged from standard edition. 160pp. 5³⁄₁₆ x 8¼. 26870-5 Pa. $1.00

GREAT WEIRD TALES: 14 Stories by Lovecraft, Blackwood, Machen and Others, S. T. Joshi (ed.). 14 spellbinding tales, including "The Sin Eater," by Fiona McLeod, "The Eye Above the Mantel," by Frank Belknap Long, as well as renowned works by R. H. Barlow, Lord Dunsany, Arthur Machen, W. C. Morrow and eight other masters of the genre. 256pp. 5⅜ x 8½. (Available in U.S. only.) 40436-6 Pa. $8.95

THE BOOK OF THE SACRED MAGIC OF ABRAMELIN THE MAGE, translated by S. MacGregor Mathers. Medieval manuscript of ceremonial magic. Basic document in Aleister Crowley, Golden Dawn groups. 268pp. 5⅜ x 8½. 23211-5 Pa. $9.95

NEW RUSSIAN-ENGLISH AND ENGLISH-RUSSIAN DICTIONARY, M. A. O'Brien. This is a remarkably handy Russian dictionary, containing a surprising amount of information, including over 70,000 entries. 366pp. 4½ x 6⅛. 20208-9 Pa. $10.95

HISTORIC HOMES OF THE AMERICAN PRESIDENTS, Second, Revised Edition, Irvin Haas. A traveler's guide to American Presidential homes, most open to the public, depicting and describing homes occupied by every American President from George Washington to George Bush. With visiting hours, admission charges, travel routes. 175 photographs. Index. 160pp. 8¼ x 11. 26751-2 Pa. $11.95

NEW YORK IN THE FORTIES, Andreas Feininger. 162 brilliant photographs by the well-known photographer, formerly with *Life* magazine. Commuters, shoppers, Times Square at night, much else from city at its peak. Captions by John von Hartz. 181pp. 9¼ x 10¾. 23585-8 Pa. $13.95

INDIAN SIGN LANGUAGE, William Tomkins. Over 525 signs developed by Sioux and other tribes. Written instructions and diagrams. Also 290 pictographs. 111pp. 6⅛ x 9¼. 22029-X Pa. $3.95

PHOTOGRAPHIC SKETCHBOOK OF THE CIVIL WAR, Alexander Gardner. 100 photos taken on field during the Civil War. Famous shots of Manassas Harper's Ferry, Lincoln, Richmond, slave pens, etc. 244pp. 10⅝ x 8¼. 22731-6 Pa. $10.95

FIVE ACRES AND INDEPENDENCE, Maurice G. Kains. Great back-to-the-land classic explains basics of self-sufficient farming. The one book to get. 95 illustrations. 397pp. 5⅜ x 8½. 20974-1 Pa. $7.95

SONGS OF EASTERN BIRDS, Dr. Donald J. Borror. Songs and calls of 60 species most common to eastern U.S.: warblers, woodpeckers, flycatchers, thrushes, larks, many more in high-quality recording. Cassette and manual 99912-2 $9.95

A MODERN HERBAL, Margaret Grieve. Much the fullest, most exact, most useful compilation of herbal material. Gigantic alphabetical encyclopedia, from aconite to zedoary, gives botanical information, medical properties, folklore, economic uses, much else. Indispensable to serious reader. 161 illustrations. 888pp. 6½ x 9¼. 2-vol. set. (Available in U.S. only.) Vol. I: 22798-7 Pa. $9.95
Vol. II: 22799-5 Pa. $9.95

HIDDEN TREASURE MAZE BOOK, Dave Phillips. Solve 34 challenging mazes accompanied by heroic tales of adventure. Evil dragons, people-eating plants, blood-thirsty giants, many more dangerous adversaries lurk at every twist and turn. 34 mazes, stories, solutions. 48pp. 8¼ x 11. 24566-7 Pa. $2.95

LETTERS OF W. A. MOZART, Wolfgang A. Mozart. Remarkable letters show bawdy wit, humor, imagination, musical insights, contemporary musical world; includes some letters from Leopold Mozart. 276pp. 5⅜ x 8½. 22859-2 Pa. $7.95

BASIC PRINCIPLES OF CLASSICAL BALLET, Agrippina Vaganova. Great Russian theoretician, teacher explains methods for teaching classical ballet. 118 illustrations. 175pp. 5⅜ x 8½. 22036-2 Pa. $6.95

THE JUMPING FROG, Mark Twain. Revenge edition. The original story of The Celebrated Jumping Frog of Calaveras County, a hapless French translation, and Twain's hilarious "retranslation" from the French. 12 illustrations. 66pp. 5⅜ x 8½. 22686-7 Pa. $3.95

BEST REMEMBERED POEMS, Martin Gardner (ed.). The 126 poems in this superb collection of 19th- and 20th-century British and American verse range from Shelley's "To a Skylark" to the impassioned "Renascence" of Edna St. Vincent Millay and to Edward Lear's whimsical "The Owl and the Pussycat." 224pp. 5⅜ x 8½. 27165-X Pa. $5.95

COMPLETE SONNETS, William Shakespeare. Over 150 exquisite poems deal with love, friendship, the tyranny of time, beauty's evanescence, death and other themes in language of remarkable power, precision and beauty. Glossary of archaic terms. 80pp. 5$^{3}/_{16}$ x 8¼. 26686-9 Pa. $1.00

BODIES IN A BOOKSHOP, R. T. Campbell. Challenging mystery of blackmail and murder with ingenious plot and superbly drawn characters. In the best tradition of British suspense fiction. 192pp. 5⅜ x 8½. 24720-1 Pa. $6.95

THE INFLUENCE OF SEA POWER UPON HISTORY, 1660–1783, A. T. Mahan. Influential classic of naval history and tactics still used as text in war colleges. First paperback edition. 4 maps. 24 battle plans. 640pp. 5⅜ x 8½. 25509-3 Pa. $14.95

THE STORY OF THE TITANIC AS TOLD BY ITS SURVIVORS, Jack Winocour (ed.). What it was really like. Panic, despair, shocking inefficiency, and a little heroism. More thrilling than any fictional account. 26 illustrations. 320pp. 5⅜ x 8½. 20610-6 Pa. $8.95

FAIRY AND FOLK TALES OF THE IRISH PEASANTRY, William Butler Yeats (ed.). Treasury of 64 tales from the twilight world of Celtic myth and legend: "The Soul Cages," "The Kildare Pooka," "King O'Toole and his Goose," many more. Introduction and Notes by W. B. Yeats. 352pp. 5⅜ x 8½. 26941-8 Pa. $8.95

BUDDHIST MAHAYANA TEXTS, E. B. Cowell and others (eds.). Superb, accurate translations of basic documents in Mahayana Buddhism, highly important in history of religions. The Buddha-karita of Asvaghosha, Larger Sukhavativyuha, more. 448pp. 5⅜ x 8½. 25552-2 Pa. $12.95

ONE TWO THREE . . . INFINITY: Facts and Speculations of Science, George Gamow. Great physicist's fascinating, readable overview of contemporary science: number theory, relativity, fourth dimension, entropy, genes, atomic structure, much more. 128 illustrations. Index. 352pp. 5⅜ x 8½. 25664-2 Pa. $9.95

EXPERIMENTATION AND MEASUREMENT, W. J. Youden. Introductory manual explains laws of measurement in simple terms and offers tips for achieving accuracy and minimizing errors. Mathematics of measurement, use of instruments, experimenting with machines. 1994 edition. Foreword. Preface. Introduction. Epilogue. Selected Readings. Glossary. Index. Tables and figures. 128pp. 5³/₈ x 8¹/₂. 40451-X Pa. $6.95

DALÍ ON MODERN ART: The Cuckolds of Antiquated Modern Art, Salvador Dalí. Influential painter skewers modern art and its practitioners. Outrageous evaluations of Picasso, Cézanne, Turner, more. 15 renderings of paintings discussed. 44 calligraphic decorations by Dalí. 96pp. 5⅜ x 8½. (Available in U.S. only.) 29220-7 Pa. $5.95

ANTIQUE PLAYING CARDS: A Pictorial History, Henry René D'Allemagne. Over 900 elaborate, decorative images from rare playing cards (14th–20th centuries): Bacchus, death, dancing dogs, hunting scenes, royal coats of arms, players cheating, much more. 96pp. 9¼ x 12¼. 29265-7 Pa. $12.95

MAKING FURNITURE MASTERPIECES: 30 Projects with Measured Drawings, Franklin H. Gottshall. Step-by-step instructions, illustrations for constructing handsome, useful pieces, among them a Sheraton desk, Chippendale chair, Spanish desk, Queen Anne table and a William and Mary dressing mirror. 224pp. 8⅛ x 11¼. 29338-6 Pa. $13.95

THE FOSSIL BOOK: A Record of Prehistoric Life, Patricia V. Rich et al. Profusely illustrated definitive guide covers everything from single-celled organisms and dinosaurs to birds and mammals and the interplay between climate and man. Over 1,500 illustrations. 760pp. 7½ x 10⅛. 29371-8 Pa. $29.95

Prices subject to change without notice.

Available at your book dealer or write for free catalog to Dept. GI, Dover Publications, Inc., 31 East 2nd St., Mineola, N.Y. 11501. Dover publishes more than 500 books each year on science, elementary and advanced mathematics, biology, music, art, literary history, social sciences and other areas.

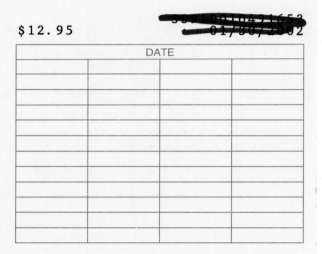